中国—东盟法律评论

China–ASEAN Law Review

第五辑 2015年
2015 Volume

■ 主编　　张晓君

Chief Editor：
Zhang Xiaojun

■ 主办方
中国法学会中国—东盟法律研究中心
中国西南政法大学

Sponsors：
China–ASEAN Legal Research Center of China Law Society
Southwest University of Political Science and Law of China

中国—东盟法律评论

韦柠滨

Bình luận pháp luật Trung quốc—Asean.

越南—中国—东盟法律信息咨询中心主任陈大兴用越南文字为
《中国—东盟法律评论》题写刊名

Journal Undang Undang Asean-China

冯正仁

马来西亚联邦法院前大法官、第五届"中国—东盟法律合作与发展高层论坛"
组委会主席冯正仁先生以马来语为《中国—东盟法律评论》题写刊名。

柬埔寨司法部大臣昂翁·瓦塔纳用高棉语为《中国—东盟法律评论》题写刊名

中国—东盟法律研究

中心：

法学之花盛开！

徐步
驻东盟大使
二〇二四年三月七日

图书在版编目(CIP)数据

中国—东盟法律评论.第 5 辑/张晓君主编.—厦门:厦门大学出版社,2016.3
ISBN 978-7-5615-5877-5

Ⅰ.①中…　Ⅱ.①张…　Ⅲ.①法律-中国、东南亚国家联盟-文集
Ⅳ.①D92-53②D933-53

中国版本图书馆 CIP 数据核字(2016)第 008608 号

出 版 人	蒋东明
责任编辑	甘世恒　邓　臻
装帧设计	蒋卓群
电脑制作	张雨秋
责任印制	许克华

出版发行	厦门大学出版社
社　　址	厦门市软件园二期望海路 39 号
邮政编码	361008
总 编 办	0592-2182177　0592-2181406(传真)
营销中心	0592-2184458　0592-2181365
网　　址	http://www.xmupress.com
邮　　箱	xmupress@126.com
印　　刷	厦门市金玺彩印有限公司

开本	720mm×1000mm　1/16
印张	22
插页	2
字数	380 千字
版次	2016 年 3 月第 1 版
印次	2016 年 3 月第 1 次印刷
定价	60.00 元

本书如有印装质量问题请直接寄承印厂调换

厦门大学出版社
微信二维码

厦门大学出版社
微博二维码

中国—东盟法律研究中心理事会人员名单

■中国

名誉理事长

陈冀平	中国法学会党组书记　中国法学会常务副会长

理事长

张鸣起	中国法学会副会长

副理事长

刘学普	重庆市委政法委书记、重庆市法学会会长
谷昭民	中国法学会对外联络部主任
付子堂	西南政法大学校长

《中国—东盟法律评论》顾问委员会委员

■中国 （中方）

张鸣起	中国法学会副会长
刘学普	重庆市委政法委书记、重庆市法学会会长
谷昭民	中国法学会对外联络部主任
张国林	西南政法大学党委书记
付子堂	西南政法大学校长
吴志攀	北京大学常务副校长
杨国华	清华大学法学院教授
王　瀚	西北政法大学副校长

■东盟国家

占·索斯威	柬埔寨司法部国务秘书
克拉罗·阿莱兰诺	菲律宾司法部总检察长
王科林	文莱仲裁协会会长
哈利芬·东巴	印度尼西亚最高法院院长
帕查拉吉迪亚帕	泰国公主
麦特瑞·苏塔帕古	泰国中央知识产权与国际贸易法院院长

Advisory Committee

■China

Zhang Mingqi	Vice-president of China Law Society
Liu Xuepu	President of Chongqing Law Society
Gu Zhaomin	Director-General of China Legal Exchange Center
	Director of the Department for Overseas Liaison of China Law Society
Zhang Guolin	Secretary of CPC of Southwest University of Political Science and Law
Wu Zhipan	Vice-Chancellor of Beijing University
Fu Zitang	Chancellor of Southwest University of Political Science and Law
Yang Guohua	Professor, School of Law, Tsinghua University, Bejing, China
Wang Han	Vice-Chancellor of Northwest University of Politic Science and Law

■ASEAN Countries

Chan Sotheavy	Secretary of State of Ministry of Justice of Cambodia
Claro A. Arellano	The Prosecutor General of Department of Justice of Philippines
Colin Ong	President of Arbitration Association of Brunei Darussalam
Harifin A. Tumpa	President of the Supreme Court of Indonesia
Patcharakitiyapa	Princess of the Kingdom
Maitree Sutapakul	Chief Judge of the Central Intellectual Property and International Trade Court
Soltoni Mohdally	Senior Justice of Supreme Court of Indonesia
Tan Sri James Foong	Justice of the Federal Court of Malaysia
Win Myint	Deputy Attorney General of the Union, Republic of the Union of Myanmar
Chaleuan Yapaoher	President of Lao National Academy of Science

目　录

Contents

编 者 按

  本期《中国—东盟法律评论》为东盟国家法律制度专刊,开设了三大栏目,包括共建21世纪海上丝绸之路的法律问题、亚洲基础设施银行(AIIB)相关法律问题研究、东盟国家国别网络空间立法与制度问题研究三个专题,主要收录了参加"中国—东盟法律培训基地"第八期东盟研修班的,来自柬埔寨、印尼、老挝、马来西亚、缅甸、菲律宾、泰国、越南等东盟国家的法律法学界专家,在"中国东南亚南亚法律合作磋商会暨21世纪海上丝绸之路法律研讨会"上的论文共计20篇,突出反映东盟法律学者顺应时代潮流在"一带一路"大背景之下对本国法治发展中存在问题的反思与建议,同时为21世纪海上丝绸之路的建设提供前沿性的研究成果与智力支持。

  在"共建21世纪海上丝绸之路的法律问题"中,中国—东盟法律研究中心秘书长张晓君教授与西南政法大学国际法硕士生王俞人提出,中国需要充分发挥主导作用,促进沿线国家共同协商、相互学习,努力构建区域性统一适用的海运法律制度体系,为21世纪海上丝绸之路的建设创造稳固的海运法律保障;印度尼西亚西爪哇省普瓦卡它地区法院法官 Indah Wastukencana Wulan 认为应从国际条约和争端解决机制入手解决法律冲突分歧是21世纪海上丝绸之路设想的一项重要问题;老挝中部人民法院干部 Thipphavanh Chanthavongsa 详细分析了中国对老挝社会经济发展做出的贡献及其深远影响并重点指出中国与老挝之间保持睦邻友好关系与经济文化合作对老挝的发展十分关键;马来西亚志豪联合律师事务所合伙人 Lai Chee Hoe 说明了铁路运输在重建丝绸之路中的重要地位,并提出当所有成员国搁置政治利益、共同致力于用铁路连通各国的美好前景时,法律协调可以实现;缅甸最高检察院法律官员 Sithu Swe Tun 着重阐述了市场经济和开放政策在国际化和区域化形势中对缅甸十分关键,并强调中国在此进程中的重要作用;泰国中央知识产权与国际贸易法院审判支持部法律官员 Maneenuch Sangsuwannukul 指出东盟国家和泰国都应在顺应全球经济发展之下发展自身并修改相关法律以有效应对将来可能的贸易投资从而为自己带来最大的实质利益;越南国家5号律师事务所法律顾问 Nguyen Thi Thao 简要介绍了越南在国际贸易方面的相关法律规定并指出在21世纪海上丝绸之路背景下中国和越南应当通过降低关税和实现贸易自由化促进两国经济合作,实现双方共赢;越南黄丹国际法律事务所法律顾问 Nguyen Thi Thu Thuy 详细分析了中国和越南如何通过实现贸易便利化促进两国贸易自由和经济发展并指出贸易便利化在全球经济发展中的重要作用及其对经济的促进作用。

在"亚洲基础设施银行(AIIB)相关法律问题研究"中,柬埔寨司法部国际关系部法律官员 Dy Molany 认为亚洲基础设施投资银行应该参考私人投资模式建立一个全新的融资模式;柬埔寨司法部部长秘书 Hun Sopheap 对比了中国主导的亚洲基础设施投资银行和美国主导的 TPP,认为如果能将强化治理作为发展的必要条件,则亚投行具有成功的可能;马来西亚郑今智及莎丽娜律师馆合伙人 Teh Tai Yong 和重庆大学国际法硕士生赵以通过对伊斯兰金融体系与银行的运作的介绍,指出建设中的海上丝绸之路也可以考虑建立伊斯兰金融体系;马来西亚梁潘及黄律师事务所法务助理 Tan Poh Hui 以在亚洲基础设施投资银行建设过程可能存在的问题,如融资、基础设施建设、港口建设、招标程序、争议解决、环境问题等为视角,认为不同行业的专家在亚洲基础设施投资银行的设立过程中应该通过对话和协商的方式更多参与进来;菲律宾安加拉·阿贝罗·雷加拉·克鲁斯律师事务所高级法务助理 Lee Everlene Ong 认为 AIIB 可以利用现有多边机构丰富的信息资源及其解决此类问题的经验教训,寻找最佳方案,保证所有相关国家都能从这一建设项目中有所收益。

在"东盟国家国别网络空间立法与制度问题研究"中,柬埔寨司法部国际关系部法律官员 Dy Molany 介绍了柬埔寨关于网络安全的法律体系与规定,并对网络法草案做了重点评述;印度尼西亚巴厘省班戈利地区法院法官 DwiRezki Sri Astarini 认为尽管印度尼西亚政府为了保证信息安全做了很多努力并采取了许多相关措施,但是正确的看待理想环境和现实环境才会帮助改变现在的情况;老挝司法部外国法律研究中心主任 Phimchanthaphone Sinthavong 通过介绍老挝网络服务的发展和网络的使用情况系统阐明了老挝的网络服务;马来西亚李素桦律师事务所法务助理 Charlie Ng Zheng Hui 认为,只要在实践中能够严格执行,马来西亚的网络立法在现阶段基本可以应对打击网络犯罪的需要;缅甸塔姆威法院法官 Kay Thee Hlaing 主要通过对《计算机科学发展法》、《电子交易法》和《电信法》三部法律相关规定的介绍,阐明了当前缅甸互联网的发展情况和网络立法情况;菲律宾安加拉·阿贝罗·雷加拉·克鲁斯律师事务所高级法务助理 Everlene O. Lee 介绍了菲律宾在网络法和网络犯罪方面的法律体系并对《电子商务法》及《2012 年网络犯罪防范法》的相关规定做了重点介绍;泰国中央知识产权与国际贸易法院法官 Yanaphak Mantarat 以泰国互联网法和相关法律的内容与执行问题为视角,建议在打击网络犯罪方面应该加强国际合作;越南文瀚法律办公室罗杰·谭律师事务所法律助理 Pham Thi Minh Hau 认为尽管越南在网络法规的相关规定散见于不同的法律和法令,但是足以调整和保证互联网相关的活动,越南的互联网也会在这样的法律体系内得以进一步发展。

《中国—东盟法律评论》编辑部
2015 年

Editor's Note

"China-ASEAN Law Review"(CALR) is special journal for the legal system of the ASEAN countries and three columns, where 20 law articles are recorded, are set up in this book (volume V Oct. 2015 Number 1) including Legal issues on the collaborative construction of the 21st-century maritime Silk Road, related legal issues about the Asian Infrastructure Investment Bank (AIIB), and some researches about cyberspace legislation and system of individual ASEAN countries. The 20 law articles of this book are mainly collected from the law scholars of Cambodia, Indonesia, Laos, Malaysia, Myanmar, Philippine, Thailand and Vietnam, which present in the "Legal Seminar on China-Southeast & South Asia Cooperation and 21st Century Maritime Silk Road" for the Graduation Ceremony of the 8th"Training Programmes China-ASEAN Legal Training Base". Those law articles reflect that law scholars of ASESN, who comply with the21st Century Maritime Silk Road, give their own thoughts and suggestions on the problems existing in the development of the rule of law in ASESN countries,and provide intellectual supports for the settlement of 21st Century Maritime Silk Road according their latest great extent reflect research achievements.

In the column of "Legal issues on the collaborative construction of the 21st-century maritime Silk Road",Professor Zhang Xiaojun and Wang Yuren of School of International Law, SWUPL consider that China needs to play the leading role to promote the common consultation and mutual learning with other countries,and make every effort to build a regional unified maritime transport legal system. Indah W. Wulan, judge at Purwakarta District Court in West Java, states that it is important for establishment of the 21st century Maritime Silk Road to solve law conflict starting by International A-greement and Dispute Settlement. ThipphavanhChanthavongsa, academic staff of the People's Supreme Court (Civil Chamber) of the Laos, analyses the significance of China's contribution to the socio-economic development of the Lao PDR and concludes that the cooperation and good relations between the two countries are essential for the development of the Lao PDR. Lai Chee Hoe, partner of Chee Hoe A Associates, detailedly discusses the importance of rail transportation in rebranding Maritime Silk Road and points out that the legal harmonization is a dream achievable when all the member countries can set aside their political interests and work towards the vision of connecting the countries by rail. Sithu Swe Tun, staff officer at the Union Attorney General's Office, show clearly that a market economy and open-door policies are crucial for Myanmar in the new situation of trade and economic cooperation and emphasises the role of China in this transition. Maneenuch Sangsuwannukul, legal officer of the Central Intellectual Property and International Trade Court, points out that both the ASEAN countries and Thailand need to amend relevant laws to develop themselves in order to be able to cope efficiently with future investment. Nguyen Thi Thao, legal counsellor from the National No. 5 Law Firm, introduces the related laws and regulations of Vietnamese on international trade, and then focuses upon how to enhance economic cooperation through the elimination of tariffs as well as the facilitation of trade between China and Vietnam in the context of building Maritime Silk Road. Nguyen Thi Thu Thuy, legal consultant at the Hoang Dam and Global Partnership Law Firm, discusses how to achieve the trade facilitation works in the field of the China-Vietnam economic trade and cooperation, furthermore, the author states the importance and benefits of trade facilitation.

In the column of " related legal issues about the Asian Infrastructure Investment Bank (AIIB)" Dy Molany, legal official of the Ministry of Justice of Cambodia, gives a recommendation to build a new finance model upon private infrastructure investment. Hun Sopheap, secretary of the Minister of Justice of Cambodia, compares the AIIB to the TPP and points out that the AIIB might be a success as a regional institution. Teh Tai Yong, partner of the Teh Kim Teh, Salina & Co., and ZhaoYi, postgraduate student of Chongqing University, introduce Islamic finance system and banking capital operation believes that construction of "the 21st Century Maritime Silk Road" could consider adopting such a finance system to realise its objectives. Tan Poh Hui, legal Associate at Jeff Leong, Poon & Wong, focuses upon the funding problems of the AIIB, the construction of infrastructure and ports, the bidding process, dispute settlement, environment issues, and other potential undeniable problems that may emerge in the establishment process of the AIIB. The author, therefore, suggests that experts from different industries, for example legal, finance, and all other relevant industries should be more involved in this process. Everlene O. Lee, senior associate of Angara Abello Concepcion Regala & Cruz Law Offices, points out that AIIB can hopefully tackle these issues before they start major infrastructure support and activities, based on the pitfalls experience.

In the column of "some researches about cyberspace legislation and system of individual ASEAN countries", Dy Molany, legal official of the Ministry of Justice of Cambodia, introduces Cambodia's legal framework to secure internet security, and focuses upon the draft of Cyber Law. Dwi Rezki Sri Astarini, judge of the Bangli District Court in Indonesia, concludes that although Indonesian government has attempted to address internet security problems by many different measures, including international cooperation, a better understanding of the current condition and ideal condition would help to improve the situation. Phimchanthaphone Sinthavong, head of Division of Research (foreign legal), Ministry of Justice in Laos, gives a brief introduction to the internet usage and discusses internet policies and regulation in Laos. Charlie Ng Zheng Hui, legal Associate of Lee Sok Wah & Co, concludes that the provisions at the moment are thorough enough to cope with cyber crimes, as long as they are properly implemented. Kay Thee Hlaing, additional township judge of the Tarmway Township Court, gives a brief introduction of the law in relation to internet in Myanmar according to the three acts: the Computer Science Development Law, the Electronic Transactions Law and the Telecommunications Law. Everlene O. Lee, senior associate of Angara Abello Concepcion Regala & Cruz Law Offices, examines the legal framework of cyber law and cyber crime law in Philippine. It mainly covers legal provisions from the E-Commerce Act and the Cybercrime Prevention Act of 2012. Yanaphak Mantarat, judge of the Central Intellectual Property and International Trade Court, calls for international cooperation to combat cyber crimes from the viewpoint of the content and implementation of Thailand's internet related provisions. Pham Thi Minh Hau, associate of Vinh An Law Office – Rajah & Tann LCT Lawyers, points out that the Vietnamese legal system contains sufficient provisions on internet law, despite being scattered in various legal instruments, and the development of the internet and activities performed via internet through this system are progressively being improved.

Editorial Board of China-ASEAN Law Review
2015

共建21世纪海上丝绸之路的法律问题

LEGAL ISSUES ON THE COLLABORATIVE CONSTRUCTION OF THE 21ST – CENTURY MARITIME SILK ROAD

21 世纪海上丝绸之路建设背景下海运法律问题研究

张晓君* 王俞人**

摘要 建设 21 世纪海上丝绸之路将是一个多元、开放的务实合作进程,中国与沿线各国以经济合作为中心,利用现有合作机制和平台照顾各方关切,共同推进海上丝绸之路的建设进程。建设 21 世纪海上丝绸之路,将有利于增强中国与沿线国家互助互信,打造稳定的合作环境,为丝路区域的长远稳定与繁荣发展创造新的机遇。海运是 21 世纪海上丝绸之路的基础和核心,但从目前的国际海运实践来看,沿线各国在经济制度、法律传统文化、现行立法规定以及司法审判实践等方面不可避免地存在较大差异,这无疑加大了海上丝绸之路沿线国家之间海运法律冲突的解决难度。因此,我国需要充分发挥主导作用,促进沿线国家共同协商、相互学习,努力构建区域性统一适用的海运法律制度体系,为 21 世纪海上丝绸之路的建设创造稳固的海运法律保障。

关键词 21 世纪海上丝绸之路;海运;法律冲突;区域性海运法律体系

一、建设 21 世纪海上丝绸之路战略的提出及必要性

2013 年 10 月 3 日,在印度尼西亚首都雅加达,国家主席习近平在印度尼西亚国会发表演讲时表示"中国愿同东盟国家加强海上合作,使用好中国政府设立的中国—东盟海上合作基金,发展好海洋合作伙伴关系,共同建设 21 世纪海上丝绸之路"。[①] 习近平主席的讲话为 21 世纪海上丝绸之路的建设指明

---

* 中国—东盟法律研究中心秘书长,西南政法大学国际法学院院长、教授、博士生导师。

** 西南政法大学国际法硕士生。

① 参见《习近平主席在印尼国会发表重要演讲》(2013-10-03)。

了前进方向。加强海上合作是 21 世纪海上丝绸之路建设的优先领域和重点任务,具有基础性和示范性效应。2013 年 11 月 12 日,中共十八届三中全会通过《关于全面深化改革若干重大问题的决定》,提出"加快同周边国家和区域基础设施互联互通建设,推进丝绸之路经济带、海上丝绸之路建设,形成全方位开放新格局"。① 2014 年两会期间,李克强总理在《政府工作报告》中提出"将继续高举和平发展合作共赢的旗帜;抓紧规划建设丝绸之路经济带和 21 世纪海上丝绸之路,推进孟中印缅、中巴经济走廊建设,推进一批重大支撑项目,加快基础设施互联互通"的倡议,并将"抓紧规划建设一带一路、拓展国际经济技术合作创新空间"作为重点工作。② 2014 年 6 月 20 日,李克强总理在出席中希海洋合作论坛发表演讲时表示,"我们愿同世界各国一道,通过发展海洋事业带动经济发展、深化国际合作、促进世界和平,努力建设一个和平、合作、和谐的海洋"。③ 2014 年 11 月,APEC 峰会在北京召开,会议以"共建面向未来的亚太伙伴关系"为主题,中央政府借此契机阐述我国对于推动亚太地区互联互通与一带一路建设的主张,并在此基础上开启设立丝路基金、进一步建设亚洲基础设施投资银行等崭新命题。2015 年 3 月 28 日,发改委、外交部与商务部联合发布了《推动共建丝绸之路经济带和 21 世纪海上丝绸之路的愿景与行动》,表明海上丝绸之路的建设问题已然上升至国家战略层面,并且被纳入顶层设计之中。④

21 世纪海上丝绸之路建设将涉及 20 多个国家和地区,其建设将是一个多元、开放的务实合作进程,中国与沿线各国以经济合作为中心,利用现有合作机制和平台照顾各方关切,共同推进海上丝绸之路的建设进程。实际上,21 世纪海上丝绸之路的沿线区域地缘政治关系错综复杂,沿线国家规模不一,利益诉求不同,在历史传统、民族宗教、语言文化等方面也具有较大差异。因此,21 世纪海上丝绸之路的建设必须做到求同存异,包容不同国家的不同需求,

---

① 参见《中共十八届三中全会关于全面深化改革若干重大问题的决定》(2013-11-12)。

② 参见李克强总理在 2014 年第十二届全国人大会议第二次会议上作出的《政府工作报告》(2014-03-05)。

③ 参见《努力建设和平、合作、和谐之海——李克强总理在中希海洋合作论坛上的讲话》(2014-06-20)。

④ 参见发改委、外交部与商务部联合发布的《推动共建丝绸之路经济带和 21 世纪海上丝绸之路的愿景与行动》(2015 年)。

照顾不同国家的不同特点,创新合作模式,夯实合作基础。①

建设 21 世纪海上丝绸之路这个构想一经提出,就引起世界普遍关注。俄罗斯总统普京,斯里兰卡总统拉贾帕克萨,印度前总理辛格,巴基斯坦总理纳瓦兹谢里夫,马来西亚总理纳吉布,老挝总理通邢塔马冯,希腊总统帕普利亚斯等政要纷纷表示愿意积极参与 21 世纪海上丝绸之路建设。中国国家主席习近平,在多种场合发表过有关建设 21 世纪海上丝绸之路的讲话。这些讲话涵盖了 21 世纪海上丝绸之路的基本内容,其中包括加强政策沟通、道路联通、贸易畅通、货币流通、民心相通。政策沟通旨在加强友好交流,道路联通旨在加强道路互联互通,贸易畅通旨在加强通商和产业投资,货币流通旨在加强资金流通,民心相通旨在加强人文交流。② 这些内容切合丝路沿线区域经济社会的实际,既指出了目标,也明确了道路,既是对历史的总结,也是对未来的指引。

中国提出建设 21 世纪海上丝绸之路的倡议,顺应时代发展潮流,具有和平、发展、合作、创新、开放等特征,它以和谐海洋为愿景,以"人海和谐、和平发展、安全便利、合作共赢"为目标,以开放创新为路径。推进 21 世纪海上丝绸之路建设,将有利于增强中国与沿线国家互信互助,打造稳定的合作环境,为丝路区域的长远稳定与繁荣发展创造新的机遇。

二、21 世纪海上丝绸之路建设面临的挑战及其海事法律体系构建的困境

(一)21 世纪海上丝绸之路建设面临的挑战

从上述分析可以看出,21 世纪海上丝绸之路是中国与沿线国家实现海运畅通、经济合作、政治合作以及文化交流的重要途径,蕴含着不可估量的发展机遇。一方面,它将促进沿线国家互信互助,加快亚太区域经济一体化进程,助力沿线国家共同构建更为紧密的命运共同体、利益共同体和责任共同体,实

---

① 刘赐贵.发展海洋合作伙伴关系推进 21 世纪海上丝绸之路建设的若干思考[J].国际问题研究,2014(4):4.

② 参见发改委、外交部与商务部联合发布的《推动共建丝绸之路经济带和 21 世纪海上丝绸之路的愿景与行动》(2015 年)。

现"一加一大于二"的互利共赢效果。① 另一方面,通过21世纪海上丝绸之路的构建,有利于促进我国参与国际规则的制定,积极应对美国主导的跨太平洋伙伴关系协议(TPP)、跨大西洋贸易与投资伙伴协议(TTIP)产生的影响,实现对区域经济贸易主导权的掌控,构建国际新秩序。但我们也应该认识到,在抓住巨大机遇的同时,21世纪海上丝绸之路建设所面临的挑战不容小觑。首先从我国自身条件分析,我国尚处于向海洋强国转型的初期阶段,软实力等内在因素仍然十分欠缺;其次从外部环境分析,沿线国家在领土主权等方面也仍然存在诸多不利于区域协同发展的争端和矛盾。② 实际上,中国要想通过实施21世纪海上丝绸之路战略建立、维持与沿线国家的合作伙伴关系,需要相应法律制度的引领、推动和保障,需要中国塑造、制定并实施相应的国际合作法律法规。因此,法律制度的设计和实施是建设21世纪海上丝绸之路的基础性问题。③

(二)构建21世纪海上丝绸之路海事法律体系的困境

构建统一的基础性法律体系并非易事。21世纪海上丝绸之路发端于中国,辐射范围涵盖东南亚、南亚、西亚、中亚和欧非地区,共涉及20多个国家和地区。沿线各国在法律文化、现行立法规定以及司法审判实践等方面不可避免地存在较大差异,这无疑加大了海上丝绸之路沿线国家之间海事法律冲突的解决难度。

目前,21世纪海上丝绸之路无论是在实体法还是在冲突法方面都没有形成统一适用的区域性海商事法律制度。这种困境形成的原因主要来源于两大层面。首先,从各国国内法的层面来看,沿线国家存在各自独立的国内法律体系,尤其在冲突规范、法律适用等实体法方面的规定各有迥异。例如,针对船舶碰撞这一侵权行为的法律适用问题,不同国家的规定就有所不同。《越南民法典》第773条规定,飞机、轮船在国际空域或国际海域造成损害的赔偿,适用飞机、轮船所属国籍国家的法律。而我国《海商法》就这一问题针对不同情况

---

① 刘赐贵.发展海洋合作伙伴关系推进21世纪海上丝绸之路建设的若干思考[J].国际问题研究,2014(4):1.

② 楼春豪.21世纪海上丝绸之路的风险与挑战[J].印度洋经济体研究,2014(5):4.

③ 韩永红,石佑启.论21世纪海上丝绸之路法律保障机制的构建[J].国际经贸探索,2015,31(10):62.

提供了多种系属公示,不仅包括船旗国法,还包括侵权行为地法和法院地法。[①] 这不仅是制度上的差异,更是在国际法基本理念等问题上的不同,其所导致的各国立法差异,会使涉外民商事纠纷的当事人在解决纠纷前进行比较,采取"择地诉讼"的战略,适用对其最有利的国家的法律,这显然不利于公平地保护各方当事人的合法利益。

其次,从国际法的层面来看,又可以从统一实体法和统一冲突法两个角度进行分析。就实体法而言,由于现有的国际海商事统一实体法公约本身在数量上就十分有限,同时又在调整对象、调整领域等方面受到限制,加之各公约的参加国也不尽相同,使得现有的国际海商事统一实体法的规范效力和作用受到了不利影响。表现为海上丝绸之路沿线各国在涉外海商事法律制度的某些具体问题上难以达成一致意见,影响构建沿线区域统一适用的区域性公约。就冲突法而言,区域性统一冲突法的缺失,使得"同案不同判"的现象愈加显著,即使海事纠纷具备相同的因素,其争议解决结果也因不同国家的法院依据不同的冲突规范所指引的准据法的不同而差异明显。这些都将极大地削弱法律的保障机能,阻碍 21 世纪海上丝绸之路的建设。[②]

三、21 世纪海上丝绸之路海运法律问题的具体表现

海运和建设 21 世纪海上丝绸之路之间具有密切的联系。一方面,近年来,我国和海上丝绸之路沿线各国之间的进出口量大幅度增长,海运在 21 世纪海上丝绸之路建设中的基础和核心地位愈加凸显。另一方面,21 世纪海上丝绸之路建设也激发了沿线各国的货物需求潜力,极大地促进了国际海运的发展。海运的实现需要船舶的承载和航运。由于作为国际海上货物运输工具的船舶经常需要来往于不同国家港口之间,而各国在海运方面的国内法规定以及加入的国际海事公约却不尽相同。因此在海上丝绸之路建设进程的加快的同时,涉外海运纠纷案件的数量也在持续攀升,沿线国家之间的海运法律冲

---

① 参见《中华人民共和国海商法》第十一章涉外关系的法律适用,第 273 条:"船舶碰撞的损害赔偿,适用侵权行为地法律。船舶在公海上发生碰撞的损害赔偿,适用受理案件的法院所在地法律。同一国籍的船舶,不论碰撞发生于何地,碰撞船舶之间的损害赔偿适用船旗国法律。"

② 佟尧,王国华.21 世纪海上丝绸之路背景下的海事法律冲突解决机制研究[J].中国海上法研究,2015(2):21.

突日益显现。

目前,国际海上运输方面重要的国际海运公约主要有《海牙规则》、《海牙—维斯比规则》、《汉堡规则》和《鹿特丹规则》,这些公约在承运人责任期间、归责原则、免责事由、单位责任限制等方面的规定存在诸多差异。虽然不同公约的规定不同,但是各国却有权决定自己加入哪个公约,适用哪种规则。有的国家选择性地加入了其中的一个公约;有的国家通过国内立法使公约国内法化;有的国家根据某个公约的基本精神,对其国内法进行了相应的修改以延续该公约的精神。在丝路区域,新加坡、菲律宾、埃及等国家均为《汉堡规则》的缔约国。而我国目前没有加入上述任何一个公约,但是现行的海商法在立法设计上同时吸纳了《海牙规则》、《海牙—维斯比规则》和《汉堡规则》的主要内容。由此可见,沿线各国因适用不同海运国际公约所造成的法律冲突在所难免。

四、解决 21 世纪海上丝绸之路海运法律问题的建议

(一)构建区域性统一适用的海事法律体系

构建区域性统一适用的海事法律体系不同于现存的《海牙规则》、《汉堡规则》等国际海运公约,在宏观层面上应涉及沿线各国广泛参与的海事海商领域的区域性公约以及被各国转化为国内法的法律规范体系;在微观层面上,应涵盖对船舶和海上运输关系当事人实体权利和义务的调整、涉外海事冲突规范以及国际海事诉讼与仲裁等规定,从而形成海商统一实体法规则与程序法规则相辅相成的区域性海事法律框架。以这种方式构建的区域性海事法律体系能够促进沿线国家海事法律制度的趋同,有利于保证跨国海事纠纷处理的确定性和可预见性。但是,构建区域性统一适用的海事法律体系绝非易事,需要从多方面综合考虑。

1.综合考量沿线不同国家的法律基础和法律文化,形成具有包容性的区域海事法律体系

21 世纪海上丝绸之路沿线国家的法律基础具有明显的差异。就我国和东盟国家的法律体系比较而言,我国是社会主义法律体系,越南的法律亦带有社会主义色彩。新加坡、马来西亚、孟加拉国基本属于英美法系,因而其法律

体系受到了英美法系的影响,其海事法律原则多体现在判例当中。[①] 印度尼西亚、泰国、老挝一般认为属于大陆法系。另外,部分东盟国家的立法也受到了宗教传统的影响,如马来西亚、文莱的伊斯兰法律,泰国、缅甸的佛教法律等。因此,在构建区域性海事法律体系的过程中,必须充分考虑沿线国家不同的法律基础和法律传统文化,建立"和而不同"的具有包容性的法律体系。在这一过程中,我国作为 21 世纪海上丝绸之路的倡导国和起点国家,应该充分发挥主导性作用,在组织专家学者深入研究和比较分析不同国家法律基础和文化的前提下,同沿线各国共同建立区域性公约起草专门法律机构。在编纂区域性海事法律制度时,首先将各国具有共性的海运法律规范吸收进区域性海事法律体系当中。其次对于各国分歧较大的其他海运法律规范可以采取磋商或谈判的方式,选择符合 21 世纪海上丝绸之路实际情况的最先进、被各国普遍接受的法律原则和规范作为区域性海事法律制度的内容。

2.纳入区域性统一适用的涉外海事冲突规范和海事司法管辖权冲突协调解决机制[②]

正如上文提到的,海上丝绸之路沿线国家的法律制度存在不同程度的差异性,涉外海事冲突规范的不同,使得不同国家即使面对相同的涉外海事法律关系也会因所援引的准据法有差异而做出差异化的裁决。因此,有必要设计一套在海上丝绸之路区域内统一适用的涉外海事冲突规范,避免"同案不同判"的现象频繁出现,实现法律"定纷止争"的权威性。

当然,在统一适用的涉外海事冲突规范下,也有可能发生海事司法管辖权冲突。海事司法管辖权冲突包括积极冲突和消极冲突。在 21 世纪海上丝绸之路海运法律领域,比较常见的是海事司法管辖权的积极冲突,即涉外海运法律纠纷所涉及的两个或两个以上沿线国家均主张其对案件享有管辖权。结合目前国际海运法律冲突解决的实践,以及国际通行的司法管辖权冲突解决原则,可以考虑采用以下原则处理海事司法管辖权冲突:

(1)尊重当事人意思自治原则。即若涉外海运法律纠纷的当事人达成合意,选择某一法院对案件行使管辖权,则应将案件提交该法院管辖。

(2)尊重沿线国家的专属管辖权。即若根据某一沿线国家的法律,该涉外

----

① 申华林.东盟国家法律概论[M].南宁:广西民族出版社,2004:2.

② 李仁达,邹立刚.中国—东盟共建新海上丝绸之路法律机制研究[J].中国海商法研究,2015(3):11.

海运法律纠纷属其国内专属管辖的案件类型，如涉及公共秩序保留等，则案件应移交该国法院管辖。但若出现多国均拥有专属管辖权的情况时，则可以考虑适用最先受理的法院行使管辖权的原则。

（3）遵循一事不再理原则。即若一国法院已经对某一涉外海运纠纷案件进行了审理并作出了生效判决，则该案当事人不得就同一诉讼请求再次进行诉讼或仲裁，他国法院也不应对该案再次立案管辖。

（4）合理援引"不方便法院"原则。"不方便法院"原则是指，若拥有管辖权的一国法院认为其行使管辖权对当事人及案件的审理均极不方便，且有其他法院对该诉讼的审理更为方便时，可以将案件交由其他更为方便的法院审理。① "不方便法院"原则的目的，是为了找到司法公正的法院，并且在该法院进行该诉讼更有把握实现司法公正。

（二）建立多元化海商事纠纷解决机制

1. 现有的国际或区域海事争端解决机制与创新的海上丝绸之路沿线区域统一海商事争端解决机制相结合

构建 21 世纪海上丝绸之路沿线区域内的海事争端解决机制并非从零开始。目前，无论是从国际层面还是在沿线区域内部都已经存在一定的海事纠纷解决机构和制度。从国际层面来看，国际海洋法法庭和国际法院是目前解决国际海事争端的主要组织和机构，但在解决私人主体之间的涉外海商事争端方面则具有较大的局限性。从区域层面来看，中国已通过自由贸易协定（FTA）或双边投资协定（BIT）同海上丝绸之路沿线多国建立了涵盖海商事纠纷解决的争端解决机制。例如，中国已同东盟十国建立了自由贸易区，形成了缔约国争端解决条款②和投资者—缔约国争端解决条款③相结合的争端解决机制。但这种争端解决机制仅具有双向适用性，不同 FTA 或 BIT 的争端解决条款也会存在一定差异，对于区域内多边海事法律冲突仍然无能为力。

因此，有必要在保留现有的国际和区域争端解决机制，继续遵守国际海商事法律基本原则和基本制度的前提下，创新性地建立海上丝绸之路沿线区域国家统一适用的涉外海商事争端解决机制，制定海上丝绸之路沿线区域海商

---

① 参见《中华人民共和国国际私法示范法》第 51 条。

② 参见《中国—东盟全面经济合作框架协议争端解决机制协议》。

③ 参见《中国—东盟全面经济合作框架协议投资协议》第 14 条缔约方与投资者间争端解决。

事争端解决协议,统一沿线国家解决区域内海商事法律冲突的程序法律依据;设立常设的争端解决机构或中心,保障争端解决程序的顺利进行,提高争端解决的效率。

2.海事仲裁与海事审判相结合

一般来说,国际争端解决机制并非仅涵盖单一的争端解决方式,通常允许争端当事人在多种方式中进行选择。海上丝绸之路沿线区域的争端解决机制也应如此。具体来说,建议可以进行如下安排:

(1)允许当事人在对涉外海商事案件有管辖权国内法院寻求当地救济,但不将"用尽当地救济"作为当事人寻求其他救济方式的前提条件。

(2)允许当事人选择相应的国际仲裁机构或国际审判机构解决涉外海商事争端。

(3)在建立海上丝绸之路沿线区域内常设争端解决机构或中心(诉讼或仲裁)的前提下,允许当事人将涉外海商事争端诉诸该常设机构寻求救济。

(三)创新沿线国家之间的海事司法协助机制

随着21世纪海上丝绸之路建设进程的加速,沿线国家之间的交流也愈加频繁,涉外海商事案件不断体现出新的时代特点,对海事司法协助也提出了新的要求。妥善、及时、公平地处理涉外海商事纠纷,既关系到涉案当事人的切身利益,也关系到沿线国家的司法公信力。消极、滞后的海事司法协助体系会阻碍海上丝绸之路沿线国家海商事法律纠纷的解决成效,甚至阻碍海上丝绸之路的建设进程。因此,有必要在21世纪海上丝绸之路沿线区域内创新性地构建统一、高效、便捷的海事司法协助机制。

具体来说,海事司法协助主要包括域外海事司法文书送达、域外调查取证、传唤涉案外籍当事人、涉案域外财产保全、外国判决和仲裁裁决的承认与执行等。中国应该加强同沿线各国的海事司法协助,积极缔结双边或多边海事司法协助协定。同时倡导沿线各国广泛参与,逐步构建海上丝绸之路沿线区域统一适用的海事司法协助制度。

(四)修改完善我国《海商法》,做好国内法的配套升级

21世纪海上丝绸之路海事法律体系需要国内法的有力支撑。上文提到,我国目前的《海商法》是结合了《海牙规则》、《海牙—维斯比规则》和《汉堡规则》三者的产物,但随着国际海上运输领域的飞速发展,目前《海商法》的许多规定都呈现出了一定的被动性和滞后性。因此,亟需修改完善《海商法》及配

套法律法规的规定，顺应国际海商法立法的潮流，吸收国外有益的海商法经验，逐步趋与国际先进的海商法律制度接轨。

(五)加强综合型法律人才的培养

正如上文提到的，21世纪海上丝绸之路沿线国家的法律基础和法律文化存在显著差异，在宗教文化方面也各有特点，加之各国天然的语言差别等，使沿线各国在沟通与信息交流方面存在一定的障碍，在很大程度上束缚21世纪海上丝绸之路建设的有序推进。因此需要我国充分发挥主导作用，积极开展中国与沿线国家法律的比较研究，并结合21世纪海上丝绸之路建设的实际需要，针对特定领域设立定向培训基地并提供专业且充足的培训条件，培养既具有专业法律素养和水平，同时又熟知沿线国家法律制度、法律文化，并了解中国同沿线国家海运领域来往内容(如对外贸易、海上运输知识)的综合性涉外法律人才。另外，中国也可以同沿线国家增进涉外法律人才培养合作。如签署双向涉外法律人才培养协议，加强双边和多边进修、访问、留学等相关专向法律人才培养计划[①]；定期开展学术交流活动，举办沿线国家法律研讨会、学术论坛等。

五、结语

建设21世纪海上丝绸之路是深化中国与亚非欧国家地区间合作、打造命运共同体、利益共同体和责任共同体的重要战略构想。从海运贸易角度来看，由于沿线国家的海事法律各有不同，且海上丝绸之路沿线区域尚缺失配套的区域性统一海商实体法以及海事冲突法律制度，使21世纪海上丝绸之路的建设在海运领域问题频发，面临着巨大的法律风险和挑战。中国作为21世纪海上丝绸之路的倡导国家，应该充分发挥主导作用，在进一步完善中国与沿线各国间法律协调机制的基础上，努力同沿线国家一道创设区域性统一适用的海商海运法律体系，培养综合型法律人才，为21世纪海上丝绸之路的建设提供坚实的海运法律保障。

---

① 李仁达，邹立刚.中国—东盟共建新海上丝绸之路法律机制研究[J].中国海商法研究，2015(3):12.

参考文献

[1]习近平主席在印尼国会发表重要演讲[N].新华网,2013-10-03.

http://www.xinhuanet.com/world/xjpynghyj/wz.htm.

[2]中共十八届三中全会关于全面深化改革若干重大问题的决定[R].2013-11-12.

http://news.xinhuanet.com/2013-11/15/c_118164235.htm.

[3]李克强总理作政府工作报告[R].2014-03-05.

http://www.gov.cn/zhuanti/2014gzbg_yw.htm.

[4]努力建设和平、合作、和谐之海——李克强总理在中希海洋合作论坛上的讲话[N].2014-06-20.

http://news.xinhuanet.com/politics/2014-06/21/c_126651068.htm.

[5]推动共建丝绸之路经济带和21世纪海上丝绸之路的愿景与行动(2015年第一版)[R].2015-03-28.

http://www.fmprc.gov.cn/ce/cevn/chn/sghkt/t1251121.htm.

[6]刘赐贵.发展海洋合作伙伴关系推进21世纪海上丝绸之路建设的若干思考[J].国际问题研究,2014(4):4.

[7]楼春豪.21世纪海上丝绸之路的风险与挑战[J].印度洋经济体研究,2014(5):4.

[8]韩永红,石佑启.论21世纪海上丝绸之路法律保障机制的构建[J].国际经贸探索(International Economics and Trade Research),2015,31(10):62.

[9]佟尧,王国华.21世纪海上丝绸之路背景下的海事法律冲突解决机制研究[J].中国海上法研究,2015(2):21.

[10]屈广清.海事法律冲突的新理论[M].北京:人民出版社,2013:119.

[11]申华林.东盟国家法律概论[M].南宁:广西民族出版社,2004:2.

[12]李仁达,邹立刚.中国—东盟共建新海上丝绸之路法律机制研究[J],中国海商法研究,2015(3):12.

[13]袁利华."丝绸之路经济带"次区域经济合作法律保障探析[J].兰州商学院学报,2014,30(4):32-35.

Study on the Legal Issues of Maritime Transportation Under the Background of the 21st-Century Maritime Silk Road

Zhang Xiaojun *, Wang Yuren**

Abstract　The construction of the 21st-Century Maritime Silk Road is a process of pluralistic, open and pragmatic cooperation. China and other countries along the road will jointly center on economic cooperation, take care of all parties concerned, and promote the construction of the road under the use of the existing cooperation mechanisms and platforms. Jointly building the 21st-century Maritime Silk Road is in the interest of the world community. Reflecting the common ideals of human societies, it is a positive endeavor to seek new models of international cooperation and global governance, and will inject new positive energy into world peace and development. Maritime transportation is the basis and core of the 21st-century Maritime Silk Road. However, in terms of international maritime transportation practice currently, the economic system, traditional legal culture, current legislation, judicial practice as well as legal system of maritime affairs involving foreign elements vary from country to country inevitably. There is no doubt that this kind of situation will increase the difficulty of settling the conflicts of maritime transport law between the countries along the 21st-century Maritime Silk Road. Hence, in order to create a

---

　＊　The Secretary-General of China-ASEAN law Research Centre, Dean of International Law School, SWUPL.

　＊＊　Postgraduate of International Law School, SWUPL.

solid legal safeguard of maritime transportation under the construction of the 21st-century Maritime Silk Road, China needs to play the leading role to promote the common consultation and mutual learning with other countries, and make every effort to build a regional unified maritime transport legal system.

Keywords: the 21st-Century Maritime Silk Road; maritime transportation; conflicts of law; regional maritime transport legal system

I. THE PROPOSAL AND NECESSITY OF THE CONSTRUCTION OF THE 21st-CENTURY MARITIME SILK ROAD

In October 3, 2013, Jakarta, the capital of Indonesia, Xi Jinping, Chairman of China, expressed in his speech that "China will strengthen the maritime cooperation with the ASEAN countries and make good use of the China-ASEAN Fund on Maritime Cooperation established by the Chinese Government to develop a good partnership on maritime affairs and jointly build the 21st-century Maritime Silk Road". [1] His speech for the construction of the 21st-century Maritime Silk Road pointed out the way forward. Strengthening the maritime cooperation is a priority field and key task of the construction of 21st-century Maritime Silk Road, which has a fundamentality and demonstration effect. On November 12, 2013, the 3rd Plenary Session of the 18th CPC Central Committee passed "The Decision on Some Major Issues Concerning Comprehensively Deepening the Reform" to propose "speeding up the construction of infrastructure connectivity with surrounding countries and regions and accelerating the construction of the Silk Road Economic Belt and the Maritime Silk Road, to form a new all-round opening-up pattern." [2] During the National People's Congress the Chinese Political Consultative Conference (NPC&CPPCC) in 2014, Li

---

① See *Chairman of China, Xi Jinping delivered speech in Indonesian Parliament*, China Daily, 3, October 2013.

② See *The Decision on Some Major Issues Concerning Comprehensively Deepening the Reform*, adopted at the Third Plenary Session of the 18th Central Committee of the Communist Party of China on November 12, 2013.

Keqiang, Premier of the State Council presented "Report on the Work of the Government", "We'll keep holding high the banner of peaceful development and win-win cooperation; intensify the planning and construction of the Silk Road Economic Belt and the 21st-century Maritime Silk Road; promote the construction of the Bangladesh-China-India-Myanmar Economic Corridor and the China-Pakistan Economic Corridor as well as launch a number of major support projects to speed up infrastructure connectivity". [1] In June 20, 2014, Li Keqiang, Premier of the State Council presented at the China-Greece Maritime Cooperation Forum that "We stand ready to work with other countries to boost economic growth, deepen international cooperation and promote world peace through the ocean and to foster peace, cooperation and harmony in the ocean". [2] In November, Beijing hosted the 2014 Asia-Pacific Economic Cooperation conference from Nov 5 to 12, which aimed at building the Asia-Pacific Partnership for the future. During the conference, Chinese Government illustrated the claims of speeding up the Asia-Pacific area's connectivity and constructing the "One Belt One Road", as well as opening new propositions on setting up the fund of Silk Road and the construction of the Asian Infrastructure Investment Bank. In March 28, 2015, the National Development and Reform Commission, Ministry of Foreign Affairs, and Ministry of Commerce of the People's Republic of China, with State Council authorization issued the "Vision and Actions on Jointly Building Silk Road Economic Belt and 21st-Century Maritime Silk Road", which showed that the issue of constructing the Maritime Silk Road had risen to national

---

① See *Report on the Work of the Government*, delivered at the Second Session of the Twelfth National People's Congress on March 5, 2014, by Li Keqiang, Premier of the State Council.

② See *For Peace, Cooperation and Harmony in the Ocean—Remarks at the China-Greece Maritime Cooperation Forum*, by H. E. Li Keqiang, Premier of the State Council of the People's Republic of China, Athens, 20, June 2014.

strategic level and had been incorporated in the top-level design. ①

The construction of the 21st-Century Maritime Silk Road is a process of
pluralistic, open and pragmatic cooperation which involves more than 20
countries and regions. It centers on economic cooperation, takes care of all
parties concerned, and be promoted jointly by China and the countries along
the road under the use of the existing cooperation mechanisms and
platforms. In fact, the area along the 21st-century Maritime Silk Road is
complex in the geopolitical relationship and the notion of the national scale,
interest demand, historical tradition, national religion, language culture and
so on other aspects vary from country to country. Hence, the 21st-century
Maritime Silk Road must be constructed based on the above differences,
contain the different needs of different countries, take care of the different
characteristics of different countries and innovate cooperation modes at the
same time to alignment and consolidate cooperation basis②.

The conception of the 21st-century Maritime Silk Road attracted the
world's attention upon its first announcement. Putin, President of Russia,
Rajapaksa, President of Sri Lanka, Singh, Former Prime Minister of India,
Nawaz Sharif, Prime Minister of Pakistan, Najib, Prime Minister of
Malaysia, Thongsing Thammavong, Prime Minister of Laos, Papoulias,
President of Greece and other politicians all agreed to participate the
construction of the 21st-century Maritime Silk Road actively. Xi Jinping,
Chairman of China, delivered speeches about building the 21st-century
Maritime Silk Road on many occasions. These speeches contained the basic
contents of the 21st-century Maritime Silk Road, including strengthening
policy communication, road connection, trade smoothness, currency
circulation, and popular support. Policy communication aims at strengthening

---

① See *Vision and Actions on Jointly Building Silk Road Economic Belt and 21st-Century Maritime Silk Road*, issued by the National Development and Reform
Commission, Ministry of Foreign Affairs, and Ministry of Commerce of the People's
Republic of China, with State Council authorization, 28, March 2015. (First Edition 2015)

② See Cigui Liu, *Some Thoughts on Developing Maritime Partnership Cooperation
and Promoting the Construction of the 21st-Century Maritime Silk Road*, International
Studies, No. 4, 2014, at p4.

friendly exchanges. Road connection aims at enhancing road connection. Trade smoothness aims at strengthening commercial intercourse and industrial investment. Currency circulation aims at promoting the flow of capital. Popular support aims at strengthening cultural exchanges. [1] These contents, in line with the regional economical and social reality along the Silk Road, not only indicate the target, but also clear the way. They are not only the summaries of history, but also the guidelines of the future.

China's initiative to jointly build the 21st-century Maritime Silk Road, with the characteristic of peace, development, cooperation, innovation and open, keeps up with the trend of modern development and embraces the trend towards a multipolar world, economic globalization, cultural divers greater IT application. It designed to uphold the global free trade regime and the open world economy in the spirit of open regional cooperation. It is aimed at promoting orderly and free flow of economic factors, highly efficient allocation of resources and deep integration of markets; encouraging the countries along the 21st-century Maritime Silk Road to achieve economic policy coordination and carry out broader and more in-depth regional cooperation of higher standards; and jointly creating an open, inclusive and balanced regional economic cooperation architecture that benefits all. Jointly building the 21st-century Maritime Silk Road is in the interest of the world community. Reflecting the common ideals of human societies, it is a positive endeavor to seek new models of international cooperation and global governance, and will inject new positive energy into world peace and development.

---

[1] See *Vision and Actions on Jointly Building Silk Road Economic Belt and 21st-Century Maritime Silk Road*, issued by the National Development and Reform Commission, Ministry of Foreign Affairs, and Ministry of Commerce of the People's Republic of China, with State Council authorization, 28, March 2015. (First Edition 2015)

II. THE CHALLENGE FOR THE CONSTRUCTION OF THE 21st-CENTURY MARITIME SILK ROAD AND THE PRESENT DILEMMA OF ESTABLISHING ITS MARITIME LEGAL SYSTEM

A. The Challenge For the Construction of the 21st-Century Maritime Silk Road

As can be seen from the above analysis, the 21st-century Maritime Silk Road is an important way by which China can realize smooth maritime transportation, economic cooperation, political cooperation and culture exchange with most countries along the route. It contains immeasurable development opportunities. On the one hand, it will promote countries along the Road to trust and help each other, to accelerate the process of economic integration in the Asia-Pacific region, to jointly build more closely a community of destiny, a community of interests, and a community in responsibility, and finally to achieve the mutually beneficial and win-win results which have an effect of "one plus one is greater than two". [1] On the other hand, the construction of the 21st-century Maritime Silk Road is beneficial for China to actively cope with the effects from TPP & TTIP. In the meanwhile, it can also promote China to participate in the formulation of international rules, to realize the control of regional economic and trade leadership, and then to build a new international order. However, we should also recognize that, at the same time of seizing those huge opportunities, the challenges exist in constructing the 21st-century Maritime Silk Road shall never be little account of. First of all, from the analysis of country's own conditions, China is still at the early stage of the transition to the Maritime Power and still lacks internal factors such as soft power. Secondly, from the analysis of external environment, among countries along the Road still exist many disputes and contradictions about

---

[1] See Cigui Liu, *Some Thoughts on Developing Maritime Partnership Cooperation and Promoting the Construction of the 21st-Century Maritime Silk Road*, International Studies, No. 4, 2014, at p1.

national sovereignty and so on,which is bad for regional cooperative development. [1] In fact, if China want to build and maintain the partnership cooperation with countries along through the construction of the 21st-century Maritime Silk Road,it needs legal system to lead,to promote and to safeguard the construction. It also requires China to shape, formulate and implement relevant international rules. Therefore，the design and implementation of the legal system is the fundamental issues of constructing the 21st-century Maritime Silk Road. [2]

B. The Present Dilemma of Establishing the Maritime Legal System of the 21st-Century Maritime Silk Road

It is not easy to establish a basic legalsystem. The 21st-century Maritime Silk Road originates in China,its radiant scope covers Southeast Asia,South Asia,West Asia,Central Asia,some African areas and Europe regions,which encompasses more than 20 countries and regions. The legal culture, current legislation,judicial practice as well as legal system of maritime affairs involving foreign elements vary from country to country inevitably. There is no doubt that this kind of situation will increase the difficulty of settling the conflicts of maritime law between the countries along the 21st-century Maritime Silk Road.

At present, the 21st-century Maritime Silk Road doesn't form any maritime legal system， which can be applied to this region uniformly,no matter in the aspect of substantive law or conflict law. The causes of this dilemma mainly come from two level. In the first place,from the countries' domestic law level,countries along have formed their independent domestic legal system,the difference exists in the rules of the conflict law and the application of laws in particular. For instance,in terms of application of law of infringing act which refers to collision of ships, different country has

---

[1] See Chunhao Lou, *The Risks and Challenges of Maritime Silk Road*, International Ocean Economic and Political Review,No. 5,2014,at p4.

[2] See Yonghong Han, Youqi Shi, *The Construction of the Legal Safeguard Mechanism of the 21st-Century Maritime Silk Road*. International Economics and Trade Research,Vol. 31,No. 10,Oct. 2015,at p62.

different rules. The *Vietnam Civil Code*, Article 773 provides that, the compensation for damages caused by planes and ships in total the airspace or international waters, shall apply to the nationality law of the country which the planes and ships belong to. But in *Maritime Code of the People's Republic of China*, there are different formula of attribution applies to different situation of infringing act which only refers to collision of ships. Namely, the formula of attribution here not only refers to the law of the flag State, but also contains the law of the place where the infringing act is committed and the law of the place where the court hearing the case is located. ①This is not only the legal system difference, but even also the difference in the basic idea of international law. The difference in countries' legislation will make the parties of a foreign-related civil and commercial dispute take the strategy of "Forum Shopping" and select the most beneficial law to apply, which will be obviously partial to protect the interests of all parties.

In the second place, from the international law level, it can be analyzed from two aspects, namely, unified substantive law and unified conflict law. In terms of the substantive law, the number of existing international maritime conventions on unified substantive law is very limited itself, and these existing conventions are limited in the adjustment object, regulative sphere and so on at the same time. In addition, Members of these conventions are different. These causes have produced negative impacts on the normative force of the existing international maritime conventions on unified substantive law. The negative impacts could be manifested as divergence of views on many specific issues of foreign-related maritime law rules between countries along the 21st-century Maritime Silk Road, and might influence the establishment of regional unified convention along the Road. In terms of the

---

① See *Maritime Code of the People's Republic of China*, Article 273: "The law of the place where the infringing act is committed shall apply to claims for damages arising from collision of ships. The law of the place where the court hearing the case is located shall apply to claims for damages arising from collision of ships on the high ses. If the colliding ships belong to the same country, no matter where the collision occurs, the law of the flag State shall apply to claims against one another for damages arising from such collision. "

conflict law, the absence of the unified regional conflict law makes the phenomena of "The same case with different decisions" more and more remarkable. Even if maritime disputes have the same elements, the dispute solution results might have discrepancy, because the courts of different countries will apply to different applicable law which is guided by different conflicts rules. All these will weaken the safeguard function of law to a large extent, and will hinder the construction of the 21st-century Maritime Silk Road. [①]

Ⅲ. CONCRETE MANIFESTATION IN LEGAL ISSUES OF MARITIME TRANSPORTATION OF THE 21st-CENTURY MARITIME SILK ROAD

There is a close contact between maritime transportation and the construction of the 21st-century Maritime Silk Road. On the one hand, in recent years, the import and export volume between China and other countries along is increasing by a big margin, and the basic and core position of maritime transportation in the construction of the 21st-century Maritime Silk Road is more and more highlighted. On the other hand, the construction of the 21st-century Maritime Silk Road also has stimulated the potential demands of goods of the countries along, which greatly promotes the development of international maritime transportation. The realization of maritime transportation needs the load bearing and shipping of vessels. As a result of, vessels, which as the means of international transport by sea, often need to sail between the ports of different countries, and countries' domestic regulations on maritime transportation and the international conventions which countries had joined into are different as well. Hence, with the speeding up of the construction process, the number of the disputes about

---

① See Yao Tong, Guohua Wang. *Study on the Resolution Mechanism of Maritime Law Conflicts Under the Background of the 21st-Century Maritime Silk Road*. Chinese Journal of Maritime Law, Vol. 26, No. 2, Jun. 2015, at p19.

maritime transportation involving foreign elements continues to rise, and the
legal conflicts of maritime transportation between countries along are prominent
day by day.

Currently, important international conventions for maritime transportation
mainly refer to the *Hague Rules*, the *Hague-Visby Rules*, the *Hamburg Rules* and
the *Rotterdam Rules*. These conventions are different in period of responsibility of
carrier, doctrine of liability fixation, exemptions, package limitation and so
on. Although different convention has its different rules, every country has
its right to decide which convention to join and to select which rules to obey.
Some countries selectively joined one of these conventions, and some
countries chose to make one of these conventions or at least several rules of
these conventions become domestic law through domestic legislation or a-
mendment of domestic laws. In the region of the 21st-century Maritime Silk
Road, Singapore, Philippines, Egypt and so on had become the contracting
party of the *Hamburg Rules*. China haven't joined any of the above
conventions until now, but the legislative design of the *Maritime Code of the
People's Republic of China* absorbed the contents of the *Hague Rules*, the
Hague-Visby Rules, and the *Hamburg Rules* at the same time. Thus it can
be seen that it is inevitable to cause conflicts of law as a result of applying
different international maritime transportation conventions.

IV. SUGGESTIONS ON SOLVING THE LEGAL ISSUES OF MARITIME TRANSPORTATION OF THE 21st-CENTURY MARITIME SILK ROAD

A. To Build A Regional Maritime Legal System Uniformly

A regional maritime legal system which could be applied uniformly is
different from the existing international maritime transport conventions such
as the *Hague Rules*, the *Hamburg Rules* and so on. On the macro level, it
shall involve both the regional conventions on maritime affairs which the
countries along participate widely, and these countries' domestic legal system
that converted from the international conventions. On the micro level, it shall
encompass adjustments to parties' entity rights and obligations relating to

the ship and maritime transportation relationship, conflict rules of foreign-related maritime legal relationship, the international maritime litigation and arbitration rules etc. to formulate the regional legal framework which synthesizes both substantive law and procedural law. The regional maritime legal system that is built in this way will promote the convergence of the maritime legal system of countries along, and benefit for guaranteeing the certainty and predictability of handling international maritime disputes. However, there is no easy to build such a regional unified maritime legal system. It needs to be considered in several ways.

1. Considering the legal basis and legal culture in different countries comprehensively to form a inclusive regional maritime legal system

The legal basis of countries along the 21st-century Maritime Silk Road have obvious difference. In terms of the comparison between China's legal system and ASEAN countries' legal system, the legal system of China is the system of socialist laws, and Vietnam's law also has a characteristic of socialist law. The legal systems of Singapore, Malaysia, Bangladesh etc. are common law system, so their maritime legal principles usually reflect in precedents. [①]The legal system of Indonesia, Thailand, Laos etc. belong to civil law system. In addition, legislation of some ASEAN countries are also influenced by religious tradition. For example, Malaysia, Brunei have Islamic laws, and Thailand, Burma have Buddhist laws. Hence, in the process of building the regional maritime legal system, we must fully consider the different legal basis and the legal culture of countries along to build a inclusive legal system "harmony in diversity". As a starting point of the 21st-century Maritime Silk Road, China shall play a leading role in organizing experts and scholars to study and analysis different legal basis and legal culture, and in setting up a law of agency to draft the regional convention with other countries along the Road. When compiling regional maritime legal system, we can absorb countries' maritime transport legal rules which have

---

① See Hualin Shen. Introduction to the Law of ASEAN Countries. Nanning, Guangxi Nationalities Publishing House, 2004:2.

some in common in the regional maritime legal system at first. For the large divergence in other maritime transport rules, we can take the ways of consultations or negotiations, and finally select the most advanced legal principles and norms which are accepted by countries and consist with the actual situation of the 21st-century Maritime Silk Road, to be the contents of the regional maritime legal system.

2. Bring into regional unified conflict rules of foreign-related maritime legal relationship and judicial settlement mechanism of jurisdiction conflicts on maritime affairs[①]

As mentioned above, there are different laws among countries along the Maritime Silk Road. Because of the differences in foreign-related maritime conflict rules, different country will quote different proper law and make differentiated verdicts even in the face of the same foreign-related maritime legal relationship. Therefore, it is necessary to design a regional unified conflict rules on foreign-related maritime affairs, which will contribute to avoid the phenomena of different verdicts under the same legal nexus and to fulfill the legal authority of ending disputes.

Without doubt that there are also maritime jurisdiction conflicts even under the unified foreign-related maritime conflictrules. Jurisdiction conflicts on maritime affairs include positive conflicts and negative conflicts. Under the background of the 21st-century Maritime Silk Road, the positive jurisdiction conflicts on maritime affairs are more common. Namely, two or more than two countries involved in the foreign-related maritime transport disputes are claiming it has jurisdiction over the case. In combination with the practice of dispute settlement of international maritime transport conflicts and the internationally accepted principles of jurisdiction conflicts resolution, we can consider to adopt the following principles to deal with the jurisdiction conflicts on maritime affairs:

---

① See Renda Li, Ligang Zou. A Study on the Legal Mechanism For the Co-construction of the New Maritime Silk Road by China and ASEAN. Chinese Journal of Maritime Law. Vol. 26, No. 1, Mar. 2015:11.

（1）Respect for the principle of party autonomy. Namely, if the parties of foreign-related maritime transport disputes have reached on an agreement and chose a court of one country to exercise the jurisdiction over the case, the case shall be submitted to such court of jurisdiction.

（2）Respect for the exclusive jurisdiction of the countries along the Road. Namely, if according to the law of a country, such foreign-related maritime transport disputes fall within the exclusive jurisdiction of the courts in this country, such as cases referring to reservation of public order, etc. such cases shall be handed over to the jurisdiction of the courts of this country. However, if more than one country has exclusive jurisdiction in the case, the principle of First-seized could be considered to decide which court to exercise jurisdiction.

（3）Follow the principle of non bis in idem. Namely, if a country's court have trialed the foreign-related maritime transport dispute and made an effective judgment, parties of such disputes shall not institute any litigation or arbitration in terms of the same cause of action, and the courts of other countries shall not accept such case again.

（4）Quote the principle of "Forum Non Convenience" reasonably. Namely, if a court of one country which has the jurisdiction over the case think it is inconvenient for both the parties and the case to trial, and there is other court more convenient for trialing such case, it could transfer the case to such convenient court.[1] The object, under the words "forum non convenience" is to find that forum which is the more suitable for the ends of justice, and is preferable because pursuit of the litigation in that forum is more likely to secure these ends.

B. To Establish Diversified Maritime Dispute Settlement Mechanism

1. The existing international or regional maritime dispute settlement mechanism combined with the innovation of regional unified maritime dispute settlement mechanism of the Maritime Silk Road

---

[1]　See *Demonstration Law of Private International Law of the People's Republic of China*, Article 51.

Building the regional unified maritime dispute settlement mechanism of
the 21st-century Maritime Silk Road is not starting form scratch. Up till the
present moment, there are certain maritime dispute settlement mechanism
and legal systems both from the international level and within the area along
the Road. From the international level, the International Tribunal for the
Law of the Sea(ITLOS) and the International Court of Justice(ICJ) are main
organizations and institutions to solve international maritime disputes
currently, but there are limitations when they solve foreign-related maritime
disputes between private parties. From the regional level, China has
established some kind of dispute settlement mechanism covering maritime
affairs with many countries along the Maritime Silk Road through Free
Trade Agreement (FTA) and Bilateral Investment Treaty (BIT). For
example, China has established FTA with ASTAN countries, and designed
the dispute settlement mechanism which is the combination of disputes
between parties[1] and investment disputes between a party and an investor[2].
But this kind of dispute settlement mechanism only has a two-way
applicability. In addition, different FTA or BIT has different dispute
settlement clauses to some extent. As a result, this kind of dispute
settlement mechanism is still powerless for regional multilateral maritime
conflict of laws.

Therefore, it is necessary to establish a regional unified maritime dispute
settlement mechanism of the Maritime Silk Road under the premise of
reserving the existing international and regional dispute settlement
mechanism and keeping on obeying the basic legal principle and legal system
of international maritime laws. It contains drawing up the regional maritime
dispute settlement agreement in Maritime Silk Road area to unify the

---

① See the *Agreement on Dispute Settlement Mechanism of the Framework
Agreement on Comprehensive Economic Co-Operation Between the People's Republic of
China and the Association of Southeast Asian Nations*.

② See *Agreement on Investment of the Framework Agreement on Comprehensive
Economic Co-Operation Between the People's Republic of China and the Association of
Southeast Asian Nations*, Article14[Investment Dispute between a Party and an Investor].

procedural law of countries along the Road in solving regional maritime law conflicts; setting up a permanent dispute settlement body or center to ensure the smooth operation of the dispute settlement procedure and to improve the efficiency of dispute settlement.

2. Maritime arbitration combined with maritime trial

Ingeneral, international dispute settlement mechanism rather than covers the single dispute resolution, it usually allows the parties of disputes to choose in a variety of ways. The dispute settlement mechanism of the Maritime Silk Road shall also be designed in this way. Specifically, it can be arranged as follows:

(1) Allow the parties to look for local relief in domestic courts which have the jurisdiction for foreign-related maritimeaffairs. But the "exhaustion of local remedies" is not the premise of the parties to seek other remedy;

(2) Allow the parties to choose international arbitration institution or international justice institution to solve foreign-related maritime disputes;

(3) Allow the parties to look for relief (in the way of litigation or arbitration) of foreign-related maritime disputes in standing body under the premise of establishing the regional standing dispute settlement body or center of the Maritime Silk Road.

C. To Innovate the Maritime Judicial Assistance Mechanism Between Countries Along the 21st-Century Maritime Silk Road

As the acceleration of the construction process of the 21st-century Maritime Silk Road, the interaction between countries along the road is increasingly frequent. In addition, cases of foreign-related maritime affairs continually reflect the characteristics of the new era, which bring up new demands for maritime judicial assistance. How to handling foreign-related maritime dispute properly, timely and impartially, not only concerns the vital interests of the parties involved, but also concerns the public credibility of the judiciary of the countries along the Road. The maritime judicial assistance system which is negative and lagging will hinder the solution effect of maritime legal disputes, and will even impede the construction process of the 21st-century Maritime Silk Road. Hence, it is necessary to build a maritime judicial assistance mechanism, which is unified, high-efficiency and convenient.

To bespecific, maritime judicial assistance refers to extraterritorial
service of maritime judicial documents, extraterritorial investigation and
evidence collection, summon foreign parties, extraterritorial property
preservation, recognition and enforcement for judgment and awards of
foreign court, recognition and enforcement of foreign arbitration award and
so on. China shall strengthen the maritime judicial assistance with countries
along the Road by negotiating bilateral or multilateral agreement of maritime
judicial assistance energetically. In the meanwhile, China shall advocate the
broad participation of countries, and build the maritime judicial assistance
system which is unified in the area of the Maritime Silk Road step by step.

**D. To Modify and Perfect the *Maritime Code of the People's Republic of
China*, and To Update the Other Domestic Laws**

Maritime legal system of the 21st-century Maritime Silk Road needs the
strong support of domestic laws. As mentioned above, the *Maritime Code
of the People's Republic of China* absorbed the contents of the *Hague
Rules*, the *Hague-Visby Rules*, and the *Hamburg Rules* at the same time.
But with the rapid development of international maritime transport sector,
many rules of the *Maritime Code of the People's Republic of China*
currently have appeared the passivity and hysteresis quality to some extent.
Therefore, it urgent needs to modify and perfect the *Maritime Code of the
People's Republic of China* and other set of laws and regulations, which will
keep up with the trend of the legislation of international maritime laws,
absorb foreign beneficial experience in maritime law, and conform with the
most advanced maritime legal institutions around the world stage by stage.

E. To Strengthen the Cultivation of Comprehensive Legal Talent

As mentioned above, there are obvious divergence in legal basis and
legal culture, among the countries along the 21st-century Maritime Silk
Road. In the aspect of religious culture, they also have their own
characteristics. All these differences combined with the different language in
nature, constitute the obstacles in communication and information exchange
between countries, which constraint the building process of the 21st-century
Maritime Silk Road. Therefore, China needs to play the leading role and to

carry out the comparative study of laws. In the meanwhile, combined with the practical need of constructing the 21st-century Maritime Silk Road, China needs to set up training bases for a special field and provide professional training conditions in order to cultivate comprehensive foreign-related legal talents that both have professional legal accomplishment and know the legal system and legal culture of the countries along, and with the understanding of the contents of maritime affairs between China and other countries (such as foreign trade, maritime transport etc.) as well. In addition, China can also enhance the cooperation of international legal talents training project with other countries. For example, China can carry out the legal talent training scheme by signing the two-way international legal talents training agreement, strengthening bilateral, multilateral study[①], conducting academic exchange activities regularly, hosting legal seminar or academic BBS among countries and so on.

V. Conclusion

The construction of the 21st-century Maritime Silk Road is a significant strategic concept to deepening cooperation among China, Asian, African and European countries and making a community of destiny, a community of interest, and a community of responsibility. From the perspective of maritime transportation, because most countries along the Road has different maritime law and there is no matched unified maritime substantive law as well as conflict law at the regional level, the construction of the 21st-century Maritime Silk Road faces legal risks and challenges in the area of maritime transportation. As the animateur, China shall play the leading role on the basis of perfecting legal coordination mechanism among China and other countries, make every effort to build the regional unified maritime transport

---

① See Renda Li, Ligang Zou. A Study on the Legal Mechanism For the Co-construction of the New Maritime Silk Road by China and ASEAN. Chinese Journal of Maritime Law. Vol. 26, No. 1, Mar. 2015:12.

legal system jointly, and strengthen the cultivation of comprehensive legal talents as well to provide a solid legal safeguard of maritime transportation for the 21st-century Maritime Silk Road.

References

[1] Chairman of China Xi Jinping delivered in Indonesian Parliament, Xinhuanet, 3, October 2013.

[2] *The Decision on Some Major Issues Concerning Comprehensively Deepening the Reform*, adopted at the Third Plenary Session of the 18th Central Committee of the Communist Party of China on November 12,2013.

[3] *Report on the Work of the Government*, delivered at the Second Session of the Twelfth National People's Congress on March 5,2014,by Li Keqiang,Premier of the State Council.

[4] *For Peace, Cooperation and Harmony in the Ocean*——*Remarks at the China-Greece Maritime Cooperation Forum*, by H. E. Li Keqiang,Premier of the State Council of the People's Republic of China, Athens,20,June 2014.

[5] *Vision and Actions on Jointly Building Silk Road Economic Belt and 21st-Century Maritime Silk Road*, issued by the National Development and Reform Commission, Ministry of Foreign Affairs,and Ministry of Commerce of the People's Republic of China,with State Council authorization,28,March 2015. (First Edition 2015)

[6] Cigui Liu, "Some Thoughts on Developing Maritime Partnership Cooperation and Promoting the Construction of the 21st-Century Maritime Silk Road", *International Studies*,No. 4, 2014, p. 4.

[7] Chunhao Lou, "The Risks and Challenges of Maritime Silk Road", *International Ocean Economic and Political Review*,No. 5,2014, p. 4.

[8] Yonghong Han, Youqi Shi, "The Construction of the Legal Safeguard Mechanism of the 21st-Century Maritime Silk Road", *International Economics and Trade Research*, Vol. 31, No. 10, Oct. 2015,p. 62.

[9] Yao Tong, Guohua Wang. "Study on the Resolution Mechanism of Maritime Law Conflicts Under the Background of the 21st-Century Maritime Silk Road", *Chinese Journal of Maritime Law*,Vol. 26,No. 2,Jun. 2015,p. 19.

[10] Guangqing Qu. New Theory on Conflicts of Maritime Laws. Beijing: The People's Press, 2013,p. 119.

[11] Hualin Shen. Introduction to the Law of ASEAN Countries. Nanning, Guangxi Nationalities Publishing House,2004,p. 2.

[12] Renda Li,Ligang Zou. "A Study on the Legal Mechanism For the Co-construction of the New Maritime Silk Road by China and ASEAN", *Chinese Journal of Maritime Law*, Vol. 26, No. 1, Mar. 2015,p. 11.

[13] Lihua Yuan. "Exploration on the Legal Protection of the Sub-regional Cooperation of the Silk Road Economic Belt", *Journal of Lanzhou Commercial College*, Vol. 30, No. 4, Aug. 2014, p. 32-35.

Legal Issues on Trade and Economic Cooperation on Building the 21st-Century Maritime Silk Route: Indonesia's Perspective

IIndah W. Wulan[*]

Abstract   China's recent proposal to build 21st-Century Maritime Silk Road has marked an important issues in the development of China and its relations with ASEAN countries. On October 2013, Chinese President Xi Jinping announced to put forward the strategic conception of building the "Silk Road Economic Belt" and the "21st-Century Maritime Silk Road" in Jakarta, in front of Indonesia's People Parliament.

In this background thinking, the proposal of the "Silk Road Economic Belt" and the "21st-Century Maritime Silk Road" then become interesting idea and become an interesting discussion about how it could be applied. How the 21st-Century Maritime Silk Road will give benefit to support regional production network and bridge economic gaps between ASEAN countries since one of the 21st-Century Maritime Silk Road program is to build China-ASEAN Maritime Cooperation Fund and help to secure the area along the route for traders.

This essay will elaborate the idea of the 21st-Century Maritime Silk Route from Indonesia's Perspective. This essay contains of 4 part. The fist part is about Introduction. The second part is about Prospects of the 21st-Century Maritime Silk Route for Indonesia. The third part is about Legal

---

* Doctor of Laws, judge at Purwakarta District Court, West Java, Indonesia.

Issues Concerning Conflicts and Divergencies. The last part is Conclusion.

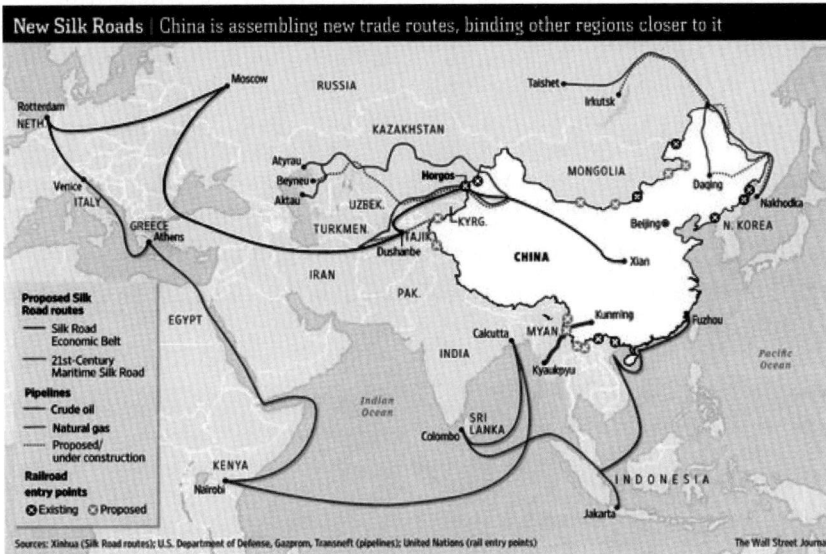

New Silk Roads | China is assembling new trade routes, binding other regions closer to it

Proposed Silk
Road routes
— Silk Road
Economic Belt
— 21st-Century
Maritime Silk Road
Pipelines
— Crude oil
— Natural gas
······ Proposed/
under construction
Railroad
entry points
⊗ Existing ○ Proposed

Sources: Xinhua (Silk Road routes); U.S. Department of Defense, Gazprom, Transneft (pipelines); United Nations (rail entry points)   The Wall Street Journal

A. Introduction

China's recent proposal to build 21st-Century Maritime Silk Road has
marked an important issues in the development of China and its relations
with ASEAN countries. On October 2013, Chinese President Xi Jinping
announced to put forward the strategic conception of building the "Silk Road
Economic Belt" and the "21st-Century Maritime Silk Road" in Jakarta, in
front of Indonesia's People Parliament.

So why is it so important?

There are so many reasons why people or countries doing international
trading. In fact, international trading had become a backbone to support for
a country to have their prosperity, welfare and strength. It had been proven
by history. The glory of the countries in the world came from their
international trade activities. The glory of China in ancient time was the
effect of its trade government policy known as *"the Silk Route"*. *Silk Route*
was a route used by Chinese traders to do their trading with traders from
other countries around the world. Not to mention glory of Spanish with its

33

Spanish Conquistadors, Britain with its *The British Empire*, the Dutch with its *VOC*, etc. All the glory of these countries came from their government policy to do the international trade.

Generally speaking, we can see the purpose of international trade from preamble of GATT (*General Agreement on Tariffs and Trade*, 1947) which is:

1. To achieve a stable international trade environment and to avoid national trading activities which can caused damage to other countries;

2. To increase international trade volume by creating an interesting trade and achieve economic development for all countries;

3. To increase human living standard;

4. To increase job opportunities;

5. To develop international trading system which can be useful to all countries;

6. To increase products and trading activities.

The rules of international trading, at the end, will create peace and international secure. Because if two or more countries related and doing a trading transaction and they gain profit from the trading then automatically the world would be better. It meant, the situation and the world condition would be more conducive. This is similar with Immanuel Kant, father of international law, once said in his journal *On Eternal Peace* that: "*spirit of trade could not co-exist with war*".

In this background thinking, the proposal of the "Silk Road Economic Belt" and the "21st-Century Maritime Silk Road" then become interesting idea and become an interesting discussion about how it could be applied.

B. Prospects of 21st-Century Maritime Silk Route for Indonesia

The increasing regionalism in East Asia is due to economic and political reasons. Firstly, intra-regional trade has increased substantially among the East Asian countries. East Asia's share of global exports increased by more than three-fold between 1975 and 2001. During the same period, intraregional exports grew even faster. Hence, to further promote trade among them, initiative has been taken to integrate the economies in the region. Those countries liberalized their economies in order to attract more foreign direct investment and to create more job opportunities. The idea of the 21st-Century Maritime Silk Road also paves the path towards East Asian economic cooperation.

It is true that trade liberalization has been progressive in China and ASEAN countries. In ASEAN, different countries took initiatives to liberalize among themselves. China, on the other hand, has committed a comprehensive package of market liberalization with different countries by promoting the 21st-Century Maritime Silk Route. Liberalization has resulted in a large increase of both exports and imports of ASEAN and China with the rest of the world. At the same time, ASEAN-China economic relations have grown dramatically, there is strong potential for further increase in trade and better investment relationship between ASEAN and China due to their geographical proximity and a strong economic growth.

Thus, trade relations between China and ASEAN countries have become increasingly important in recent years. With sluggish economic performance in the major markets of US and Japan, China has become an alternative market to ASEAN's exports and to support the future growth of the region. Hence, China has posed for ASEAN, the potential for economic cooperation and mutual gains between ASEAN and China is enormous. Moreover, with their geographical proximity and growth in complementary sectors, ASEAN and China should consider each other as natural trading partners.

The 21st-Century Martime Silk Road Further Promotes Bilateral Trade between Indonesia and China

It is noted that China has been Indonesia's important trading partner in recent years. Moreover, trade flows between them exhibited increasing trend from year to year. Trade between them is expected to further expand in the future with the opening of their markets if the 21st-Century Maritime Silk Road. This optimistic forecast is the result of China's dynamic growth.

If the ideas of 21st-Century Maritime Silk Route can be applied, the regional framework abolishing trade barriers will facilitate trade flows among member countries and also encourage more economic cooperation, thereby lowering trade friction among the countries concerned and finally, result in an increase of trade among member nations.

Indonesia will benefit from it if there is net trade creation. Theoretically, trade creation will most likely be greater after the 21st-Century Maritime Silk Route coming into effect. Countries that trade heavily with each other stand to gain the most. With China increasing its share in Indonesia's total trade, it is likely that Indonesia will gain from the trade integration of China and ASEAN countries.

Greater Market Access Opportunities for Malaysian Manufacturers

The fact that China is emerging as a major economic power means that it will demand a greater variety of products. Even though China has many resources, it cannot specialize in everything. The law of comparative advantage still applies, just as it applied to all countries. The huge population of China is an obvious indicator of market potential. Moreover, Chinese consumers' rising purchasing power makes it an appealing market. Opening trade with China benefits consumers as the country has been seen as the "factory of the world" and the source of cheap products such as garments and shoes. Furthermore, removal of tariffs and non tariff barriers will result in lower transaction costs and enable free flow of products in the region; consumers now have a wider choice of products in the market, with each member country offering different products for tariff reduction. When the negotiation processes are completed, products under tariffs reduction lists will eventually be increased.

In addition, enlarging the market creates intense competition. Companies become committed to improve their quality of products to expand sales; consumers then will now have a wide choice of quality products.

Reduction in Exports Over-Dependence on Developed Countries

The 21st-Century Martime Silk Road will not only enlarge the trade between Indonesia and China, it will also reduce its exports dependence on developed countries. Although trade between Indonesia and China and ASEAN countries had increased greatly, Indonesia's exports are heavily

dependent on developed countries such as the United States, Japan and EU.
However, growth in exports to China and ASEAN countries will offset the
decline of Indonesia's share in its key market with the formation of the free
trade. Hopefully, Indonesia's exports market will be widening with China
and other ASEAN countries within this 21st-Century Martime Silk Road.
These would gradually reduce Indonesia's over-dependence on the developed
countries.

Considering these factors, it leaves greater room for the future
development and expansion in trade between Indonesia, China and other
ASEAN countries. In the context of global economic slowdown, and years of
recession of the regional economic power, Japan, these countries by
enhancing trade flows of the member countries will be especially beneficial.

Promote Economic Efficiency and Productivity

The 21st-Century Maritime Silk Road will open a Free trade with a
larger, dynamic partner like China should result in improved efficiency and
productivity for Indonesia. Reduced costs should lead to lower transaction
costs and enable products to flow freely within the region. The minimizing of
these transaction costs should also result in cheaper prices for consumers and
larger profits for firms.

It may increase the intensity of competition, which will induce
companies to eliminate internal inefficiencies and raise productivity level.
Besides, productivity may also increase as the companies learn from each
other through cooperation. These learning processes typically include work
methods, plan layouts, incentive programs and management techniques.

Overall Implications for the Indonesian Economy

By building the 21st-Century Maritime Silk Road will benefit Indonesia
through increasing market access to China's huge market. Indonesia's
exports to China will increase, while imports from China will increase too.
With such more simple mechanism, individual country will source its
demands from the cheaper producer in China. Meanwhile, the reduction in
trade barriers will encourage more exports to flow into China's huge market.
This will change the trade flows of member countries as the shifts in demand
and supply will be more inclined towards China.

C. Legal Issues Concerning Conflicts and Divergences

This is an important issue relating with the idea of opening the 21st-Century Maritime Silk Road. Actually, these issues had been realized by the United Nations in its resolution Number 2102 (XX) which said: *"Conflicts and divergences arising from the laws of different states in matters relating to international trade constitute anobstacle to the development of world trade."*

International Agreement

To answer these issues, there are 3 techniques can be done. *Firstly*, the countries agrees not to apply their national law. On the other hand, they applies international trade law to control trade relations among them. *Secondly*, if there is no international trade rules or if the countries doesn't come to an agreement then the national law from a country can be applied. Method to choose which law is going to applied is using the *choice of laws principles*. *Choice of Laws Principles* is a choice of law clauses which agreed by the parties and written in international contract they made. *Thirdly*, is using unification and harmonization of laws technique which combines all the essences of the international trade rules. This last technique is the most efficient because it can avoid conflicts from different law systems among each countries.

An international agreement binding to all parties made the agreement. So, an international trade agreement also binding for countries in the agreement. An international agreement that had been ratified will be the country's national law.

An international trade agreement usually contains of:

a)*Liberalization of trade*

Countries member in an international agreement put-off their national laws and rules which can hampers international trade transactions.

b)*Economic Integration*

Countries member in an international agreement try to achieve economic integration throughout customs union, free trade zone, or an economic union.

c)*Law Harmonization*

Main goal of law harmonization is to find the unity or meeting-points from different fundamental principles from various legal systems (to be harmonized).

d)*Unification of Law*

In unification of law, the uniformity includes the removal and replacement of a legal system with a new legal system. Examples: rules about intellectual property rights, patent, industry design, etc.

e)*Models of Law and Legal Guides*

This form of law usually chosen if there is no agreement which law is going to be applied. So that they made this Model of Laws which is usually not binding. Models of Laws makers hope that the models can become a guide for countries to make their national laws or rules. Famous model of law known is *UNCITRAL Model Law on International Commercial Arbitration* of 1985.

Despite all, national law had an important role as a law source in international trade law. The role of national law starts when the dispute arise in implementation of a contract. A national law's role is very wide and important, not just about ruling an international trade contract. Significant role of a national law born from jurisdiction of the nation. This nation authority is absolute and exclusive. Namely, there is no exclusion and no one can bother this authority.

This national jurisdiction includes international trade transactions includes tax laws, customs, intellectual property rights regulation, import-export licenses etc.

Dispute Settlement

The idea of the 21st-Century Maritime Silk Road which accommodates traders between countries must be prepared by dispute settlements since the dispute can arise between countries.

Transactions or trade relationships has many of forms. It can be sell and buy activities, delivery, production of goods and services etc. according to the contract. All the transaction full and potentially rising a dispute. Firstly, a dispute settlementusually proceeded by negotiation. If it failed, then they come with other ways such as through arbitration or the court.

D. Conclusion

The 21st-Century Maritime Silk Road will give benefit because it support regional production network and bridge economic gaps between ASEAN countries. One of the 21st-Century Maritime Silk Road program is build China-ASEAN Maritime Cooperation Fund and help to secure the area along the route for traders.

Indonesia doesn't have to worry about the idea of 21st-Century Maritime Silk Road because of these three reasons. *Firstly*, Indonesia is not China's enemy. In fact, China considers Indonesia is the most important partner in Southeast Asia. *Secondly*, Indonesia can synergize its maritime development policy with the 21st-Century Maritime Silk Road ideas. *Thirdly*, the idea of building 21st-Century Maritime Silk Road is fair because China has the right to develop programs to support its continuing economic development.

The most important thing is 21st-Century Maritime Silk Road programs cannot be decided only by China's government but there has to be a dialogue and agreement with ASEAN countries as well. These things have to be accommodated by China if they want the 21st-Century Maritime Silk Road ideas supported by other countries. For that, it has to be stressed too that the 21st-Century Maritime Silk Road won't be used by China as justification to strengthen its army forces.

For the ASEAN countries, the 21st-Century Maritime Silk Road ideas can be a remedy for *land-connectivity policy* which had been announced few years ago. Land connectivity can also had been planned to accelerate transportation and logistics supply between cities in South China and ASEAN countries.

建设 21 世纪海上丝绸之路中贸易与经济合作的法律问题：印度尼西亚视角世纪海上丝绸之路建设

Indah W. Wulan[*]

孙晓丹　译

摘要　中国国家主席习近平于 2013 年 10 月在雅加达的印度尼西亚国会上正式提出建设"丝绸之路经济带"和"21 世纪海上丝绸之路"，这对中国，对东南亚国家联盟（ASEAN）各国关系而言，都意义重大。"一带一路"的倡议，引起了各国广泛兴趣，而如何将这一概念落到实处则成为热点话题。21 世纪海上丝绸之路内容之一，是建立中国—东盟海上合作基金，保护丝绸之路覆盖区域，确保贸易顺利进行，问题是，如何支持区域生产网络的运行，如何沟通中国与东盟各国。文章从印度尼西亚视角出发，介绍 21 世纪海上丝绸之路的理念。

一、21 世纪海上丝绸之路的重要性

商人或政府从事国际贸易，有多种因素驱动，其中之一，便是国际贸易能为国家创造财富，提升国力，保障人民福利。历史上有许多国家就是因国际贸易取得显著的国际地位。中国古代政府曾利用"丝绸之路"沟通各国，推行国际贸易政策。西班牙建立殖民地，英国建立日不落帝国，荷兰建立东印度公司等，都是因政府推行国际贸易之故。

从关税与贸易总协定序言（GATT），可一窥国际贸易之目的：

1. 建立国际贸易的稳定环境，防止一国贸易活动危及他国；

---

[*]　法学博士，印度尼西亚西爪哇省普瓦卡它区法院法官。

New Silk Roads | China is assembling new trade routes, binding other regions closer to it

2.创造贸易机会,实现各国经济发展,提高国际贸易总量;

3.提高人民生活水平;

4.提供就业岗位;

5.建立惠及世界的国际贸易体系;

6.增加商品贸易。

国际贸易规则归根结底,是能够构建和平环境,保障贸易安全。而贸易双方或多方进行国际贸易活动,从贸易中获取利润,也利于构建和谐世界,改善国际环境与贸易条件。正如国际法之父伊曼努尔·康德在《永久和平论》中所说:"贸易的精神能够抑制战争"。

二、21世纪丝绸之路下印度尼西亚的前景

东亚区域化进程加快,有其经济、政治原因。首先,东亚各国在东亚区域内的交易量大幅增加。1975—2001年间,东亚在世界出口量中所占的比例增长了三倍多,区域内同期出口量增速更快。因此,为进一步促进东亚区域贸易,建立区域一体化经济提上日程。东亚各国致力于实现经济自由,以吸引外来投资,创造就业机会。21世纪海上丝绸之路,能够促进东亚各国间的经济合作。

中国与东盟各国也在推进贸易自由化。东盟内部,就有不同的国家提出

过实行东盟自由化的倡议,而中国则通过推动建设 21 世纪海上丝绸之路,推行了市场自由化的全面配套方案。自由化能促进东盟和中国与其他国家进出口贸易的大幅增加。同时,在东盟—中国经济联系更加紧密的基础上,东盟与中国的地缘关系和经济的迅速增长,还可能促进二者贸易与投资关系的发展。

因此,近年来,中国与东盟的贸易关系日益重要。加之美国与日本疲软的市场状况,中国已经成为东盟另一个出口市场,支撑着东南亚未来的经济发展。正如中国的提议,东盟与中国之间有很大的合作共赢空间,而且由于地缘亲密和诸多互补领域的存在,双方都是彼此天然的贸易伙伴。

1. 21 世纪海上丝绸之路能够推动印度尼西亚与中国的双边贸易

近年来,中国已经成为印度尼西亚的重要贸易伙伴,双方贸易量呈现逐年增长态势,21 世纪海上丝绸之路运行之后,双方贸易有望进一步增加,这是基于中国经济的迅速增长所做的乐观估计。

如果 21 世纪海上丝绸之路的设想得以实现,在区域内废除贸易壁垒的框架得以建立,成员国之间的贸易流动会更加便捷,这也会鼓励经济合作,减少贸易双方之间的摩擦,最终使各国实现贸易增长。

如果出现贸易净增长,印度尼西亚即可从中获益。理论上讲,21 世纪海上丝绸之路建好之后,贸易量极有可能大幅增长,参与到贸易中的国家也能获取更多利益。中国与印尼之间的贸易总量与日俱增之下,中国—东盟一体化更有利于印尼发展。

2. 马来西亚制造商将获得更多进入市场的机会

中国正成长为一个巨大的经济体,对各类商品都会有大量需求。中国地大物博,却也不能样样自足,相对优势法则依然适用。中国人口众多,显示了巨大的市场潜力,中国人民的消费能力提高,中国市场更具吸引力。中国也被称作"世界工厂",制造出的服装和鞋子价格低廉,与中国开展开放贸易,消费者可以获益。加上关税与非关税壁垒的消除,交易成本会更加低廉,产品的区域自由流动会更加顺畅;每个成员国针对不同产品提供关税减让的同时,消费者能获得更多市场选择。磋商结束后,享受关税减让的产品也会增加。

此外,市场扩大,竞争会更加激烈。企业为提高销量,会提升产品质量;消费者将能买到更多高质量产品。

3. 出口过度依赖发达国家的状况将有所缓解

21 世纪海上丝绸之路,不仅会扩大中国与印尼之间的贸易,还可以减轻印尼在出口上对发达国家的依赖。印尼和中国的贸易虽然已有大幅增长,但其出口仍严重依赖美国、日本、欧盟等发达国家。对中国及其他东盟国家出口的增加,能抵消印尼在自由贸易中失去的发达国家份额。印尼希望通过21世纪海上丝绸之路,扩大与中国及东盟诸国的出口市场,进而减轻自己对发达国家的过度依赖。

因此,印尼与中国及东盟各国之间的贸易合作和发展空间很大。在全球经济放缓,区域经济大国日本连年衰退的背景下,各成员国之间通过促进贸易自由能够实现共赢。

4.提高经济效率与生产力

21世纪海上丝绸之路让印尼能够与中国这样更大更具经济活力的国家开展自由贸易,进而提升本国经济效率和生产力。成本降低能够减少交易成本,使产品在区域内部自由流动。交易成本最小化,也能让消费者买到更便宜的产品,让企业得到更多利润。

21世纪海上丝绸之路也可能加剧竞争,迫使企业消除内部效率低下的因素,提升生产力。企业可以在合作中相互学习借鉴,也能够提高生产力,这样的学习借鉴一般涉及工作方法、方案设计、激励项目和管理制度。

5.对印尼经济的总体影响

21世纪海上丝绸之路为印尼创造了进入中国大市场的机会。印尼向中国出口量增加的同时,进口也将有所提高。这样的简单机制下,东盟各国都能在中国找到价格更加低廉的产品,同时,贸易壁垒的减少将能够鼓励对中国出口,各国的供给和需求会更倾向于中国,进而改变贸易动向。

三、法律间的冲突分歧

法律间的冲突分歧是21世纪海上丝绸之路设想的一项重要问题。联合国决议第2102(XX)号就谈到过:"不同国家之间关于国际贸易的法律冲突与分歧,是世界贸易发展的障碍。"

(一)国际条约

解决此类法律冲突的途径有三,一是国家之间缔结条约,约定禁止国内法的适用,而在关系各方贸易关系时,适用国际贸易法;二是在国际贸易规则出现空白,或者在各国不能达成协议时,可以适用国内法,国内法的选择采用法律选择规则,即各方达成协议,写入国际条约中的规则;三是在法律间追求统一与和谐,融合国际贸易规则的精华。最后一种方法因为能够避免不同国家法律体系之间的冲突,因而效率最高。

国际条约对缔约各方具有约束力。国际条约经批准能够转化为国内法。国际条约通常包含以下内容：

a）贸易自由化

缔约各方不得适用不利于国际交易的国内法或规则。

b）经济一体化

缔约方通过实施关税一体、自由贸易或者经济一体实现经济一体化。

c）法律间协调

法律间协调的主要目标，是在不同法律体系、不同基本原则中，找到共同点。

d）法律统一

法律统一指的是以新的法律体系替代旧的法律体系，例如知识产权规则、专利规则、工业产品设计规则等。

e）示范法和法律指导

贸易相关方之间没有法律适用的约定时，往往会选择示范法和法律指导。示范法不具有约束力，制定者期望其能够在各国制定国内法律和规则时提供指导。1985 年 UNCITRAL 国际商事仲裁示范法就是一例。

尽管如此，国内法仍是国际贸易法的重要法律渊源，合同履行中出现争议时得以适用。国内法不只规范国际贸易合同，它的作用重要而深远。其重要性源于绝对的、排他的国家管辖权，内容涉及国际贸易中的税法、关税、知识产权规则、进出口许可证等。

（二）争端解决

涉及不同国家贸易方的 21 世纪丝绸之路必须为可能产生的争端做好准备。

交易或贸易关系形式多样，根据合同类型包括买卖、运输、商品和服务的提供等。任何交易都可能产生争端，进而引起磋商，若磋商失败则通过仲裁或判决等其他方式解决。

四、结论

21 世纪海上丝绸之路能够支持区域生产网络，减少东盟国家之间的经济差距。这一设想之一是建立中国—东盟合作基金，保证区域贸易方交易安全。

21 世纪海上丝绸之路的建设上印尼无须担心，第一，印尼与中国没有敌对关系,中国把印尼看做自己在东南亚最重要的贸易伙伴;第二,印尼能够将本国海上发展政策与21世纪海上丝绸之路结合;第三,中国依靠该项目促进经济继续发展,会保证公平公正。

最重要的一点是,21世纪海上丝绸之路不凭中国一国决定,而应与东盟各国开展对话,订立合约。中国要得到各国支持,协商是必然选择。因此必须强调,中国不会利用21世纪海上丝绸之路来加强其军事力量。

对东盟国家而言,建设21世纪海上丝绸之路,能够帮助落实其在数年前宣布实行的地缘联系政策,即加快东盟各国与中国南方交通和物资供给的政策。

Trade and Economic Cooperation between Lao PDR and China

Thipphavanh Chanthavongsa[*]

Introduction

The Lao People's Democratic Republic (Lao PDR) is a landlocked country situated in the center of the Indochina Peninsula where it shares borders with China, Vietnam, Cambodia, Thailand and Myanmar. The country covers an area of 236,800 Km², much of which is mountainous, forested, and covered by rivers. It has a population of 5.7 million people and a population density of 22 persons/Km². An estimated 49 ethnic groups live in Lao PDR. Its economy is basically agricultural; about 80% of the population is engaged in farming.

In 1986, the Lao government adopted a relatively comprehensive reform program called the New Economic Mechanism to shift from a centrally planned economy to a market-oriented one. Despite its political regime, the government of Lao PDR has developed a good relationship with all countries in the world, with the ultimate goal of attaining development through cooperation and collaboration with international communities. In 1992, Lao PDR joined a sub-regional economic cooperation program known as the Greater Mekong sub-region (GSM). In 1997, it became a full member of the

* Academic Staff, The People's Supreme Court (Civil Chamber), Lao PDR.

Association of Southeast Asian Nations (ASEAN).

Cognizant of the importance of international cooperation, Lao PDR has forged diplomatic relations with 128 countries worldwide to date (Ministry of Foreign Affairs, 2008). Foreign direct investment (FDI), foreign trade, and official development assistance (ODA) have all been addressed as important factors for development of the Lao economy, especially in the implementation of the country's annual plan and five year plan. The government recognizes economic growth as the primary means by which income can be raised and poverty reduced, both of which must happen if the country is to achieve its vision of graduating from the list of Least Developed Countries (LDCs). Although the government considers investments as the most important source of growth, the country looks to foreign investments to help it attain its macro development goals because of limited domestic investments.

The foreign sector, through FDI, international trade development, and ODA, has played a significant role in the socioeconomic development of Lao PDR. One of the country from the East Asian region is China, have been particularly dominant in those three areas. China has contributed to approximately one-fourth of the total aid that Lao PDR receives yearly. China has also made significant investments in the country's public infrastructure and contributed to the development of its private sector.

On the other hand, China has been one of the large source of total FDI value in Lao PDR since the early 2000s. The value of the investments China has made in Lao PDR's industrial development has contributed to the country's growth. The current dynamism of China's economy is also seen as an important opportunity for the development of Lao production through the expansion of trade and economic ties between these two countries.

This paper aims to review the significance of China's contributions to the socioeconomic development of Lao PDR as part of analyzing the role of this country. The paper focuses on the economic aspect, Social and Economic Relation between Lao PDR and China, in order to analyze the characteristics of this country in the development in Lao PDR. The paper starts with an overview of the country's Regional Economic Integration and Trade

Facilitation Policies in Lao PDR. An analysis of the relationship between Lao PDR and China is in the Section Two. Section three presents a comparison of the characteristics of the relationships, followed by the conclusion and some policy recommendations.

I. Regional Economic Integration

The regional economic integration policy of Lao PDR started in 1986 with the introduction of a comprehensive reform program called the NEM, which was intended to facilitate the shift from the central planned economic model to a market-oriented one and which would consequently lead to the open-door policy in the 1990s.

Since the introduction of the NEM, Lao PDR has been gradually promoting regional integration and cooperation and became a full member of the Association of Southeast Asian Nations (ASEAN) in 1997 together with Cambodia, Vietnam, and Myanmar. Consequently, Lao PDR joined the ASEAN Free Trade Area (AFTA). It thus took on an obligation to facilitate trade with other ASEAN member countries. The ASEAN expanded its cooperation and free trade area (FTA) by introducing several programs. The ASEAN+3 (ASEAN + Japan, South Korea, and China) program expands cooperation and free trade with China. In November 2001, the ASEAN and China agreed in Phnom Penh to launch negotiations for the ASEAN-China Free Trade Area (ACFTA). In 2002, the parties signed the Framework A- greement on Comprehensive Economic Cooperation, which aims to: (1) strengthen and enhance economic trade and investment cooperation between the ASEAN and China; (2) progressively liberalize and promote trade in goods and services as well as create a transparent, liberal, and facilitative in- vestment regime; (3) explore new areas and develop appropriate measures for closer economic cooperation between both parties; and (4) facilitate a more effective economic integration of newer ASEAN members and bridge the development gap among the parties.

In 2004, the ASEAN and China signed the Agreement on Trade in Goods. According to this agreement, the six original ASEAN members

(Thailand, Malaysia, Indonesia, Philippines, Singapore, and Brunei) and China should reduce tariff on 90 percent of their products by 2010 while the new ASEAN members (Cambodia, Laos, Myanmar, and Vietnam) will have to implement the agreement in 2015.

The ACFTA will be fully implemented by 2015. However, Article 6 of the Framework Agreement requires the implementation of tariff reduction and tariff elimination on certain agricultural products ahead of schedule, supposedly to enable the parties to enjoy the early benefits of the FTA. The Early Harvest Program (EHP), for example, includes a total of 562 products. However, it allows for an exclusion list whereby a party can have certain products exempted from the program's coverage and a request list for the inclusion of certain products not covered by the program but mutually agreed upon by China and the concerned ASEAN member. Brunei and Singapore, whose economies are nonagricultural, fully subscribed to the provisions of EHP with no exemption. Vietnam and Cambodia submitted their exclusion lists in 2002 prior to the signing of the framework agreement. Malaysia followed suit before the March 2003 deadline. Indonesia and Thailand had no exclusion list but had request lists. Indonesia's request list (as agreed upon with China) included coffee, palm oil, coconut oil, vegetable oil and fats, cocoa powder, soap, vulcanized rubber, glass for cathode-ray tubes (CRTs), and wooden furniture. Aside from including anthracite and coke of coal on its request list, Thailand earlier agreed with China in June 2003 to implement zero tariffs on fruits and vegetables. Lao PDR did not submit an exclusion list or request list. Consequently, the Lao-China EHP automatically includes all 562 agriculture product items. This means that reduced import tariffs will be imposed on Lao PDR's agricultural exports to China. Until recently, however, there has been no study on the effects of the EHP on the Lao-China trade flow.

In addition, Lao PDR is working toward its acceptance to the World Trade Organization (WTO). When it becomes a member of the WTO, it will gain access to foreign markets and opportunities to get more investments and technological advancements, which are important factors in stimulating economic growth and reducing poverty in the long term.

However, to get the real benefits of WTO accession, the country has to stimulate its production capacities, enhance productivity, and improve the quality of its products in order to increase its competitiveness in the international market.

Moreover, Lao PDR signed a bilateral and multilateral trade and transportation agreement with Thailand, Vietnam, and China. This includes the following:

(1) Agreement to Exchange Traffic Rights and Implementation of the Customs Transit System in Lao PDR, Thailand, and Vietnam on June 11, 2009. This agreement facilitates cross-border transportation along the East-West Corridor (EWC). To ensure the continuity of the integration policy and facilitate cross-border transportation, the governments of Lao PDR, Thailand, and Vietnam agreed on June 11, 2009 to: (a) facilitate a vehicle's passage across national borders through the exchange of traffic rights; (b) permit vehicles to forgo the need to unload and reload goods at each border crossing through the customs transit guarantee system; and (c) allow minimum inspection of goods at border checkpoints within a reasonable amount of time via a single-stop and single-window inspection facility.

(2) Bilateral Transportation Agreement with Thailand, Vietnam, China, Cambodia, and Myanmar. Lao PDR signed a bilateral transportation agreement with its neighboring countries to facilitate the movement of people and goods. The bilateral transportation agreement allows trucks from Lao PDR entry to and exit from neighboring countries with reloading rights. The agreement allows trucks from neighboring countries the same privileges. The bilateral transportation agreement facilitates trade and cooperation between Lao PDR and its neighbors.

However, it should be noted that Lao PDR does not have any specific bilateral agreement on agricultural trade with foreign countries. Instead, its exports of agricultural products are facilitated by regional and multilateral trade agreements. The lack of bilateral agreements on agricultural trade (which would facilitate the export of specific agricultural products to specific markets) seems to indicate that the country has no specific policy and strategy on agricultural trade. A specific policy and strategy would help agricultural development because the country has many constraints in agricultural production (e. g. , land constraints, limited financial and human resources). It would also help Lao PDR enhance its productivity and competitiveness.

Ⅱ. Trade Promotion Policies in Lao PDR

Recognizing the role of external trade in the country's economic growth and poverty reduction efforts, the government facilitates exports and imports through several policies, such as:

(1) One-Stop Service Policy. On October 13, 2004, the MOIC enacted Order Number 962 (Implementing Decree Number 205/PM on the Establishment of One-Stop Service) in an effort to facilitate exports and imports. This policy directs all export-related and import-related agencies in all provinces and the nation's capital, Vientiane, to establish offices at all border checkpoints and to abolish export-import licenses (except for gold, copper, vehicles, vehicle spare parts, petroleum, gas, diamonds, and other prohibited goods requiring import licenses from the MOIC). A study conducted by NERI in 2008 showed that the implementation of the One-Stop Service policy facilitates cross-border trade by reducing time and costs.

(2) Border Trade Facilitation Policy. In 2001, the MOIC issued Instruction Number 948 on the Management of Border Trade. This policy aims to promote small-scale commercial production and exports as well as create jobs and income-generating activities for people living on the country's borders. It also classifies border areas into two types: remote areas and non-remote areas. Remote areas have no access to, or have difficulty in accessing, domestic markets while non-remote areas have good access to domestic markets. People in remote areas can export and import all kinds of products necessary for production and consumption while those in non-remote areas can export all their products but import only the necessary production inputs. People living in non-remote areas have to buy consumer products from the domestic market.

(3) Special Economic Zone and Border Trade Area Establishment

Policy. To facilitate trade and promote investment, the government implements policies governing special economic zones (SEZs) and establishing border trade. To date, one SEZ and three border trade areas have already been established. Additional incentives and facilitating measures are necessary to attract more investment and trade in the border areas and SEZs. For example, investors at the SAVAN-SENO SEZ enjoy privileges such as exemption from turnover and utilization and minimum tax andother incentives. These incentives include: (a) tax exemption during the early stages of investment and tax reduction based on sector and condition; (b) dividend tax of only 5 percent, which is lower than the normal rate; (c) profit tax of 5 percent, which is also lower than the normal rate; (d) transferable deficit within five years; (e) exemption from import taxes on raw materials, construction materials, equipment, machinery, transport vehicles, spare parts, and semi-finished products and end products for use in or assembly at the SEZ; and (f) reduced minimum registration capital based on investment sector. Investors at the Lao-China border trade area also enjoy various incentives, including (a) exemption from taxes on profit and income for the first four years of operation and a 50 percent reduction in said taxes for an agreed period when the four years are up; (b) seven-year exemption from land taxes; and (c) 10 percent reduction in import tax. If investors use domestic raw materials in their production processes, the import tax levied on the final products coming from the border trade area into the Lao domestic market is reduced based on the percentage cost of the domestic raw materials used vis-a-vis the total production cost. For example, the import tax for an investor who uses domestic raw materials costing 30 percent of the total production cost will be reduced by 30 percent when the final products are imported into the domestic market.

Ⅲ. Social and Economic Relations between Lao PDR and China

This section describes the bilateral relation between Lao PDR and China as neighbors that share a 500-kilometer border with each other. Lao PDR and

China officially established diplomatic relations on April 25, 1961 and have long historical ties, especially the three northern provinces of Lao PDR (Phongsaly, Luangnamtha and Oudomxay) that share a border with China's southern province of Yunnan. However, it is not only these three provinces of Lao PDR, but all of its other northern provinces that have established business relationships with Chinese traders. This section will also present official figures of Chinese investment, trade relation and ODA.

· **Chinese Investment in Lao PDR**

Currently, Chinese investment in Lao PDR ranks second in terms of total value after Thailand. Tables 3 and 4 indicate that FDI from China accounts for almost 80% of the totalinvestment value in the industry sector or more than 50% of the total number of projects. Chinese investment in Lao PDR increased gradually in the 1990s and then grew dramatically beginning in the 2000s. In the period 1991—2000, total FDI from China was only about US$127 million spread out over 71 projects. From 2001—2008, the total value of Chinese investment grew to about US$1. 4 billion covering a total of 244 projects. The figure shows more than a tenfold increase in the past eight years compared to the previous decade. The total value of FDI from China in the past eight years accounted for over 91% of total Chinese investment value in Lao PDR from 1991—2008.

Table 3: Total FDI from China to Laos USD (1991-2008)

Year	Projects	Agriculture	Projects	Industry	Projects	Service	Projects	Total
1991			2	2,209,600	1	500,000	3	2,709,600
1992			4	16,000,000	4	1,095,631	8	17,095,631
1993	2	1,227,475	5	3,012,000	9	5,395,000	16	9,634,475
1994			7	20,911,000	5	3,625,000	12	24,536,000
1995	1	997,000			1	7,500,000	2	8,497,000
1996	1	400,000	2	2,000,000	2	600,000	5	3,000,000
1997			2	3,102,000	2	708,838	4	3,810,838
1998			3	4,077,610	2	2,138,900	5	6,216,510
1999	1	878,763	5	41,534,813			6	42,413,576
2000	1	2,000,000	5	6,982,800	4	423,000	10	9,405,800
2001	1	1,550,000	5	2,120,000	3	1,345,000	9	5,015,000
2002			7	54,482,796	3	870,000	10	55,352,796
2003	2	2,000,000	13	16,922,046	8	4,236,000	23	23,158,046
2004	1	800,000	23	23,016,380	9	2,579,908	33	26,396,288
2005	5	7,970,000	20	42,545,280	3	600,500	28	51,115,780
2006	21	37,730,040	24	494,220,000	11	8,397,651	56	540,347,691
2007	14	22,240,118	10	367,223,135	14	113,470,465	38	502,933,718
2008	7	66,199,998	26	87,877,232	14	17,340,000	47	171,417,230
Total	57	143,993,394	163	1,188,236,692	95	170,825,893	315	1,503,055,979

Source: Dept. of Investment, MPI, 2009

Table 4: Total FDI from China to Lao PDR (1991-2008)

Year	Agriculture		Industry		Service		Total		(%)
	Projects	Value (USD)	Projects	Value (USD)	Projects	Value (USD)	Projects	Value (USD)	
1991-2000	6	5,503,238	35	99,829,823	30	21,986,369	71	127,319,430	8.5
2001-2008	51	138,490,156	128	1,088,406,869	65	148,839,524	244	1,375,736,549	91.5
1991-2008	57	143,993,394	163	1,188,236,692	95	170,825,893	315	1,503,055,979	100

Source: Dept. of Investment, MPI, 2009

From the time China started investing in Lao PDR, its FDI was allocated to the secondary and tertiary sectors. The third five-year plan of the country, therefore, showed Chinese investors contributing to the development of the industry and service sectors. More than 67% of the total investment value went to the industry sector, about 29% to servicesector, and only about 3% to the agriculture sector. While there was not much change in the FDI value from China during the implementation of the fourth five-year plan (1996—2000), the allocation for agriculture stayed at the same level as the previous years, that for the service sector decreased, and the allocation for the industry sector dramatically improved and accounted for almost 90% of total investment value in that period.

Table 5: FDI from China to Laos (1991-1995)

Year	Agriculture		Industry		Service		Total		(%)
	Projects	Vale (USD)	Projects	Vale (USD)	Projects	Vale (USD)	Projects	Vale (USD)	
1991			2	2,209,600	1	500,000	3	2,709,600	4
1992			4	16,000,000	4	1,095,631	8	17,095,631	27
1993	2	1,227,475	5	3,012,000	9	5,395,000	16	9,634,475	15
1994			7	20,911,000	5	3,625,000	12	24,536,000	39
1995	1	997,000			1	7,500,000	2	8,497,000	14
1991-1995	3	2,224,475	18	42,132,600	20	18,115,631	41	62,472,706	100

Source: Dept. of Investment, MPI, 2009

FDI from China significantly increased more than three times in terms of investment value and projects during the period covered by the fifth five-year plan (2001—2005). The industry sector accounted for more than 85%, while service and agriculture sectors accounted for about 8% and 6% of

Table 6: FDI from China to Laos (1996-2000)

Year	Agriculture		Industry		Service		Total		(%)
	Projects	Vale (USD)	Projects	Vale (USD)	Projects	Vale (USD)	Projects	Vale (USD)	
1996	1	400,000	2	2,000,000	2	600,000	5	3,000,000	5
1997			2	3,102,000	2	708,838	4	3,810,838	6
1998			3	4,077,610	2	2,138,900	5	6,216,510	10
1999	1	878,763	5	41,534,813			6	42,413,576	65
2000	1	2,000,000	5	6,982,800	4	423,000	10	9,405,800	15
1996-2000	3	3,278,763	17	57,697,223	10	3,870,738	30	64,846,724	100

Source: Dept. of Investment, MPI, 2009

total investment value respectively. The growth rate of FDI from China during this period was about 148% compared to the past period. Agriculture grew by 276%, while industry and service was 141% and 149%, respectively.

Table 7: FDI from China to Laos (2001-2005)

Year	Agriculture		Industry		Service		Total		(%)
	Projects	Vale (USD)	Projects	Vale (USD)	Projects	Vale (USD)	Projects	Vale (USD)	
2001	1	1,550,000	5	2,120,000	3	1,345,000	9	5,015,000	3
2002			7	54,482,796	3	870,000	10	55,352,796	34
2003	2	2,000,000	13	16,922,046	8	4,236,000	23	23,158,046	14
2004	1	800,000	23	23,016,380	9	2,579,908	33	26,396,288	16
2005	5	7,970,000	20	42,545,280	3	600,500	28	51,115,780	32
2001-2005	9	12,320,000	68	139,086,502	26	9,631,408	103	161,037,910	100

Source: Dept. of Investment, MPI, 2009

The figure for the first half of the sixth five-year plan (2006—2010) shows a dramatically increased amount of FDI from China to Lao PDR. In 2006 alone, total FDI increased by almost five times compared to the entire period covered by the previous five-year plan (2001—2005). It was even approximately double the total FDI value in the past 15 years (1991—2005). The average growth rate of investment during the past three years is almost 300% per year, in which agriculture, industry, and service grew at about 177%, 320% and 822% per year, respectively. Table 8 shows that the total

56

FDI value from China in the first half of the sixth five-year plan (2006—2010) was about US$1.2 billion covering 141 projects. The industry sector accounted for about 78%, service about 11.5% and agriculture 10% of total investment value.

Table 8: FDI from China to Laos (2006-2008)

Year	Agriculture		Industry		Service		Total		(%)
	Projects	Vale (USD)	Projects	Vale (USD)	Projects	Vale (USD)	Projects	Vale (USD)	
2006	21	37,730,040	24	494,220,000	11	8,397,651	56	540,347,691	44
2007	14	22,240,118	10	367,223,135	14	113,470,465	38	502,933,718	41
2008	7	66,199,998	26	87,877,232	14	17,340,000	47	171,417,230	14
2006-2008	42	126,170,156	60	949,320,367	39	139,208,116	141	1,214,698,639	100

Source: Dept. of Investment, MPI, 2009

Table 9 presents FDI from China broken down per five-year plan and the first three years of the sixth five-year plan (2006—2010). Clearly, Chinese investment in Lao PDR has significantly increased in recent years across all sectors(industrial, service and agriculture) and accounts formore than 80% of total investment value in the period 1991—2008. FDI from China has invested not only in the central and southern regions but also the northern region, which has very poor infrastructure compared to other regions in the country. Due the situation of infrastructure, northern region does not very attractive for FDI from other regions of the world, but as a geographical advantage northern region could benefit from Chinese investment and vice versa.

Table 9: Total FDI from China to Lao PDR by Five Year Time

Year	Projects	Agriculture	Projects	Industry	Projects	Service	Projects	Total	(%)
1991-1995	3	2,224,475	18	42,132,600	20	18,115,631	41	62,472,706	4.2
1996-2000	3	3,278,763	17	57,697,223	10	3,870,738	30	64,846,724	4.3
2001-2005	9	12,320,000	68	139,086,502	26	9,631,408	103	161,037,910	10.7
2006-2008	42	126,170,156	60	949,320,367	39	139,208,116	141	1,214,698,639	80.8
1991-2008	57	143,993,394	163	1,188,236,692	95	170,825,893	315	1,503,055,979	100

Source: Dept. of Investment, MPI, 2009

Overall, the total value of Chinese FDI accounted for about 8.6% of total FDI value in Lao PDR during the period 1989—2008. The top five sectors that received FDI from China were hydropower, handicraft, mining, service and agriculture. The FDI received by the hydropower-electricity sector accounted for approximately 6.3% of total FDI in the country's electricity sector. This made it the top sector in term of clinching the bulk of investment funds from China. The industry and handicraft sectors took second place and accounted for about 17.8% of total FDI in their sector. Mining, which was the most invested in area in 2006, was the third to recipient of Chinese FDI, accounting for about 14.3% of total FDI. Service and agriculture took the fourth and fifth spots, respectively, with service accounting for almost 20% of total FDI and agriculture about 7%.

Table 10: Total FDI and Chinese Investment in Lao PDR (1989-2008)

No	Sectors	Projects		Value of FDI (USD)		(%)
		Total	Of Chinese	Total	Of Chinese	
1	Electricity Generation	47	9	9,845,791,585	623,204,400	6.33
2	Agriculture	260	51	1,571,455,899	108,296,394	6.89
3	Mining	177	55	1,165,674,715	166,578,335	14.29
4	Industry & Handicraft	308	78	1,805,706,193	320,799,160	17.77
5	Services	278	36	643,492,893	126,690,376	19.69
6	Trading	178	22	317,509,429	17,416,303	5.49
7	Construction	62	12	424,807,707	16,970,300	3.99
8	Hotel & Restaurant	103	18	275,195,254	7,263,714	2.64
9	Wood Industry	65	11	159,769,822	36,819,600	23.05
10	Banking	22	0	171,235,535	0	0.00
11	Telecom	10	2	227,770,980	800,000	0.35
12	Garment	74	10	67,778,289	11,957,000	17.64
13	Consultances	57	7	2,893,622	1,450,000	50.11
	TOTAL	**1,649**	**311**	**16,691,931,511**	**1,438,245,582**	**8.62**

Source: Department of Investment, MPI, 2009

The general observation is that amount of FDI from China has dramatically increased in recent years. These investments are mostly in the natural sector, which includes electricity, agriculture and mining. Collectively, these investments account for almost 60% of total investment in terms of value. While there are also many projects for the handicraft, service, trading, hotel and restaurant and wood industries, there are none for banking sector presumably because inflow of Chinese FDI started only in the past few years. Another aspect worth nothing is that FDI from China has contributed to the development of the country's northern region due to that region's proximity to China. This is regarded as an important source of income and means for poverty reduction for the people living in that region.

· **Trade Relations between Lao PDR and China**

Foreign trade has been considered a significant source of economic growth for an important sector in the country. Lao PDR's implementation of the open-door policy in the late 1980s spurred growth in foreign trade. Although it has trade relations with more than 60countries worldwide, most of its trade activity is conducted with the other countries within the region, particularly with its neighboring countries. This situation is attributed to Lao PDR's being landlocked and the fact that intraregional trade seems to be more competitive for the country than trade outside of the region.

The overall trend of trade relation between the two countries (Lao PDR and China) has increased although it fluctuated during early 2000s. From 2004 onward, it improved dramatically in the growth of both imports and exports. However, data show that imports have grown faster than exports, which constitutes a deficit in the trade balance with China. Although the overall trade balance gradually improved during late 2000s, the trade deficit has nevertheless continued these past few years.

However, looking at the percentage of exports and imports to and from China to the total trade figure (total exports and imports of the country), the average component of exports to China has significantly grown from only about 3%—4% during the early 2000s and up to about 8%—9% of total export value in late 2000s. The component of imports from China in Lao PDR's total import value has stabilized at 2% to 4% in the period 2000—2008.

Another interesting issue related to trade between Lao PDR and China involves cross-border trade, especially in the border areas like Luangnamtha and Oudomxay province in Northern Laos. Cross-border trade has both positive and negative effects on the social and economic activities of the

Figure1 : Trading between Lao PDR and China (2000-2008)

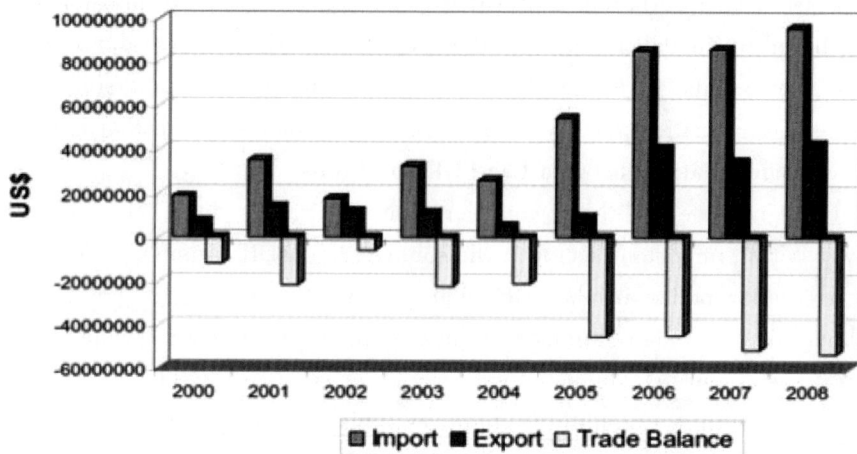

Source: Ministry of Industry and Commerce, 2009

Figure2 : Percentage of Export and Import to and from China to Total Export and Import of Lao PDR

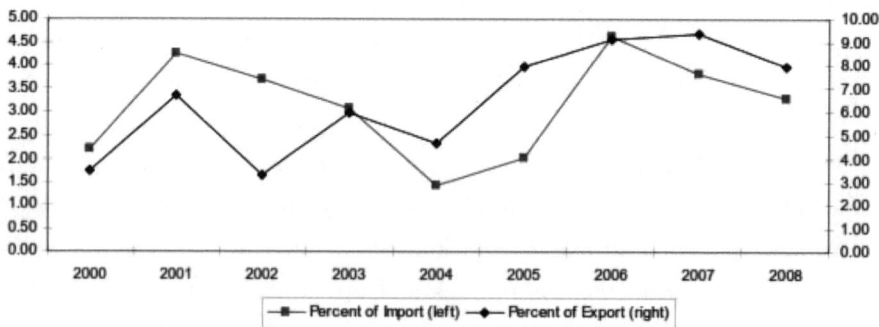

Source: Ministry of Industry and Commerce, 2009

people in these areas. The positive aspects include changes in the livelihood system, opportunities for employment, improvement in income and trade as well as other social benefits like education and healthcare. However, there are also other social issues related to cross-border trade such as: foreign labor problem.

• **Chinese ODA in Lao PDR**

ODA has played a crucial role in the socioeconomic development of Lao PDR. Source of ODA for the country include multilateral communities and international organizations such as the World Bank, the United Nations, WTO and bilateral countries, especially the high-income or developed countries in the world. The International Monetary Fund (IMF) and International Nongovernment Organizations (INGOs) have also contributed significantly to the development of rural areas through technical and grant assistance.

Official statistics indicate that Chinese ODA to Lao PDR started in early 2000s and has steadily flowed inward thereafter. In term of value, it fluctuates yearly, but the average from 2000—2008 was about US $ 18 million per year. On average, Chinese ODA accounted for about 7% to 8% of total ODA inflow value annually from 2000—2008.

Figure 3: Value of ODA from China to Lao PDR

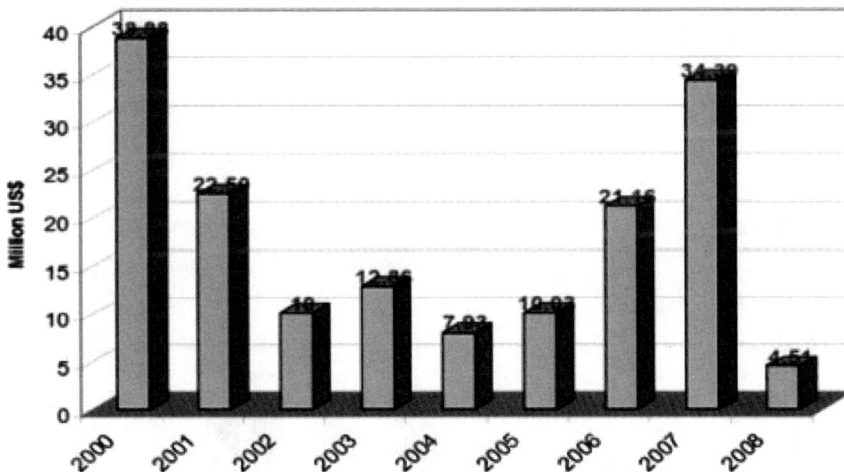

Source: Depat. of International Cooperation, MPI, 2009

In general, Chinese ODA has been concentrated in a few areas suchas health, rural development, social development, education/human resource development and transportation. Chinese ODA for transportation has been

61

Figure 4: Percentage of Chinese ODA in Lao PDR

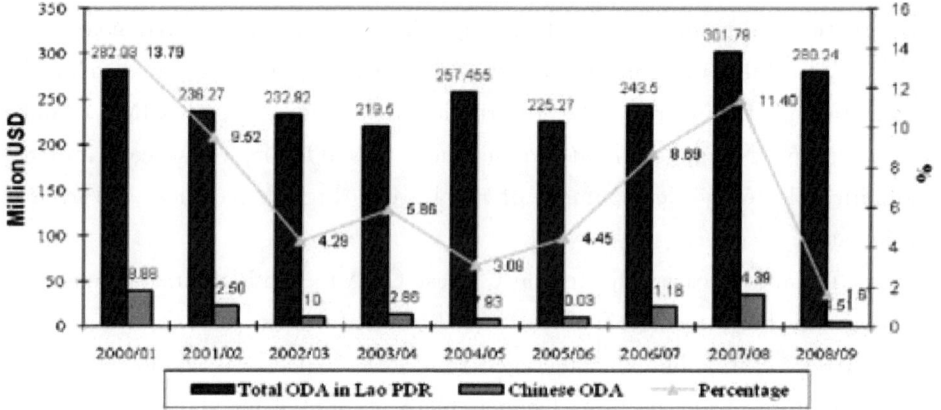

Source: Dept. of International Cooperation, MPI, 2009

used to improve links from Lao PDR to some Chinese provinces such as Yunnan and Nanning and develop transportation infrastructure in urban areas as well as some of the country's rural northern provinces. In 2004—2006, the bulk of Chinese ODA was concentrated in the transportation sector followed by education/human resource development. The latter took the form of the Chinese government providing approximately 200 scholarships annually to Lao students to help them study in China.

Figure 5 : Chinese ODA and Sector of Working in Lao PDR

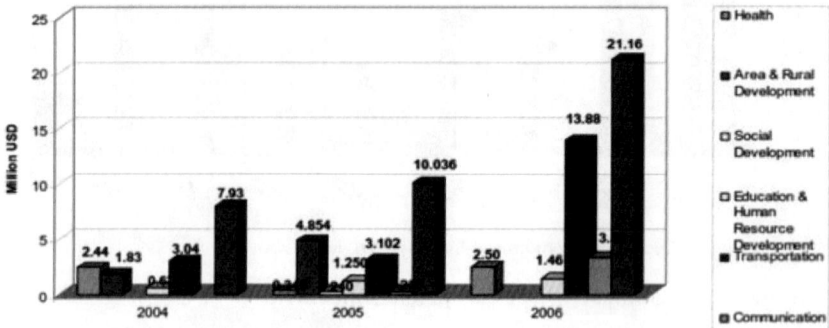

Source: Dept. of International Cooperation, MPI, 2008

IV. Conclusion

FDI, foreign trade and ODA are considered important factors for the development of Lao PDR since we are considered as the primary means by which to achieve the macroeconomic goals of growth, poverty reduction and graduation from the status of LDC by 2020. These finance vital investment projects stimulate the growth of Lao economy. In the country's annual and five-year plans, these external sectors have been directly identified as significant factors for ensuring the achievement of Lao PDR's strategic goals for socioeconomic development.

Besides the ASEAN, the East Asian region is acknowledged to be an important source of financial and technical assistance for the social and economic development of Lao PDR. China is the country's most important partner in this region, providing substantial funding for many priority projects in the private business sector as well as for public investment.

China has focused more on FDI and trade relations with Lao PDR. It ranks top three in terms of the value of FDI, and it has engaged in many huge private investment projects, especially in the northern provinces, including the Boten-Dankham project in Luang namtha province and Ton Pheung project in Bokeo province, among others. China has also been a significant trade partner, being a source of many of the consumer products the Lao people use in their daily life and the products used as a means of production in factories and farms, especially in the remote northern rural areas.

Border trade in the northern provinces has also been identified as significant contributor to the development of the local people, especially in terms of employment opportunities, incomegeneration, technology transfer and knowledge transfer. Many social benefits have identified as an outcome of Cross Border Trade including education opportunities and access to health care.

Therefore, the overall conclusion is that cooperation and good relations with both countries is important for the development of Lao PDR. The investment, trade relation and aid that Lao PDR receives from China are crucial for its continued social and economic development.

中国与老挝的贸易与经济合作

Thipphavanh Chanthavongsa[*]
赵　耀　译

引　言

老挝民主共和国为内陆国,位于中南半岛中部,与中国、越南、柬埔寨、泰国和缅甸接壤。国土面积 236,800 平方公里,多山地,森林、河流覆盖面广。人口 570 万,人口密度 22 人/平方公里。老挝民主共和国约有 49 个民族。经济以农业为主,约有 80% 人口从事农业生产。

1986 年,老挝政府施行推动中央计划经济向市场经济转变的新经济政策。尽管老挝政治体制与他国存在差异,但老挝政府仍积极发展与世界各国的友好关系,试图通过与国际社会的合作实现发展。1992 年,老挝共和国加入一个次区域经济合作项目——大湄公河次区域(GSM)。1997 年,老挝正式成为东盟成员。

由于充分认识到国际合作的重要性,老挝迄今为止已与世界上 128 个国家建立了外交关系。(外交部,2008)外商直接投资,对外贸易和官方发展援助(ODA)已被作为促进老挝经济发展的重要因素,特别是在国家年度计划与五年计划实施中地位尤为突出。老挝政府认识到,老挝要实现从最不发达国家(LDCs)脱离出来的愿景,就要增加收入,减少贫困。因投资是经济发展的重要因素,而老挝国内投资有限,老挝希望通过引进投资来实现经济大幅增长的目标。

外商直接投资、国际贸易发展和官方发展援助的国外投资在老挝社会经

---

[*]　老挝中部人民法院干部。

济发展中发挥着重要作用。中国是其众多东亚投资者之一,在上述三个领域处于支配地位。老挝每年收到的援助约 1/4 来自中国。中国也大量投资老挝的公共基础设施,并对老挝私营部门的发展做出了贡献。

从二十世纪早期开始,中国就成为老挝外商直接投资总值的重大来源之一。现在由于中老贸易和经济联系的扩大,中国经济的蓬勃发展也成为老挝的制造业发展的重要契机。

此篇论文将回顾中国对老挝社会经济发展做出贡献的深远意义,作为分析中国地位的部分佐证。本文将着重着笔于经济层面,中老社会与经济关系,以此来分析中国在老挝经济发展中的角色。本文将以老挝区域经济一体化与贸易促进政策的综述作为开端,中老关系分析作为第二部分,最后是结论与政策建议。

一、区域经济一体化

1986 年,老挝的区域经济一体化政策以新经济政策的推广作为开端。新经济政策的制定目标是使老挝从中央计划经济模式转变为市场经济模式,也因此引起了 20 世纪 90 年代对外开放政策的制定。

自推广新经济政策以来,老挝渐渐提升了区域一体化与区域合作的水平,并且在 1997 年与柬埔寨、越南、缅甸共同成为了东盟的正式成员。老挝也因此加入了东盟自由贸易区(AFTA),承担起了便利与其他东盟成员国贸易的义务。东盟也引入了许多项目来扩大合作与自由贸易区(FTA)。东盟＋3(东盟＋日本、韩国、中国)项目扩大了与中国的合作与自由贸易。2001 年 11月,东盟与中国在金边启动了建立中国与东盟自由贸易区(ACFTA)的系列谈判。2002 年,双方签订了全面经济合作的框架协议,目的是加强并提高中国与东盟间的经济贸易与投资合作水平,逐渐实现货物与服务贸易自由化促进新东盟成员形成更有效的经济一体化,缩小各缔约国的发展差距。

2004 年,中国与东盟签订货物贸易协议。根据此协议,东盟的六个创始成员国(泰国、马来西亚、印度尼西亚、菲律宾、新加坡和文莱)和中国应当自2010 年开始对它们 90％的产品的减免关税,东盟的新成员国(柬埔寨、老挝、缅甸和越南)将于 2015 年实施此协议。

中国与东盟自由贸易区将于 2015 年全面实施。但是,框架协议第六条规定要提前实施对特定农产品的关税减免,以此让缔约各国提前享受自由贸易区的好处。例如,早期收获计划(EHP)包含了总共 562 种产品。但是,协议也允许一方将早期收获计划范围内的某些特定产品排除在减免关税的行列,也允许一方将计划内未包含的特定产品归入减免关税的行列,前提是必须经过中国与相关同盟成员国的相互同意。文莱和新加坡属于经济非农业型的国家,那它们就要完全遵守早期收获计划(EHP)的规定,而不能排除部分特定产品不减免关税。越南与柬埔寨于2002年提交了排除在减免关税名单外的农产品名录,早于框架协议的签订。马来西亚在2003年3月的截止日期前也提交了相应名录。印度尼西亚和泰国没有提交排除名录,而是提交了纳入减免关税名录的请求名录。印尼的请求名录(与中国达成一致意见)包括咖啡、棕榈油、椰子油、植物油脂、可可粉、香皂、硫化橡胶、做阴极射线管(CRTs)的玻璃和木制家具。除了无烟煤和焦炭的请求名录,泰国早在2003年6月就与中国达成协议——对水果和蔬菜征零关税。老挝没有提交排除名录也没有提交请求名录。因此,中国—老挝早期收获计划自动地包含562种农产品。这意味着中国会减免从老挝进口的农产品关税。但是直到最近,还没有研究表明早期收获计划(EHP)对中老贸易量的确切影响。

另外,老挝正致力于加入世界贸易组织(WTO)。当其成为WTO成员国时,就可以进入海外市场,得到更多投资与促进技术进步的机会,而这些长期看来,是刺激经济增长与减少贫困的重要因素。但是,要从加入WTO中真正获得好处,老挝仍必须刺激它的生产力,提高产量和提高产品质量,以增强它在国际市场的竞争力。

老挝也与泰国、越南、中国签订了双边或多边的贸易与运输协议,包括:

(1)2009年6月11日签订的老挝、泰国、越南关于联运运输权利和海关过境制度的实施的协议。此协议促进了沿东西走廊(EWC)的跨境运输。为了保证一体化政策的延续和促进跨境运输,老挝与泰国、越南政府在2009年6月11日一致同意:①通过联运运输权利的规定,促进运输工具的跨境运输;②基于海关过境保障制度,允许运输工具在任何过境地放弃卸载和重新加载货物的需要;③在合理的时间内,通过单站和单窗检查仪器,允许在边防关卡对货物进行最小检验。

(2)老挝与泰国、越南、中国、柬埔寨和缅甸的双边运输协议。老挝与邻国签订了双边运输协议以促进旅客与货物的运输。双边运输协议允许卡车从老挝进入或离开邻国时拥有重载权,同样邻国的卡车也享有此项权利。双边运输协议促进了老挝与邻国的贸易与合作。

但是,必须指出,老挝与外国没有关于农业贸易的具体双边协议。它农产品的出口靠的是区域与双边贸易协议。农业贸易双边协议(它将会促进具体的农产品出口向具体的市场)的缺失貌似体现在老挝没有针对农业贸易的具体政策与战略。具体的政策与战略将会促进农业发展,因为老挝有很多对农业生产的限制条件(例如,土地紧张,有限的财力与人力资源)。具体的政策与战略也将有利于老挝生产力与竞争力的提升。

二、老挝的贸易促进政策

由于认识到对外贸易在国家经济发展和贫困减少中的重要地位,政府通过一些政策促进出口与进口,例如:

(1)一站服务政策。2004年10月13日,老挝工商部(MOIC)颁布了962号法令(在一站服务机构实施205/PM号法令)来促进进出口。此项政策指导各省和首都——万象的所有进出口代理处在边防关卡设立办公室,取消进出口许可证(除了黄金、铜、运输工具、运输工具零件、石油、天然气、钻石和其他工商部禁止的需要进口许可证的货物)。国民经济研究所(NERI)的研究表明一站服务政策的实施减少了时间和成本,促进了跨境贸易的发展。

(2)边境贸易促进政策。2001年,老挝工商部出台了边境贸易管理的948号指令。此项政策旨在促进小规模商业生产和出口,为生活在边境的人民创造工作机会、提供收入。边境地区被分为两类:偏远地区与非偏远地区。偏远地区没有或说很难有机会进入国内市场,而非偏远地区很容易进入国内市场。偏远地区的人可以出口和进口对生产和消费来说必要的各种产品,而非偏远地区的人可以出口任何产品,但是仅可以进口对生产投入来说必要的产品。住在非偏远山区的人们必须从国内市场购买消费品。

(3)建立经济特区和边境贸易区的政策。为了便利贸易和促进投资,老挝政府实施了管理经济特区(SEZs)、建立边境贸易区的政策。迄今为止,已有一个经济特区和三个边境贸易区建立。另外的刺激和促进措施是必要的,以此在边境地区和经济特区吸引更多的投资和贸易。例如,沙湾—色诺经济特区(SAVAN-SENO SEZ)的投资者享有一些特权,比如免交营业税和使用税、交很低的税和其他刺激手段。这些刺激方式有:①在投资的初期免税,根据部门和情况可以减税;②5%的股利税,远低于普通税率;③5%的利润税,也低于普通税率;④五年内可转让的亏损;⑤免除原材料、建筑材料、仪器设备、机器、运输工具、零件和在经济特区使用或装配的半成品、成品的进口税;⑥根据投资的领域,减少最小注册资本。在中老边境贸易区的投资者享受着各种刺激投资的方式,包括①起初运营的前四年免除利润税与所得税,满四年后在允许的一段时间内可以享受 50％的税收减免；②免除 7 年的地税；③减免 10％的进口税。如果投资人在生产过程中要用老挝国内的原材料，那么从边境贸易区进口到老挝国内市场的成品的进口税就会根据使用国内原料花费的成本与总的生产成本的百分比而减少。例如，投资人使用国内原料的成本与总生产成本的比为 30％，那么当成品进口到国内市场时进口税就会减少 30％。

三、老挝与中国的社会与经济关系

中国与老挝于 1961 年 4 月 25 日建交。两国有着长期的历史渊源，特别是老挝的北部三省（丰沙里，达南塔，乌多姆赛）与中国南部的云南省接壤。而且除老挝上述三省外的其他北部省份都与中国的商人建立了业务关系。本章也会呈现中国投资、双方贸易关系、官方发展援助的官方数据。

1. 中国在老挝的投资

现在，中国对老挝的投资总量占第二位，仅落后于泰国。来自中国的外商直接投资占工业总投资值的将近 80％，占项目总数 50％以上。中国对老挝的投资在 20 世纪 90 年代稳步增长，从 21 世纪开始迅猛增长。1991—2000 年，来自中国的外商直接投资仅约 127,000,000 美元，71 个项目以上。而 2001—2008 年，中国的投资总值超过 14 亿美元，覆盖 244 个项目。与先前的 10 年相比，过去 8 年的数字翻了 10 倍。过去 8 年来自中国的外商直接投资占了1991—2008 年中国对老挝投资总额的 91％以上。

从中国开始向老挝投资起，其外商直接投资均流向第二、第三产业，促进了老挝工业与服务业的发展。中国 67％以上的投资流向工业，约 29％流向服务业，只约 3％流向农业。中国对老挝的外商直接投资额在第四个五年计划（1996—2000）期间变化不大，对农业的投资与前几年处于同一水平，对服务业的投资减少，对工业的投资大幅上升，占总投资额的约 90％。

第五个五年计划（2001—2005）期间，来自中国的外商直接投资的投资额与项目数增长超过三倍。对工业的投资占投资总值的 85％以上，对服务业占8％，农业占 6％。与上一阶段相比，来自中国的外商直接投资增长率为148％，农业为 276％，工业 141％，服务业 149％。

第六个五年计划（2006—2010）上半叶，中国对老挝的外商直接投资迅猛增长。与上一个五年计划（2001—2005）的整个阶段相比，2006 年一年的外商直接投资总额增长了将近 5 倍，甚至大约是过去十五年（1991—2005）外商直接投资总额的 2 倍。过去三年的投资增长率的平均值约为 300％一年，其中对农业投资增长率为 177％一年,工业 320％一年,服务业 822％一年。而第六个五年计划(2006—2010)上半叶来自中国的外商直接投资总额大约是 12 亿美元,覆盖 141 个项目,工业占总投资额的 78％,服务业占 11.5％,农业占 10％。来自中国的外商直接投资打破了每一个五年计划的预计目标和第六个五年计划(2006—2010)前三年的目标。很明显,近些年中国对老挝的投资在工业、服务业和农业都大幅增长,并且在 1991—2008 年,占到了投资总额的 80％以上。来自中国的外商直接投资不仅流向中西部地区,还流向了与其他地区相比基础设施落后的北部地区。因为落后的基础设施条件,北部地区对世界其他地区的直接投资吸引力较小,但是由于北部地区的地理优势,它可与中国互惠互利。

总体上,1989—2008 年,来自中国的外商直接投资总额约占老挝总额的 8.6％。中国外商直接投资的前五个部门是水力、手工业、矿业、服务业与农业。其水力发电接受的外商直接投资大约占国家电力产业直接投资总额的 6.3％。中国的大量投资使它排名第一。工业与手工业排名第二,占他们部门外商直接投资总额的 17.8％。矿业在 2006 年是投资最多的领域,它是中国外商直接投资的第三大部门,占外商直接投资总额的 14.3％。服务业与农业分别为第四、第五名,服务业约占外商直接投资总额的 20％,农业约占 7％。

总体上,近些年来自中国的外商直接投资额迅猛增长。这些投资大多数流向自然资源领域,如电力、农业和矿业。而这些投资的投资额大约占总额的 60％。大概是由于中国对老挝的直接投资在过去几年才起步的原因,中国投资了很多手工业、服务业、贸易、旅馆和饭店、木材工业领域的项目,但是没有投资银行业。来自中国的外商直接投资促进了老挝临近中国的北部地区的发展,这成为了北部地区居民收入的重要来源与减少贫困的重要途径。

2. 中老间的贸易关系

对外贸易是老挝的重要产业,是经济增长的重要来源。20 世纪 80 年代晚期老挝实行的对外开放政策推动了对外贸易的发展。虽然它与世界上超过 60 个国家有贸易往来,但是贸易活动大多是与同区域内的国家开展,特别是与邻国开展。作为内陆国,老挝区域内贸易比区域外贸易更具竞争力。

虽然 21 世纪早期中老贸易交往的趋势有些波动,但总体上升。2004 年起,两国的进口和出口额都迅速增长。但是数据显示,老挝仍呈贸易逆差的状态。尽管 21 世纪后期贸易平衡的总趋势稳步提升,但是贸易逆差依然存在。

但是,就与中国进口或出口的贸易额和贸易总额(进出口总额)的比值看来,出口中国的比值从 21 世纪早期出口贸易总额的 3％～4％上升至 21 世纪晚期的 8%～9%。2000—2008 年，从中国进口的总额占进口贸易总额的 2%～4%。

与中老贸易有关的另一个值得注意的问题是边境贸易，特别是老挝北部达南塔省和乌多姆赛省的边境贸易问题。边境贸易对这些地区居民的社会和经济活动既有积极影响，也有消极影响。积极影响包括生活水平、就业机会、收入增加、贸易来往等方面的变化，还包括教育与医疗保障等社会福利方面的好处。但是，边境贸易也存在其他社会问题，比如外籍劳工问题等等。

3.中国对老挝的官方直接投资

官方直接投资对老挝的社会经济发展来说非常重要。老挝官方直接投资的来源有世界银行、联合国、世贸组织和双边国家（特别是高收入的国家或发达国家）等多边共同体、国际组织。国际货币基金组织和非政府间的国际组织也会通过技术援助和赠款援助来促进农村地区的发展。

官方数据表明，中国对老挝的官方直接投资起始于 21 世纪早期，投资自此之后稳步流入老挝。中国对老挝的官方直接投资额每年会有波动，但是 2000—2008 年平均每年大约有 18000000 美元资金。2000—2008 年，中国的官方直接投资平均每年占官方直接投资总额的 7%～8%。

通常中国的官方直接投资会集中于健康、农村发展、社会发展、教育（人力资源）发展和交通运输等几个领域，改善了老挝到中国部分省市（如云南，南宁）的铁路状况，发展了城市和某些北部农村地区交通运输的基础设施建设。2004—2006 年，大部分中国的官方直接投资集中于交通运输业，其次是教育（人力资源）。后者采用的方式是中国政府每年大约提供 200 个奖学金给老挝学生，资助他们在中国学习。

四、结论

外商直接投资、对外贸易和官方直接投资是老挝经济发展的重要因素，它们是老挝 2020 年实现经济大幅增长、减少贫困和脱离最不发达国家队伍目标的首要途径。这些重要的金融投资项目刺激了老挝经济的增长。在老挝的年度计划与五年计划中，这些外部因素直接被认定为保证老挝实现经济发展的战略目标的重要因素。

除了东盟，东亚地区是老挝获得促进社会和经济发展的技术与资金援助的重要来源。中国作为老挝在东亚地区中最重要的伙伴，持续为私营企业和公共投资领域的许多重点工程提供资金。

中国更专注对老挝的外商直接投资与贸易往来。中国对老挝的投资占老挝外商直接投资总额的第三位,参与了许多大型私营投资项目,特别值得一提的是在北部省份的投资,包括在达南塔(Luang namtha)省的 Boten-Dankham 工程和博胶省(Bokeo)的 Ton Pheung 工程。中国也是老挝的重要贸易伙伴,老挝人日常使用的很多消费品、供工厂和农场加工生产的产品都来自中国,这种情况在偏远的北部农村地区尤为突出。

北部地区的边境贸易为北部地区居民生活水平的提高做出了重大贡献。边境贸易带来了许多像教育机会、医疗保障这样的社会福利。

因此,两国的合作与友好关系对老挝的发展举足轻重。中国对老挝的投资、贸易往来、援助对老挝社会与经济的发展至关重要。

Legal Issues on Infrastructure Construction and Connectivity

Lai Chee Hoe[*]

Part A. Introduction

1. In ancient times, the Maritime Silk Road facilitated the trading of China's silk, ceramics and other luxuries to the world.

2. This route saw a rebranding when Chinese President Xi Jinping brought up the "Maritime Silk Road of the 21st-century" during his official visit to South-East Asia.

3. The 21st-century Maritime Silk Road is set to spawn many new infrastructure linkages and strengthen greater economic and social exchanges between China and its Asean counterparts.

4. The dream will focus on building roads, railways, ports and airports across Central and South Asia, marking a new stage for China's global presence in infrastructure.

5. Connectivity in this regard plays a very important role. Although the silk road places a lot of emphasis on maritime transport, the connectivity of the rail networks cannot be ignored.

6. When concerns were raised with regards to the adverse effects originated from the transportation networks, railways offers an efficient, safe and environmental sound mode of transport.

7. The entry into force of the inter-government agreement on the Trans-

* Partner, Chee Hoe A Associates.

Asian Railway Network in 2009 also indicates the readiness of governments to co-operate on railway projects of international importance and work together on the development of efficient rail transport corridors to serve growing trade.

8. Internally, railways play a significant role in China's economic development and improvement of its people's livelihood.

9. The ultra modern and efficient city rail transit system not only relieves the crowded passenger traffic, but also guides the development of the Chinese cities.

10. According to Wikipedia, as of 2013, China has 103,144 km of railways, the third longest network in the world, including 11,028 km of HSR, the longest HSR network in the world.

11. In the context of Malaysia, CSR ZHUZHOU ELECTRIC LOCOMOTIVE CO., LTD. (中国南车集团株洲电力机车有限公司) and CHINA RAILWAY CONSTRUCTION CORP LTD (中国铁建股份有限公司) have either secured a project or vying for projects including the Kuala Lumpur-Singapore high-speed rail (HSR) project.

12. It is no wonder that China has grand plans to build thousands of miles of track that will run through Lao, Cambodia, Thailand, Myanmar and Malaysia as well as head south to Singapore as part of a trans-Asian rail accord signed by nearly 20 Asian countries in 2006. The line will provide an alternative to the longer shipping route through the South China Sea and compliment the maritime silk road.

13. To avoid direct confrontation with maritime transport, railway may focus on the remote rural areas and the rail networks also meanwhile provide more reliability and predictability.

Part B. Existing International Organisations to promote rail co-operation

14. There are various international organisations set up and the more prominent ones are:

(a) Organisation for Co-operation between Railways ("OSJD") which was established in Bulgaria with the main objective to provide, develop and improve international transportation between Europe and Asia;

(b) International Organization for international carriage by Rail ("OTIF") which has 48 members states in Europe, North Africa and the Middle East. One of the principal objectives of OTIF is to establish a uniform system of law on various aspects;

(c) International Union for Railways ("UIC") established in Paris with a main purpose to harmonise and improve conditions for railway construction and operations;

(d) International Rail Transport Committee ("CIT") formed in 1902 to promote harmonisation of legal frameworks and support uniform implementation of laws governing railway transport;

15. There are also several regional set ups and one of which is the Singapore Kunming Rail Link which is monitored by a special working group (SWG) which meets annually. The last meeting took place in Kuala Lumpur, Malaysia in October 2013. Malaysia holds the chair of the SWG and is supported by ASEAN secretariat. At the SWG meetings, each country briefs about the work undertaken and railway developments.

Part C. Legal Challenges

16. The Trans-Asia Rail Network shows that the existing railway lines of international importance form a circular strip, generally connecting the member countries of Trans-Asia Rail. Member countries have been attempting to build new railway lines to complete the missing links. The ASEAN initiative on the Kunming-Singapore rail link will build 3 links between Northeast Asia and Southeast Asia. This will compliment the silk road connectivity and trade.

17. Theoretically, passengers and goods can then be transported throughout the land-linked regions. However in practice, international rail transport on this network only takes place partially due to economic reason and institutional barriers.

18. In general the key legal challenges to international railway transport

include:

(a) the legal requirement for the break of gauge;

(b) the legal requirement in acquiring land for purposes of building railway tracks;

(c) the technical requirements for number of tracks, distance between track centres;

(d) the legal permissible speed, axle load, maximum gradient;

(e) regulatory issues such as maximum working hours, training and benefits for rail employees;

(f) legal procedures for crossing borders;

(g) lack of harmonization in the documents required by different countries;

(h) inspection documents on both sides of border crossings;

(i) different legal specifications for braking, signaling systems;

(j) different operating rules and tariff structures;

(k) different legal requirements for train drivers and crews;

(l) different legal requirements for purposes of transmitting information across borders;

(m) lack of a legal permits for train drivers and crews when operating cross-border trains.

19. To materialise the Silk Road Connectivity by rail, a number of key issues needs to be addressed such as:

(a) participation in international railway organisations;

(b) tackling of difficulties with break of gauge;

(c) harmonization of documents;

(d) acquiring interest in land to build tracks;

(e) simplification of procedures for crossing borders;

(f) standardization of technical requirements;

(g) standardization of tariff structures.

Part D. Possible solutions

20. The international and bilateral agreements have identified these

problems and attempts of legal harmonization can be found in many of the international agreements. There are many proposed solutions but because time doesn't permit us to go through all the solutions, we extract 2 general ones as below.

(a) Advance passenger and cargo information system (Customs, immigration)

21. Delays of trains at border crossings are mostly caused by significant time required by control authorities such as Customs, immigration and quarantine to process and clear documents and inspect goods.

22. According to a survey made by OSJD 34.5% of time of international trains was spent for border crossing formalities and 11% for correction of wrong translation of documents. Such unnecessary delays can be substantially reduced with the use of advance passenger and cargo information system.

23. This system has been employed in international air and maritime transport for years. Adoption of a common standard is crucial to harmonise the legal procedures.

(b) Human Resources

24. Visa for crew and drivers should be simplified to ensure certainty. One year multiple entry visas on reciprocal basis is suggested as provided in many bilateral agreements.

25. Common system for training drivers should also be encouraged. A mutually recognised authorisation or certification may be issued by the national railway that is acceptable to other railway in the region based on a pre-agreed common training to the drivers. This will ensure that the driver is aware of the route he is operating including the legal speed limits, signalling systems and emergency procedures

Part E. Existing Legal Instruments in harmonizing international railway transport

26. In harmonising the legal requirements, there are several international conventions and agreements signed by the member states and OSJD itself has 9

different agreements which are:

(a) Agreement on the International Passenger Transport by Rail;

(b) Agreement on the International Goods Transport by Rail;

(c) Agreement on the International Passenger Tariff;

(d) Agreement on the International Railway Transit Tariff;

(e) Agreement on the Uniform Transit Tariff;

(f) Agreement on Rules of the Use of Coaches in International Tariff;

(g) Agreement on Rules for the Use of wagons in International Tariff;

(h) Agreement on the Accounting Rules in International Transport of Passengers and Goods by Rail;

(i) Agreement on Organizational and Operational Aspects of Combined Transport between Europe and Asia.

27. We will not dwell on each of the agreement but suffice to say that some of these agreements have gone through a thorough study to formulate a set of standardized rules. Further a draft convention is being prepared to integrate the basic documents of the organisation and establish a comprehensive set of rules related to international railway transport.

28. The system of the OSJD legislative documents consists of procedural rules and regulations for the OSJD, agreements concluded within the framework of the OSJD together with mandatory or recommended nature on technical issues.

29. There are many other international legal frameworks which the member countries of ASEAN can make reference to including the OTIF uniform rules, standardization platform of UIC, the Economic Co-operation Organisation (ECO) Transit transport Framework Agreement ("TFFA") which came into force in May 2006, The Protocol 6 on Railway Border and Interchange station attached to the ASEAN Framework Agreement on facilitation of goods in transit; Joint Traffic Working Agreement signed between Malaysia-Thailand Railway.

Part F. Conclusion

30. This short paper only serves to identify the various legal issues

which may face whilst developing the railway connectivity among countries to achieve the silk road dream.

31. The legal complications although can be identified and solutions be proposed and adopted by international treaty, it always boils down to the issue of harmonising within the national policies and implementing them.

32. Implementing the international standards requires a ratification through legislation and it has its own set of difficulties. Stability in the local political arena is a must and in addition a comprehensive training including the introduction of the rationale of the policies must be disseminated to the grass roots officers who work closely with the railway industry.

33. Implementation remains the key to harmonising the international rail networks policies and developing the railway connectivity. It is my view that the legal harmonization is a dream achievable when all the member countries can set aside their political interests and work towards the vision of connecting the countries by rail.

Source:

1. *Monograph Series on Transport Facilitation of International Railway Transport in Asia and the Pacific of the United Nationals ESCAP*

2. *Wikipedia.*

基础设施建设与互联互通中的法律问题

Lai Chee Hoe[*]
赵　耀　译

一、引言

习近平主席在对东南亚进行国事访问时,提出建立"21世纪海上丝绸之路"。21世纪海上丝绸之路的建设,将刺激大量基础设施的修建,加强中国与东盟的交往。

此构想主要是修建跨越中亚和南亚的公路、铁路、港口与机场,开启中国建设海外基础设施的新篇章。

这样看来,通道的建设对21世纪海上丝绸之路而言,举足轻重。海运通道在海上丝绸之路的建设中非常重要,但是铁路通道的建设同样不容忽视。铁路作为一种高效、安全、环保的交通模式,可以解决交通网络的负面问题。

2009年"泛亚铁路网"政府间协议的生效,也表明双方政府计划在具有国际重要意义的铁路工程上开展合作,共同建设高效率铁路通道。

从中国国内来看,铁路在中国经济发展与人民生活水平的提高中扮演着重要的角色。现代和高效的城市轨道交通不仅能够减轻客运压力,还可以促进中国城市的发展。

在马来西亚,中国南车集团株洲电力机车有限公司已得到一个铁路建设项目,而中国铁建股份公司正在竞标包括吉隆坡—新加坡段高铁建设工程在内的建设项目。

中国在铁路建设上规划远大,将建设途经老挝、柬埔寨、泰国、缅甸、南至

---

* 马来西亚志豪联合律师事务所合伙人,马来西亚KJ罗法律事务所合伙人。

新加坡的数千英里铁路,这是 2006 年将近 20 个亚洲国家签订的泛亚铁路协议的一部分,它也将穿越中国南海。这缩短了路线,可与海上丝绸之路媲美。

为避免与海运直接竞争,铁路可能主要在偏远的农村地区修建。

二、促进铁路合作的国际组织

众多国际组织中,较为突出的包括:

(1)铁路合作组织(OSJD)。设于保加利亚建立,目标为建设、发展和提高欧亚间的国际交通运输;

(2)国际铁路联运组织(OTIF)。48 个成员国分别来自欧洲、北美洲与中东地区。目标是在各方面建立统一的法律制度;

(3)国际铁路联盟(UIC)。于巴黎建立,目标是协调和改善铁路建设和运行的条件;

(4)国际铁路运输委员会(CIT)。成立于 1902 年,旨在促进法律框架的协调,支持管理铁路运输的法律的统一实施。

还有几个区域性组织,其中之一是监督"新加坡昆明铁路线"特别工作小组(SWG),特别工作小组每年都会会面。上一次会议是 2013 年 10 月在马来西亚的吉隆坡举行。马来西亚是特别工作小组的主席,由东盟秘书处协助。在特别工作小组的会议中,每个国家都简述了工作成果与铁路的发展状况。

三、法律上的挑战

泛亚铁路网使得具有国际重要意义的铁路线形成了一个环形带,将泛亚铁路沿线诸国相连接。目前各成员国仍致力于兴修新线路,加强彼此联系。由东盟发起建设的昆明—新加坡铁路线将会在东北亚与东南亚之间建立三个新的交通路线,这将与丝绸之路媲美。

理论上,装载乘客或货物的列车可以穿越不同国家。但是在实践中,由于经济与制度障碍等原因,国际铁路运输并没有那么顺利。

大体而论,对国际铁路运输的关键法律挑战有:

(1)换轨的法律规定;

(2)为了建设铁路获得土地的法律规定;

(3)铁轨数量、轨距长度的技术要求;

(4)法律允许的速度、轴载、最大坡度;

(5)诸如铁路员工的最长工作时长、培训、福利等监管问题；

(6)跨越国界的法律程序；

(7)不同国家要求的文件不一致；

(8)双方列车跨越国境的检查文件；

(9)国家间对制动系统与信号系统的具体的法律规定不同；

(10)不同的运营规定和关税结构；

(11)对列车司机与乘务员的不同法律要求；

(12)跨国界传送信息的不同法律规定；

(13)列车驾驶员与乘务员运营跨国界列车缺少法定许可。

为通过铁路运输实现丝绸之路的连通性，需要提出一些关键问题，例如：

(1)沿线国家参与国际铁路组织；

(2)解决换轨的难题；

(3)文件的协调一致；

(4)为建铁路获得土地权益；

(5)跨境的程序简化；

(6)技术要求的标准化；

(7)关税结构的标准化。

四、合理的解决方案

国际条约和双边协定已经认识到了这些问题，并且许多国际条约已经试图协调不同国家的法律来解决这些问题。现在已提出了许多解决方案，但我们不将所有方案一一列举，仅提出两个普遍的方案如下：

(1)改进客运和货运信息系统（海关、移民局）

列车在过境处的迟延主要因为像海关、移民局和检疫局等管控机关要花大量的时间审核、清理过境文件和检查货物。

根据铁路合作组织（OSJD）的一项调查显示，国际列车有 34.5％ 的时间花在过境手续，11％ 的时间花在更正过境文件错误的翻译上。如此不必要的迟延将在运用了先进的客运与货运信息系统后大大减少。国际航空运输与海运已运用上述系统多年。

要使各国法律程序相协调，制定统一的标准必不可少。

(2)人力资源

可以简化列车驾驶员与乘务员的签证。许多双边条约规定了基于互惠原则,可以给予一年多次入境签证。

各国应促进建立起统一的列车驾驶员的培训制度。基于各国事先议定要对驾驶员实行一致的培训,那由一国国内铁路局颁发的各国相互承认的授权书或资格证在另一国的铁路局也会得到认可。这就确保了列车司机充分了解驾驶线路的法定限速值、信号系统和应急措施等情况。

五、目前协调国际铁路运输的法律文件

为协调不同国家的法律规定,成员国签订了数个国际条约与协定,而铁路合作组织也有九个不同的协定,如下:
(1)《国际铁路旅客运输协议》;
(2)《国际铁路货物运输协议》;
(3)《国际旅客运输价格协议》;
(4)《国际铁路过境关税协议》;
(5)《统一过境关税协议》;
(6)《国际关税下的车厢使用规则协议》;
(7)《国际关税下的货车使用规则协议》;
(8)《国际铁路客运与货运会计规则协议》;
(9)《欧亚联合运输组织与操作协议》。

这些协议是经过了全面的研究才构想出一套标准化的规范,而整合了组织基本文件和一套国际铁路运输的全面规则的公约草案正在筹划中。

还有很多其他国际法律框架东盟成员国可以参考适用,包括国际铁路联运组织统一规则、国际铁路联盟标准化平台、在 2006 年 5 月生效的经济合作组织(ECO)过境运输框架协议(TFFA)、附属于东盟促进货物过境运输的框架协议的铁路边防车站与换乘车站的六号协议,由马来西亚与泰国铁路局签署的联合运输工作协议。

六、结论

这篇论文仅用来识别我们在发展国家间铁路交通以重建丝绸之路的过程中出现的各种法律问题。虽然我们已识别出复杂的法律问题,解决方案也具可行性,但最终要解决的问题是能使解决方案与国内政策相协调并得以实施。

国际标准的实施需要国内立法的承认。但实施本身就存在诸多困难——

当地政局可能不稳定。另外，全面培训，包括政策推行原因的宣传，必须要在铁路业基层人员中推广。

落实才是国际铁路运输网政策协调与铁路连通性发展的关键。我认为，当所有成员国搁置政治利益、共同致力于用铁路连通各国的美好前景时，法律协调才可以实现。

Legal Issues on Trade and Economic Cooperation in Myanmar

Si Thu Swe Tun [*]

1. Introduction

The Republic of the Union of Myanmar, at the present time, already has new Constitution and the new civilian Government. Under Section 35 of the Myanmar Constitution, Myanmar's economic system is Market Economic System. In terms of commercial relations, bilateral trade between China and Myanmar exceeds $1. 4 billion. Chinese imports to Myanmar typically focus around oil, steel and textile products, while Myanmar imports range from natural rubber to raw wood. Myanmar allows inputs such as technology, investments, machinery, raw materials, so forth, to the extent possible for changeover from manual to mechanized agriculture.

2. The 2008 Constitution

According to Section 36, Myanmar permits all economic forces such as the State, regional organizations, cooperatives, joint-ventures, private individual, so forth, to take part in economic activities for the development of National economy; protect and prevent acts that injure public interests through monopolization or manipulation of prices by an individual or group

---

* Staff Officer, the Union Attorney General's Office, Myanmar.

with intent to endanger fair competition in economic activities; strive to improve the living standards of the people and development of investments; not nationalize economic enterprises; and not demonetize the currency legally in circulation.

In 2011, when the President Thein Sein's government came to power, Myanmar embarked on a major policy of reforms including anti-corruption, currency exchange rate, foreign investment laws and taxation. Foreign investments increased from US $ 300 million in 2009—2010 to a US $ 20 billion in 2010—2011 by about 667%. Large inflow of capital results in stronger Myanmar currency, kyat by about 25%. In response, the government relaxed import restrictions and abolished export taxes. Despite current currency problems, Myanmar economy is expected to grow by about 8.8% in 2011. After the completion of 58-billion dollar Dawei deep seaport, Myanmar is expected be at the hub of trade connecting Southeast Asia and the South China Sea, via the Andaman Sea, to the Indian Ocean receiving goods from countries in the Middle East, Europe and Africa, and spurring growth in the ASEAN region.

In 2012, the Asian Development Bank formally began re-engaging with the country, to finance infrastructure and development projects in the country. The $ 512 million loan is the first issued by the ADB to Myanmar in 30 years and will target banking services, ultimately leading to other major investments in road, energy, irrigation and education projects.

3. China Economic Aid

China is providing extensive aid and helping to develop industries and infrastructure and Myanmar aims to be the chief beneficiary from cultivating Myanmar's extensive oil and natural gas reserves. It is one of the chief partners of the Myanmar regime in the project to renovate and expand the Sittwe seaport and has received rights to develop and exploit natural gas reserves in the Arakan region. China has offered loans and credit to Myanmar, as well as economic aid and investments for the construction of dams, bridges, roads and ports as well as for industrial projects. China extensively aided the construction of strategic roads along the Irrawaddy River trade route linking Yunnan province to the Bay of Bengal. Chinese firms have been involved in the construction of oil and gas pipelines stretching 2,380 km (1,480 mi) from Myanmar 's Arakan coast to China's Yunnan Province.

China National Offshore Oil Corporation and the China National Petroleum Corporation hold important contracts on upgrading Burmese oilfields and refineries andsharing of production. PetroChina is in process of building a major gas pipeline from the A-1 Shwe oil field off the coast of the Rakhine State leading to Yunnan, accessing and exploiting an estimated 2.88 to 3.56 trillion cubic feet of natural gas. A proposed Sino-Myanmar oil pipeline off the western coast of Myanmar may permit China to import oil from the Middle East, bypassing the Strait of Malacca.

4. International collaboration

Myanmar is a member of the General Agreement on Tariffs and Trade (GATT) and then the World Trade Organization (WTO). Relating to the Investment Promotion and Protection so as to keep up the investor friendly relations with foreign partners, Myanmar concluded many bilateral treaties such as Promotion and Reciprocal Protection of Investments Agreement with the Republic of the Philippines on 17th February 1998, with the Socialist Republic of Vietnam on 12th May 2000, with People's Republic of China on 12th December 2001, with the Lao People's Democratic Republic on 5th May 2003, with the Kingdom of Thailand on 14th March 2008, with the Republic of India on 24th June 2008, the Encouragement, Reciprocal Protection of Investments Agreement with the State of Kuwait on 6th August 2008, the Promotion and Protection of Investments with the Republic of Singapore and the Liberalization, Promotion and Protection of Investment with Japan on 25th December 2013 in accordance with the International Standards. And then, the Republic of the Union of Myanmar signed the trade and Investment Framework Agreement with the United States of America on 22th May, 2013.

Besides, Myanmar is trying to conclude many other bilateral agreement with other countries such as Mongolia, the People's Republic of Bangladesh, the State of Israel, the Republic of Maldives, the Republic of Korea, Japan, the Republic of Serbia, Iran, Russian Federation, the European Union and so on. In recent years, both China and India have attempted to strengthen ties with the government for economic benefit. Many nations, including the United States and Canada, and the European Union, have imposed investment and trade sanctions on Burma. The United States banned all imports fromBurma, though this restriction was since lifted. Foreign investment comes primarily from People's Republic of China, Singapore, South Korea, India, and Thailand.

The estimates of Myanmar foreign trade are highly the great volume of market trading. Myanmar remains a developing country with no improvement of living standards for the majority of the population over the past decade. The main causes for continued sluggish growth are previous government planning result. Recently, new of the recent government initiatives is to utilize Myanmar's large natural gas deposits. The Economist special report on Myanmar points to increased economic activity resulting from Myanmar's political transformation and influx of foreign direct investment from Asian neighbors.

For example, near the Mingaladon industrial Park, Japanese-owned factories have risen from the "debris" caused by "decades of sanctions and e-conomic mismanagement". Japanese Prime Minister has identified as Myanmar economically attractive market that will help stimulate the Japanese economy. Among its various enterprises, Japan is helping build the Thilawa Port, which is part of the Thilawa Special Economic Zone, and helping fix the electricity supply in Yangon.

According to the International Institute for Sustainable Development (IISD), Myanmar investment treaties that were negotiated with or through ASEAN, show some degree of consistency. In contrast, there is a very high degree of variation between Myanmar's ASEAN investment treaties and Myanmar's BITs, both in the types of provisions included in different treaties and in the drafting of provisions common to several treaties. These variations have significant legal implications for the nature and extent of Myanmar's obligations under different treaties. They also make the government's task of complying with Myanmar's existing investment treaties more complex.

Many of Myanmar's investment treaties contain most-favoured nation (MFN) clauses. The effect of these provisions is that any benefit extended to foreign investors from one country under one investment treaty may need to be extended to foreign investors covered by Myanmar's other investment treaties. As a result, Myanmar may berequired to grant a combination of benefits to foreign investors that are more generous than that provided by any one of Myanmar's investment treaties, considered individually.

Aside from the Myanmar-Philippines BIT, all of Myanmar's investment treaties allow foreign investors to bring claims under the treaty directly to investor-state arbitration. In such disputes, an arbitral tribunal will decide if the state in which the investment is located has breached the treaty. If the investor's claim is successful, the tribunal will make a binding, monetary award against the state. Because Myanmar's investment treaties are enforceable through investor-state arbitration, questions relating to the extent of Myanmar's obligations under different treaties have important practical implications.

Myanmar's investment treaties all contain provisions requiring the host state to treat foreign investment fairly and equitably. There is, however, a degree of variation in the way in which the FET provisions of Myanmar's in-vestment treaties are defined. In Myanmar's early BITs, the obligation to provide fair and equitable treatment is a "free-standing" obligation. These provisions do not tie the FET standard to international law and do not provide any clarification of what is meant by the phrase "fair and equitable". In contrast, the Myanmar-Japan BIT requires "treatment according to inter-national law, including fair and equitable treatment". This formulation limits the FET standard to the requirements of international law, but does not provide a great deal of guidance to a tribunal about what is required by inter-national law.

Also, all of Myanmar's investment treaties contain provisions dealing with the expropriation of foreign investment. These provisions allow the host state to expropriate foreign investments owned by investors of the home state only if compensation is paid to the investor. All of Myanmar's investment treaties endorse the basic principle that compensation should be equivalent to the fair market value of the investment at the time when the expropriation was announced.

For example, the ASEAN CIA holds that a host state "shall not expropriate or nationalise a covered investment either directly or through measures equivalent to expropriation or nationalisation" except on payment of compensation. As with theprovisions of Myanmar's other investment treaties this provision deals with two distinct situations. The first is "direct expropriation", which occurs when a government nationalizes or permanently takes over possession of an investment. The second is "measures equivalent to expropriation", more commonly referred to as "indirect expropriation". Indirect expropriation occurs when a government takes a measure akin to expropriation that does not involve nationalization or the ousting of the investor from possession of the investment.

5. Conclusion

Myanmar's transition toward a market economy began with a series of open-door policies. It allows private sector businesses to engage in external trade and to retain export earnings, and starts to legitimize and formalize border trade with neighbouring countries. In the context of advances in globalization and regionalization, an export-oriented and foreign investment-driven development strategy has become an orthodox and most promising policy for developing economies.

缅甸经济与贸易合作的法律问题

Si Thu Swe Tun [*]

陈诗慧 译

一、概述

缅甸联邦共和国现已通过新宪法并建立新的平民政府。缅甸宪法的第35条规定,缅甸实行市场经济体制。在商业往来方面,中缅双边贸易超14亿美元。中国主要向缅甸输入石油、钢铁及纺织品,而缅甸出口至中国的商品则包括天然橡胶和原木。缅甸允许科技、投资、机械、原材料等进入国内,以促进农业从劳动密集型向机械化转变。

二、2008年宪法

根据宪法第36条,为促进国民经济的发展,缅甸允许包括国家、区域组织、合作社、联营企业、私营企业在内的所有经济力量从事经济活动;禁止任何个人或团体采取垄断或操纵价格的手段破坏市场竞争,损害公共利益;着力提高人民生活水平,促进投资增长;禁止对企业实施国有化;允许合法货币流通。

2011年,吴登盛总统领导的政府上台,推行改革政策,改革涉及反腐败、货币外汇汇率、境外投资法以及税收。境外投资从2009—2010年度的3亿美元增至2010—2011年度的200亿美元,同比增加了667%。资本的大量流入使缅甸元势头强劲,涨幅约为25%。对此,缅甸政府放宽进口限制并取消出口关税。尽管目前有货币问题困扰,缅甸经济仍有望在2011年达到8.8%的

---

[*] 缅甸总检察长办公室法律官员。

增速。耗资580亿美元的土瓦深水港建造完毕后,缅甸将成为经由安达曼海入印度洋联结东南亚与中国南海的重要贸易枢纽,中转来自中东、欧洲和非洲等国家的货物,刺激东盟国家地区的发展。

2012年,亚洲发展银行正式向缅甸提供贷款,支持缅甸的金融设施建设和发展项目。从这笔5.12亿美元的贷款开始,亚洲发展银行将在接下来的30年里向缅甸发放贷款,针对银行服务并最终用于投资道路、能源、灌溉及教育项目。

三、中国的经济援助

中国向缅甸提供贷款,同时提供经济援助和投资用于工业项目与坝址、桥梁、道路和港口的建设。中国已获得若开地区天然气资源的开发权,在中国的大力援助下,缅甸将成为其丰富油气资源开发的主要受益者;在实兑海港的修缮扩建项目中,中国是缅甸政府主要的合作伙伴之一;中国大力援建了伊洛瓦底江(沟通云南省和孟加拉湾)沿岸的重要道路;中国公司参与建设从缅甸若开海岸至中国云南省绵延2380公里(1480英里)的油气管道。

中国海洋石油总公司与中国石油天然气集团公司均和缅甸签订了升级油田设备、改善炼油条件、实现产品共享的合同。中石油目前正在建设一条从若开邦沿海的气田通往中国云南的天然气管道,预计开采天然气2.88至3.56万亿立方英尺。中国计划沿缅甸西海岸建设一条中缅石油管道,绕过马六甲海峡直接从中东进口石油。

四、国际合作

缅甸是关贸总协定(GATT)的缔约国,世界贸易组织(WTO)的成员。为维护中外投资者友好关系,在"促进和保护投资协定"的框架下,缅甸缔结了许多双边协定,如从1998年到2013年分别与菲律宾、越南、中国、老挝、泰国、印度、科威特、新加坡、美国、日本签订的"促进和保护投资协定"。

此外,缅甸正努力与蒙古、孟加拉、以色列、马尔代夫、韩国、日本、塞尔维亚、伊朗、俄罗斯、欧盟等国家(国际组织)缔结双边协定。近几年,中国和印度都积极强化与缅甸政府的联系以促进经济发展。虽然美国、加拿大和欧盟等国家和国际组织都与缅甸有投资和贸易往来,且美国已取消了对缅甸的进口限制,但缅甸的境外投资主要来自中国、新加坡、韩国、印度和泰国。

缅甸的外贸因其巨额市场成交量被寄予厚望。然而在过去的几十年里，缅甸仍是一个发展中国家，大部分人口的生活水平并未改观。持续经济迟滞的主要原因在于往届政府的经济计划，而新政府的政策是开发利用缅甸大量的天然气储备。《经济学人》关于缅甸的特别报道指出，缅甸日趋活跃的经济活动源于其政治变动与亚洲邻国的直接投资。

例如，在明格拉东工业园附近，日资工厂摆脱了经济管制导致的经营不善。日本首相称缅甸是极具经济吸引力的市场，能够促进日本经济发展。日本在缅甸设立了各种企业，目前日本正在协助建设迪拉瓦经济特区的迪拉瓦港，此举有助于改善仰光的供电。

国际可持续发展研究所（IISD）研究发现，缅甸与东盟有关的投资协定在某些程度上具有一致性。相反地，缅甸的东盟投资协定与双边投资协定却有着很大差别，无论是在条款类型还是普适性条款的拟定上。此类区别从法律层面体现了缅甸在不同协定下义务的性质与范围，同时也使政府遵守现有投资协定的义务变得更加复杂。

缅甸许多投资协定都包含最惠国待遇（MFN）条款。此类条款的效力是，当某协定缔约国的投资者享有任何优惠待遇时，缅甸缔结的其他投资协定所涉及的投资者也应享有同等待遇。因此从个体层面看，缅甸须保障的境外投资者权益要比投资协定中规定的更多。

除了缅菲双边投资协定，缅甸缔结的所有投资协定都允许境外投资者直接向投资者所在国的仲裁机构提交仲裁申请。在此类纠纷中，仲裁庭将决定东道国是否违反协定。一旦投资者赢得仲裁，仲裁庭将对东道国做出有约束力的债务裁决。由于缅甸缔结的投资协定允许投资者以东道国为被申请人提起仲裁，有关不同协定下缅甸义务范围的问题便有着重要的实践意义。

缅甸缔结的投资协定都要求东道国公正平等地对待境外投资者。但不同投资协定中对此条款的定义却有些不同。在缅甸早期缔结的双边投资协定中，提供公平待遇的义务是独立的。这些条款并不将公平待遇标准与国际法接轨，同时不对"公正平等"做出阐释。然而缅日双边投资协定则要求"协定根据国际法包含公正待遇条款"。这种简洁的陈述将公正待遇标准限定在国际法要求范围内，但并没有向仲裁庭提供国际法规定的指导意见。

同时，缅甸缔结的所有投资协定都规定了如何处理对境外投资的征收。此类条款允许东道国在对投资者做出赔偿的前提下征收母国投资者拥有的境外投资。缅甸所有投资协定都支持了一项基本原则，即赔偿须与做出征收时投资的合理市场价一致。

例如,东盟 CIA 主张,除非支付赔偿,东道国不应直接或者通过类似征收或国有化的手段对投资实施征收或国有化。此条款与缅甸其他投资协定中的同类条款同样适用于两种不同的情形。第一种是"直接征收",发生于政府国有化或永久拥有某投资时。第二种是"类似于征收的手段",通常被称为"间接征收",发生于政府采取类似征收的手段但不涉及国有化或剥夺投资者所有权时。

五、结论

缅甸向市场经济的转变从一系列开放政策开始。市场经济允许私营企业参与对外贸易、获取进口收益,同时承认并规范化与邻国的边境贸易。在全球化与区域化的背景下,以进口为主、由外资驱动的发展战略无疑已成为发展经济的康庄坦途。

Legal Issues on Trade and Economic Cooperation: the Problems of the ASEAN Economic Community

Maneenuch Sangsuwannukul*

Abstract　The motivations for the birth of ASEAN were so that its members' governing elite could concentrate onnation building, the common fear of communism, reduced faith in or mistrust of external powers in the 1960s, and a desire for economic development. ASEAN has emphasized "three pillars" of regional cooperation: security, socio cultural integration, and economic integration. The regional group has decided to pursue economic integration by aiming to create an ASEAN Economic Community (AEC) by 2015 to establish a common market which based upon the four freedoms. The single market will ensure the free flow of goods, services, investment and skilled labour and the free flow of capital.

By creating the AEC, ASEAN would become "a single market and production base, turning the diversity that characterizes the region into opportunities ... making the ASEAN a more dynamic and stronger segment of the global supply chain." with main objectives of AEC are to create a single market and production base, highly competitive economic, region of equitable economic development, region fully integrated into the global economy. When, The benefits from the ASEAN Community are shared

---

　* LL. B, (Ramkhamhaeng University), Barrister at laws, (of the Thai Bar), LL. M, (Dhurakij Pundit University); Legal officer of The Central Intellectual Property and International Trade Court of Thailand.

among all ASEAN Member States, it is important to have an understanding
of the varying stages of their economic development and the development
gaps that exist between and among them.

Therefore, I would like to mention about two problems as follows: The
Problems of Framework Agreement on the ASEAN Investment Area and
Legal Problems and Obstacles of Economic Integration on ASEAN.

1. Overview

The Association of Southeast Asian Nations, or ASEAN, was
established on 8 August 1967 in Bangkok, Thailand, with the signing of the
ASEAN Declaration (Bangkok Declaration) by the Founding Fathers of
ASEAN. The aims and purposes of ASEAN are: [1]

—To accelerate the economic growth, social progress and cultural development in the region through joint endeavours in the spirit of equality and
partnership in order to strengthen the foundation for a prosperous and
peaceful community of Southeast Asian Nations;

—To promote regional peace and stability through abiding respect for
justice and the rule of law in the relationship among countries of the region
and adherence to the principles of the United Nations Charter;

—To promote active collaboration and mutual assistance on matters of
common interest in the economic, social, cultural, technical, scientific and
administrative fields;

—To collaborate more effectively for the greater utilisation of their agriculture and industries, the expansion of their trade, including the study of
the problems of international commodity trade, the improvement of their
transportation and communications facilities and the raising of the living
standards of their peoples.

---

[1] http://www.asean.org/asean/about-asean/overview

2. What is the ASEAN Economic Community?

ASEAN is aiming to create a community by 2015 The ASEAN Community consist of three pillar they are The ASEAN Political-Security Community (ASC), ASEAN Economic Community (AEC), and ASEAN Socio-Cultural Community (ASCC). It was the ASEAN Vision 2020 that first mapped out the concept of ASEAN Unification in three areas. By creating the AEC, ASEAN would become "a single market and production base, turning the diversity that characterizes the region into opportunities ... making the ASEAN a more dynamic and stronger segment of the global supply chain".

The ASEAN Economic Community (AEC) shall be the goal of regional economic integration by 2015. AEC envisages the following key characteristics: (a) a single market and production base, (b) a highly competitive economic region, (c) a region of equitable economic development, and (d) a region fully integrated into the global economy.

The AEC areas of cooperation include human resources development and capacity building; recognition of professional qualifications; closer consultation on macroeconomic and financial policies; trade financing measures; enhanced infrastructure and communications connectivity; development of electronic transactions through e-ASEAN; integrating industries across the region to promote regional sourcing; and enhancing private sector involvement for the building of the AEC. In short, the AEC will transform ASEAN into a region with free movement of goods, services, investment, skilled labour, and freer flow of capital. And The ASEAN Leaders adopted the ASEAN Economic Blueprint at the 13th ASEAN Summit on 20 November 2007 in Singapore to serve as a coherent master plan guiding the establishment of the ASEAN Economic Community 2015.

To ensure that benefits from the ASEAN Community are shared among all ASEAN Member States[1], it is important to have an understanding of the varying stages of their economic development and the development gaps that exist between and among them. The Initiative for ASEAN Integration (IAI) and Narrowing the Development Gap (NDG) are two of ASEAN's frameworks that aim to address these development issues. Both frameworks recognise the value of addressing subregional issues to support ASEAN-wide goals.

3. What is the ASEAN Economic Community(AEC): Market Integration

The AEC is configured from four characteristics (pillars), but its subject areas can be organized into the following five sectors : 1) market integration for the free and smooth flow of trade investment, service, capital, and skilled labor, 2) integration and cooperation (institutions and infrastructure) in transport, energy, ITC, and the like 3) a common policy for consumer protection, competition policy, intellectual property rights, and the like 4) reducing disparities, and 5) FTAs outside of ASEAN. Infrastructure and reducing disparities are also development policies.

The foundation is market integration. AFTA was mostly realized in 2010, and the free flow of goods progressed to a substantial level. However, only goods satisfying the rules of origin are targeted, and it is not the all goods can flow freely. Mutual acceptance of standards has only been for an extremely limited range of items. There is the goal of eliminating non-tariff barriers.

Trade facilitation initiatives in ASEAN are spearheaded by the implementation of the ASEAN Trade in Goods Agreement (ATIGA) and Agreement on Customs. These agreements are supported by work done by several sectoral bodies plan and execute the trade facilitation measures,

---

① The member states of ASEAN consist of Myanmar, Laos, Vietnam, Thailand, Cambodia, Philippines, Brunei, Malaysia, Singapore and Indonesia.

guided by the provisions and the requirements of ATIGA and the Agreement on Customs. The progress being made by these sectoral bodies forms the backbone for achieving the targets of the AEC Blueprint and establishing the ASEAN Economic Community by 2015.

The Coordinating Committee on the Implementation of the ATIGA (CCA) oversees the implementation of the ATIGA and supervises the implementation of the provisions of the agreement and its trade facilitation initiatives So, The flow of services is to be liberalized for all fields (sectors), but equity participation limits remain in flow of commercial presence, and it is not clear whether implementation will be to the degree of flow of service providers. Minimal restrictions will remain for investment, and the flow of people is limited to skilled labor. There is no goal of introducing common external tariffs or a common currency.

Regional integration that achieves the free flow of goods, services, capital and people is referred to as a common market, but the AEC is incomplete as a common market, and can be considered to be an "FTA plus".

1) ASEAN Plus Three

After the East Asian Financial Crisis of 1997, a revival of the Malaysian proposal was established in Chiang Mai, known as the Chiang Mai Initiative, which calls for better integration between the economies of ASEAN as well as the ASEAN Plus Three countries (China, Japan, and South Korea).

Leaders of each country felt the need to further integrate the region. Beginning in 1997, the bloc began creating organizations within its framework with the intention of achieving this goal. ASEAN Plus Three was the first of these and was created to improve existing ties with the People's Republic of China, Japan, and South Korea. This was followed by the even larger East Asia Summit, which now includes these countries as well as India, Australia, New Zealand, United States and Russia. This new grouping acted as a prerequisite for the planned East Asia Community, which was supposedly patterned after the now-defunct European Community. The ASEAN Eminent Persons Group was created to study the possible successes and failures of this policy as well as the possibility of drafting an ASEAN

Charter.

In 2006, ASEAN was given observer status at the United Nations General Assembly. As a response, the organisation awarded the status of "dialogue partner" to the United Nations.

2)Initiative for ASEAN Integration

To ensure that benefits from the ASEAN Community are shared among all ASEAN Member States[①], it is important to have an understanding of the varying stages of their economic development and the development gaps that exist between and among them. The Initiative for ASEAN Integration (IAI) and Narrowing the Development Gap (NDG) are two of ASEAN's frameworks that aim to address these development issues. Both frameworks recognise the value of addressing subregional issues to support ASEAN-wide goals.

Narrowing the Development Gap (NDG) is ASEAN's framework for addressing various forms of disparities among and within Member States where pockets of underdevelopment exist. Under NDG, ASEAN has continued coordinating closely with other subregional cooperation frameworks in the region (e. g. , BIMP-EAGA, IMT-GT, GMS, Mekong programmes), viewing them as "equal partners in the development of regional production and distribution networks" in the AEC, and as a platform to "mainstream social development issues in developing and implementing projects", in the context of the ASCC.

The IAI aims to provide support to Cambodia, Lao PDR, Myanmar and Vietnam (CLMV), ASEAN's newer and lesser developed member states. The IAI was launched in 2000 by ASEAN Heads of States to contribute to the objectives of Narrowing the Development Gap and accelerating integration of CLMV as the newer members of ASEAN. By augmenting the capacity of CLMV to implement regional agreements, the IAI hopes to accelerate the regional integration process as a whole.

---

① The member states of ASEAN consist of Myanmar, Laos, Vietnam, Thailand, Cambodia, Philippines, Brunei, Malaysia, Singapore and Indonesia.

The six-year IAI Work Plans have been developed to assist the CLMV countries as well as ASEAN's other sub-regions to ensure that the economic wheels of their economies move at an accelerated pace. IAI Work Plan I was implemented from 2002 to 2008, prior to the development of the Roadmap for an ASEAN Community (2009—2015). IAI Work Plan II (2009—2015) supports the goals of the ASEAN Community and is comprised of 182 prescribed actions, which includes studies, training programmes and policy implementation support conducted through projects supported by ASEAN-6 countries, and ASEAN's Dialogue partners and external parties. The IAI Work Plan is patterned after and supports the key programme areas in the three ASEAN Community Blueprints: ASEAN Political-Security Community Blueprint, ASEAN Economic Community Blueprint and ASEAN Socio-Cultural Community Blueprint.

The IAI Task Force, comprised of representatives of the Committee of Permanent Representatives and its working group from all ten ASEAN member states, is in charge of providing general advice and policy guidelines and directions in the design and implementation of the IAI Work Plan. All 10 ASEAN Member States are represented in the IAI Task Force, with the Task Force chaired by representatives of the four CLMV countries. Chairmanship is rotated annually in alphabetical order. The chair for 2014 is Cambodia.

The greatest difference in the principles of integration is that in the EU, national sovereignty is transferred to the EU in terms of market integration and currency integration, while ASEAN does not transfer national sovereignty and has a basis in non-interference in the domestic matters of other states. This is delaying progress in integration extending to domestic institutions and policies such as elimination of non-tariff barriers, liberalization of trade in service, and unification of rules.

4. The Problems

1)The Problems of Framework Agreement on the ASEAN Investment Area

The ASEAN Investment Area set up under the Framework Agreement on the ASEAN Investment Area is not an international organization that enjoys the status as a person. It is only an ASEAN body Set up for the development of economic cooperation among member countries within the frameworks of GATT and WTO of which most of member countries of ASEAN are members. The setting up of the ASEAN Investment Area is to be governed by the Framework Agreement on the ASEAN Investment Area, an international agreement under the operation of international law by which every member country of ASEAN is bound to accept and apply in its territory.

In practice, there are certain problems of complying with the commitments under the Framework Agreement on the ASEAN Investment Area arising from the Framework Agreement itself and from member countries, that member countries shall have to resolve together, in order for the ASEAN investment Area to achieve the purposes for which it is set up and be beneficial to trade and investment for ASEAN and Thailand.

2) Legal Problems and Obstacles of Economic Integration on ASEAN

As the States in each region have realized the importance of economic power, they integrate themselves into an economic block resulting in a linkage of relationships to attaining common profits.

The international economic integration has several levels, each of which includes difference kinds of binding and of procedures, mechanism and measures for the economic integration.

The Economic integration is almost at the level of free trade area. Only does the European region have a common market (the European Economic Community) which proved successful. The procedures of common market are as follows:

1. The Member States shall have common commercial policies among themselves and the non-member states and these policies affect the sovereignty of the Member States.

2. The Member States shall have their community laws, which directly apply to all Member States.

3. By establishing the community, the supranational organizations shall be set up, using the community laws to impose sanction on the Member States.

The Success of the common market is due to the community laws which enforce sanction on all Member States and also due to the supranational organizations which have the power of legislation, administration and punishment.

For ASEAN, they try to integrate their economy in a free trade area type, but it is not a strong integration. Agreements involved are thus flexible. Moreover, their organizations, which have the duty to administer and to assist the Member States, have no power to enforce, control and punish all Member States.

5. The Resolve and Development

The setting up of the ASEAN Investment Area may affect to ASEAN and Thailand in certain areas. ASEAN and Thailand must develop themselves and amend relevant laws in order to be able to cope efficiently with future investment in such a way as to bring about maximum and real benefits to ASEAN and Thailand.

Furthermore, where ASEAN have ASEAN VISION 2020, its purpose is to have economic integration in common market. It is essential to have their community law and to establish organizations which have full legal power directly enforceable in all Member States. Also, it is necessary to harmonize and/or approximate their internal laws. All these will affect the sovereignty of the ASEAN Member States. Therefore, in order to achieve the objectives of ASEAN VISION 2020, all Member States have to express obviously their intention by establishing their community treaty and indicate in the constitutions of all Member States to surrender some concerned parts of their sovereignty to the community and its organizations to exercise the power to monitor control and push all Member States towards their goal as described in the ASEAN VISION 2020.

6. Summary

Changes in the international economic competition coupled with the economic crisis have in no small measure directly affected foreign investment in the ASEAN Region. In view of this, the setting up of the ASEAN Investment Area by the 10-member countries, by no means a large market with its abundance of natural resources, to enhance the area's advantage in investment atmosphere in order to attract investments from countries within ASEAN itself and from outside will only be of great benefits to the region and to Thailand alike. In addition to its contribution towards the overall expansion of the investment market in the Region, to compensate for the loss of market shares resulting from the economic unification of other regions.

The ASEAN investment Area will help to strengthen the Region, making it one of the most effective investment regions and one of the most advantageous areas for trade and investment. The ASEAN Investment Area (AlA) is the grouping together of member countries of Southeast Asia or ASEAN for economic reason with the purposes to increase in this Region investment from investors from within the area and outside of it, to enhance ASEAN's industrial efficiency and ASEAN's economic sector, to make it one of the regions most favourable for investment, taking into account the differences in the levels of development and the economy of each member country within the Framework Agreement on the ASEAN Investment Area (AlA Agreement), which requires that member countries commit themselves to the opening of free industry and National Treatment (NT) by 2010 for ASEAN investors and by 2020 for other investors.

The ASEAN Investment Area set up under the Framework Agreement on the ASEAN Investment Area is not an international organization that enjoys the status as a person. It is only an ASEAN body Set up for the development of economic cooperation among member countries within the frameworks of GATT and WTO of which most of member countries of ASEAN are members. The setting up of the ASEAN Investment Area is to be governed by the Framework Agreement on the ASEAN Investment Area, an international agreement under the operation of international law by which every member country of ASEAN is bound to accept and apply in its territory.

In practice, there are certain problems of complying with the commitments under the Framework Agreement on the ASEAN Investment Area arising from the Framework Agreement itself and from member countries, that member countries shall have to resolve together, in order for the ASEAN investment Area to achieve the purposes for which it is set up and be beneficial to trade and investment for ASEAN and Thailand. The setting up of the ASEAN Investment Area may however affect ASEAN and Thailand in certain areas. ASEAN and Thailand must develop themselves and amend relevant laws in order to be able to cope efficiently with future investment in such a way as to bring about maximum and real benefits to ASEAN and Thailand.

经贸合作的法律议题：东盟经济共同体面临的问题

Maneenuch Sangsuwannukul[*]

陈诗慧　译

摘要　对社会主义的普遍恐惧、20世纪60年代对外部力量的不信任以及对经济发展的渴望催生了东盟，自此东盟成员国的政府得以致力于国家建设。东盟一直强调区域合作的"三大支柱"，即安全、社会文化交融与经济一体化。东盟决心在2015年前建成东盟经济共同体（AEC），构建基于四项自由的统一市场，以促进经济一体化，确保商品、服务、投资、人才资金的自由流动。AEC旨在创造统一市场和制造基地，促进经济充分竞争，创建平衡发展、充分融入世界经济的地区，使东盟成为"一个统一市场和制造基地，将区域多样性转化为机遇，成为全球产业链中更为活跃有力的一环"。当东盟成员国共享AEC成果时，理解不同成员国之间的发展差异至关重要。本文将讨论两个问题：东盟区域投资框架协定存在的问题，以及东盟国家经济交流的法律问题和障碍。

一、概述

随着创始国签署了《东南亚国家联盟成立宣言》（《曼谷宣言》），东南亚国家联盟或称东盟于1967年8月8日在泰国曼谷成立。东盟的目标与宗旨是：[②]

通过平等合作促进地区经济、社会与文化的发展，巩固东南亚社会和平繁

---

　　*　蓝康恒大学法学学士，泰国出庭律师，泰国博仁大学法学硕士（一年制）；泰国中央知识产权和国际贸易法庭法律官员。

　　②　http://www.asean.org/asean/about-asean/overview.

荣的基础;

遵守国家间交往的法律及规则,遵守联合国宪章的基本原则,促进区域和平与安全;

就经济、社会、文化、技术、科学及行政管理等不同领域的共同关切提高合作和互相协助的水平;

在高效利用工农业、扩大贸易包括对国际商品贸易问题的研究、改善运输通讯设施和提高人民生活水平方面进行更有效的合作。

二、何为东盟经济共同体

东盟计划在 2015 年建成东盟共同体。东盟共同体由政治安全共同体(ASC)、经济共同体(AEC)和社会文化共同体(ASCC)组成。《东盟 2020 年愿景》首次提出在这三个领域统一东盟的概念。AEC 建成后,东盟将成为"一个统一市场和制造基地,将区域多样性转化为机遇,成为全球产业链中更为活跃有力的一环"。

AEC 是 2015 年前区域经济一体化要达成的目标。AEC 预计将成为:(a)统一市场和制造基地,(b)充分竞争的经济区,(c)经济平等发展的地区,以及(d)全面融入世界经济的地区。

AEC 合作的领域包括发展人力资源和资本,实现专业资质的认可,密切探讨宏观经济和财政政策,实施贸易融资措施,加强基础设施和提高通信通达度,发展以电子东盟为平台的电子商务,加强工业区际交流以调节区域资源分布不均,以及增强 AEC 建设中的私主体参与度。简言之,AEC 将促使东盟转变为商品、服务、投资、人才资金自由流动的区域。2007 年 11 月 20 日在新加坡举行的第十三届东盟峰会上,东盟国家首脑通过了东盟经济规划,作为指导建设 AEC 的总方略。

为确保东盟成员国共享东盟共同体的成果①,理解不同成员国之间的发展差异至关重要。东盟一体化倡议(IAI)和缩小发展差距(NDG)这两大机构专门探讨了这些发展问题,它们都认为解决次区域问题有利于在东盟范围内达成目标。

---

① The member states of ASEAN consist of Myanmar, Laos, Vietnam, Thailand, Cambodia, Philippines, Brunei, Malaysia, Singapore and Indonesia.

三、何为 AEC：市场一体化

AEC 由四部分组成，但其针对的主要领域可分为以下五个部分：1）市场一体化以促进贸易投资、服务、资本和人才的自由流动，2）交通、能源、通信等领域的交流合作（机构与设施），3）消费者保护和市场竞争政策、知识产权等，4）减少分歧，以及 5）东盟区域外的自由贸易协定。基础设施和减少分歧也是发展的政策。

市场一体化是基础。东盟自由贸易区在 2010 年已基本建成，商品的自由流通已达到一定水平。但这只针对符合原产地法规的商品，而非所有商品；标准的互认仅限于极少数商品。非关税壁垒仍须消除。

东盟的贸易促进倡议始于"东盟商品贸易协定"（ATIGA）和"关税协定"的施行。这些协定有多个分支，指导贸易促进措施的实施。各分支组成的进程成为完成 AEC 规划目标、在 2015 年前建成 AEC 的支柱。

协调实施 ATIGA 委员会（CCA）监督 ATIGA 的实施以及贸易促进措施的落实。自此，所有领域的服务流通放开，但商业存在的流通仍存限制，且尚不明确流通程度是否取决于服务提供者的流动。投资仍受到一定限制，自然人流动仅限于人才流动；并未计划统一关税或货币。

商品、服务及自然人流动自由的区域一体化适用于统一市场，但 AEC 并非完全意义上的统一市场，应被视为"升级版的自由贸易协定"。

1）东盟 10＋3

1997 年亚洲金融危机后，东盟在清迈通过了马来西亚的一项提案，又称"清迈协议"，呼吁一体化不应局限于东盟内部，也应包括中日韩三国。

各国领导人都意识到需要进一步实现区域一体化。1997 年起，为实现该目标，东盟集团在其框架内建立相关组织。作为首次尝试，东盟 10＋3 创立的初衷是改善与中日韩三国的关系。紧接着是规模更大的东亚峰会，目前有印度、澳大利亚、新西兰、美国和俄罗斯等国参加峰会。这一新团体是将来东亚共同体的雏形，而东亚共同体则是仿效原来的欧共体。为研究这一政策的利弊及起草东盟宪章的可能性，东盟杰出人士小组得以组建。

2006 年，东盟获得联大观察员的地位，成为了联合国对话伙伴。

2)东盟一体化倡议

为确保东盟成员国共享东盟共同体的成果①,理解不同成员国之间的发展差异至关重要。东盟一体化倡议(IAI)和缩小发展差距(NDG)这两大机构专门探讨了这些发展问题,它们都认为解决次区域问题有利于在东盟范围内达成目标。

NDG 是东盟为研究稍落后成员国之间差异而建立的机构。NDG 下,东盟不断与地区内其他次区域合作组织协调(如东东盟经济成长区、印尼—马来西亚—泰国增长三角区、大湄公河次区域经济合作、湄公河项目),将它们视为 AEC 背景下"发展区域制造和分配网络的平等合作伙伴",同时也是 ASCC 背景下落实规划的主要社会发展事项。

IAI 致力于向较落后的东盟新成员国如柬埔寨、老挝、缅甸和越南(CLMV)提供援助。为实现 NDG 的目标并加速 CLMV 四国入盟进程,东盟各国元首在 2000 年发起 IAI。通过加强 CLMV 四国履行区域协定的能力,IAI 有意加速区域一体化进程。

IAI 六年工作计划将援助范围从 CLMV 四国扩大到东盟其他次区域以确保经济增长。IAI 第一个工作计划在 2002—2008 年期间实施,先于东盟共同体(2009—2015)的发展路线图。IAI 第二个工作计划(2009—2015)拥护东盟共同体的目标,由 182 个行动计划组成,包括教育、培训项目和由东盟六国、东盟对话伙伴及其他主体通过项目对政策落实做出的支持。IAI 工作计划借鉴并在关键领域支持了东盟共同体的三份规划:政治安全共同体规划、经济共同体规划和社会文化共同体规划。

IAI 工作组由常驻代表委员会的代表和来自东盟十国的工作团队组成,负责就 IAI 工作计划的设计和实施提供建议和政策指导。东盟十国在 IAI 工作组中均有代表,而工作组的负责人则由 CLMV 四国的代表担任,按字母顺序每年轮换,2014 年由柬埔寨轮值。

欧盟一体化原则与东盟最大的不同在于,在欧盟,国家在市场和货币一体化领域将主权让渡给欧盟,而东盟不影响国家主权并坚持不干涉他国内政的基本原则。一体化延伸至国内制度政策如消除非关税壁垒、开放服务贸易和实施统一的规则,这将是一个缓慢的进程。

---

① The member states of ASEAN consist of Myanmar, Laos, Vietnam, Thailand, Cambodia, Philippines, Brunei, Malaysia, Singapore and Indonesia.

四、存在的问题

1. 东盟投资区(AIA)框架协议的问题

AIA 框架协议的签署宣告了 AIA 的成立。建立在框架协议下的 AIA 并非享有独立地位的国际组织,其仅是东盟为促进成员国在 GATT 和 WTO (东盟多数成员国参加)框架下进行经济合作而设立的分支机构。

实践中,在 AIA 实施框架协议下达成的决议面临一些困难,有些来自协议本身,有些则来自成员国。为了实现东盟投资区设立的初衷并促进东盟与泰国的贸易投资,这些困难应由成员国共同解决。

2. 东盟经济一体化的法律问题与障碍

在认识到经济实力的重要性后,各国融入经济共同体中,积极加强联系,获取共同利益。

国际经济一体化有不同阶段,每一阶段都有不同的效果、程序机制及措施。

经济一体化正处于自由贸易区阶段。仅欧洲存在成形的统一市场(欧洲经济共同体)。统一市场的形成过程如下:

1. 成员国内部或成员国与非成员国之间存在统一的贸易政策,且这些政策足以影响成员国的主权。

2. 成员国之间应存在能够约束所有成员国的共同体法律。

3. 建立共同体,应成立超国家组织,依据共同体法律对成员国实施制裁。

统一市场成功的关键在于存在对所有成员国有约束力的共同体法律以及拥有立法、行政、惩罚权力的超国家组织。

东盟国家试图以自由贸易区的形式实行经济一体化,但这种联合并不牢固。因此,相关协定显得灵活有余效力不足。此外,负责管理、协助各成员国的组织并没有命令、控制或惩罚任何成员国的权限。

五、对策与发展

AIA 的成立或许会在某些领域影响东盟和泰国。东盟和泰国应当发展自身并修改相关法律,有效应对此类投资,从而为自己带来最大的实质利益。

此外,东盟发布《东盟 2020 年愿景》,其目的在于促进统一市场的经济一体化。通过共同体法律并建立有权直接约束各成员国的组织至关重要,同时有必要使各成员国国内法与协定保持一致。所有这些措施将影响东盟各国的主权。因此,为实现《东盟2020年愿景》的目标,各成员国须通过缔结条约明确表示其意愿,并在宪法中声明将部分主权让渡给共同体使其有权监督各成员国,促使各成员国向目标前进。

六、结语

国际经济竞争的变化伴随着经济危机对东盟地区的境外投资影响深远。作为一个在投资环境中扩大地区优势吸引东盟内外投资、拥有丰富自然资源的巨大市场,东盟十国建立的投资区将惠及东盟地区及泰国等国家。除了为区域投资市场总体扩张做出的贡献,还能弥补其他区域的经济统一导致的市场份额损失。

AIA有助于加强本地区实力,使其成为最具活力与优势的贸易投资区。AIA是东南亚国家或东盟成员国形成的联合,以吸引区域内外投资,提高工业及其他行业效率,使本区域成为最有利投资地。其考虑到各成员国经济发展水平的差异,要求成员国在2010年前向东盟投资者开放自由工业,提供国民待遇,至2020年,范围扩大到其他投资者。

AIA框架协议的签署宣告了AIA的成立。建立在框架协议下的AIA并非享有独立地位的国际组织,是东盟为促进成员国在GATT和WTO(东盟多数成员国参加)框架下进行经济合作而设立的分支机构。实践中,在AIA实施框架协议下达成的决议面临一些困难,有些来自协议本身,有些则来自成员国。为了实现东盟投资区设立的初衷并促进东盟与泰国的贸易投资,这些困难应由成员国共同解决。东盟投资区的成立或许会在某些领域影响东盟和泰国。东盟和泰国应当发展自身并修改相关法律以有效应对此类投资从而为自己带来最大的实质利益。

Legal Issues on Trade and Economic Cooperation of Vietnam on Building the 21st-Century Maritime Silk Road

Nguyen Thi Thao *

Chinese President Xi Jinping said a significant content about the 21st-Century Maritime Silk Road to restore and rebuild the ancient Silk Road. The 21st-Century Maritime Silk Road plays an important role in economic development, trade, goods and cultural exchanges together. With the significant meaning and bringing the great opportunities, China is creating all necessary conditions for building the 21st-Century Maritime Silk Road. However, besides the opportunities, it still faces important challenges during the building the Maritime Silk Road. One of these problems is the legal issues in trade and economic cooperation between China and the countries concerned, including Vietnam. Currently, China and Vietnam do not have a specific agreement on the issue of bilateral trade and economic cooperation. However, China and ASEAN signed a framework agreement about economic cooperation, such as the ASEAN-China Free Trade Area (ACFTA)... As a member of ASEAN, Vietnam has the specific legal provisions of the Agreement, and a Memorandum of Understanding between China and Vietnam. It partly also facilitates the exchange of goods, economic development and cooperation between two countries. The following essay will provide a general overview of the Vietnamese legislations involving

---

* Legal counselor, The National No. 5 Law Firm.

Vietnam and China.

A. Introduction

One year ago, President Xi Jinping put forward the strategic conception of building the "Silk Road Economic Belt" and "21st-Century Maritime Silk Road", known shortly as the "One Belt and One Road" initiatives.

Chinese President Xi said that the 21st-Century Maritime Silk Road would create a new opportunity to rejuvenate the economic and cultural ties built via the ancient Silk Road. It presents a "win-win approach" to peaceful coexistence and mutual development. The idea carries forward the spirit of the ancient Silk Road that was based on mutual trust, equality and mutual benefits, inclusiveness and mutual learning, and win-win cooperation.

It also conforms to the 21st-century norms of promoting peace, development, cooperation and adopting a win-win strategy for all. The conception organically links the "Chinese dream" to the "Global Dream" and has far-reaching strategic significance with a global impact.

By building the 21st-century maritime silk road, the countries involved are allowed to create a three-dimensional and multilayer transport network that connects them via land, sea and air. It will has an important role in the economy of many countries involved and brings new opportunities to China, ASEAN countries, such as promoting tourism cooperation as countries along the maritime route have long coastlines and beautiful landscapes, and thus boast tremendous potential yet to be unleashed. .

Infrastructure development will get a boost from the ambitious plan with better connectivity linked by waterway, road and railway, according to transport officials attending the 8th Pan-Beibu Gulf (PBG) Economic Cooperation Forum. However, the Maritime Silk Road connects between many different countries, there are many requirements and challenges on building this Silk Road.

Currently, there is no bilateral agreements on trade, economic issues or establishment on the 21st-Century Maritime Silk Road which has signed by Vietnam and China. Therefore, on Building the 21st-Century Maritime Silk

Road, there is no legal regulations on Trade and Economic Cooperation adjustment on the issues in Vietnam.

However, Vietnam is a member of ASEAN, therefore, when the ASEAN signed Trade and Economic Agreements with China, Vietnam partly is influenced by the Trade and Economic Agreements.

So far, ASEAN has signed with China a number of Trade and Economic Agreements, such as the Agreement on Comprehensive Economic Cooperation ASEAN-China, ACFTA Trade in Goods 11. 2004, ACFTA Trade in Goods-Annex1, ACFTA Trade in Goods-Annex2, ACFTA Trade in Goods-Annex3, Dispute Settlement Agreement-Framework Agreement, MOU ASEAN-China on Agriculture Cooperation Agreement on trade in goods, trade in services agreement, Agreement on Services...

B. Content

I. ASEAN—China Economic Cooperation

In 2001, the Report "Forging Closer ASEAN-China Economic Relations in the Twenty-First Century" made the following recommendations:

—Establishment of an ASEAN-China FTA within 10 years, including special and differential treatment and flexibility for CLMV countries, and an "early harvest" package of mutually agreed list of goods to be liberalized ahead of implementation of China's commitments to the WTO;

—Wide range of trade and investment facilitation measures;

—Technical assistance and capacity building to ASEAN members, particular CLMV;

—Expansion of cooperation in areas such as finance, tourism, agriculture, human resource development, small and medium enterprises, industrial cooperation, intellectual property rights, environment, forestry and forestry products, energy and subregional development. At the ASEAN-China Summit in November 2001, ASEAN and China agreed to launch negotiations for a ASEAN-China FTA (ACFTA) and to establish it within 10 years.

The details as follow: ACFTA will be established within 10 years, with tariffs reduced or eliminated by 2010 for ASEAN-6 and China and 2015 for CLMV (in consonance with the deadlines for AFTA). The ASEAN-China FTA comprises developing countries and could qualify under the WTO enabling clause for developing countries (as was the case for AFTA) rather than the more stringent GATT Article XXIV. Nevertheless, for trade in goods, ACFTA is committed to cover "substantially all trade". The tariff reduction has two tracks. Track 1 refers to the "Early Harvest" which covers a large group of agricultural products under HS1-HS8 and representing over 600 tariff line (about 10% of total), so that participating countries can benefit from increased liberalized trade before thee actual FTA enters into force. Early Harvest products will have tariffs eliminated over 3 years, with effect from 1 January 2004. The Early Harvest products highlight that agriculture is not a sensitive sector in China as it is in Japan or Korea. Track 2 goods will have tariffs progressively reduced according to a negotiated timeframe, with end-dates of 2010 for ASEAN-6 and China, and 2015 for CLMV. The Framework Agreement also covers liberalization of services and investment and economic cooperation activities.

II. Vietnamese Regulations

In 2005, Vietnam Deputy Prime Minister Vu Khoan signed Decision No. 257/2005/QD-TTg approving the Agreement on Trade in Goods ASEAN-China and the Memorandum of Understanding between Vietnam and China on a number of issues in the Agreement on Trade in Goods ASEAN-China. The Decision requests urgently Ministry of Finance issued the legislation on the tariff reduction schedule under the provisions of agreements and memoranda; to guide implementation of customs import and export management and statistical work. Ministry of Commerce and Ministry of Finance monitor and assess the overall situation of import and export between Viet Nam and China, with other countries in ASEAN and other countries; evaluation of policies related to proposed management measures synchronized in time.

Accordingly, Vietnam has made certain commitments in the ASEAN Free Trade Area-worms China (ACFTA), the summary is as follows:

1. Commitment in the field of trade in goods

The content committed tax cuts of Vietnam within ASEAN Free Trade Area and China (ACFTA) is governed by the Framework Agreement on Comprehensive Economic Cooperation ASEAN-China, which was signed on 4th November, 2002 by the leader Shanghai ASEAN summit and China in Cambodia (hereinafter referred to as the Framework Agreement), the Agreement on Trade in Goods ASEAN-China was signed on 29th November, 2004 in Laos, and MOU between Vietnam and China signed on 18th July, 2005 in China. Accordingly, the reduction and the liberalization of tariffs in Vietnam in the ACFTA is divided into three categories of goods: Early Harvest Programme, normal and sensitive list, as follows:

• Early Harvest Programme (EHP):

It consists mostly of agricultural and fishery products from Chapter 1-8 of import tariff. The item has been implemented tax cuts in 2004 and under the tariff elimination in 2008 on the following schedule:

Table 1: Roadmap reduction of EHP list

Tariff tax MFN	MFN tariff tax EHP through the years				
	2004	2005	2006	2007	2008
MFN$\geq$30%	20%	15%	10%	5%	0%
15$\leq$MFN<30%	10%	10%	5%	5%	0%
MFN<15%	5%	5%	0~5%	0~5%	0%

• **Sensitive Track (ST):**

In Vietnam, the sensitive track includes 388 commodity groups at the 6-digit HS level (Annex III of the Memorandum of Understanding), they are mainly products such as eggs, sugar, tobacco, motor vehicles (cars and motorcycles), petroleum, iron and steel, building materials, electronic products refrigeration, paper, textiles ... The items on the sensitive track have no specific tariff reduction schedule for each year, but have limited tax rate last and final year of implementation, the specific model reduction sensitive Track of Vietnam as follows:

—Sensitive goods: tax rate of 20% in 2015 and decreased to 0~5%

in 2020.

——High Sensitive goods: includes no more than 140 HS 6 digit commodity groups and the tax rate of 50% in 2018.

• Common Track (items must reduce and eliminate tariffs) of Vietnam:

including 90% of tariff lines of import tariffs, tariff reductions were implemented in 2006. The roadmap reduction of conventional category is shown in the table below.

Table 2: Roadmap reduction of conventional list (ACFTA)

X = the rate at 01/01/2003 MFN tariff rates ACFTA

at not later than 1/1 of the year

X = the tariff rates MFN at 01st January, 2003	MFN tariff rates ACFTA							
	At time is not later than 1st January of the year							
	2005	2006	2007	2008	2009	2011	2013	2015
X≥60%	60	50	40	30	25	15	10	0
45%≤X<60%	40	35	35	30	25	15	10	0
35%≤X<45%	35	30	30	25	20	15	5	0
30%≤X<35%	30	25	25	20	17	10	5	0
25%≤X<30%	25	20	20	15	15	10	5	0
20%≤ X<25%	20	20	15	15	15	10	0~5	0
15%≤X<20%	15	15	10	10	10	5	0~5	0
10%≤X<15%	10	10	10	10	8	5	0~5	0
7%≤X<10%	7	7	7	7	5	5	0~5	0
5%≤X<7%	5	5	5	5	5	5	0~5	0
X<5%	Remain							0

In addition to reducing taxes on the route, Vietnam must performs some additional commitments follows:

——To reduce the rate of at least 50% of tariff lines in the list usually 0~5%, it is not later than on 1st January, 2009.

—To eliminate tariffs of 45% of tariff lines in the list normally, it is not later than 1st January, 2013.

Table 3

Items	Tariff Commitments	
	%	Year
Trucks kind of big load	30%	2012
Trucks small payload type	45%	2014
Motorcycles	45%	2012
Motorcycle Parts	13%	2013
Iron and steel construction	15%	2014
Electronics-Appliances Refrigeration	10%~15%	2012—2013
Petrol	20%	2009

—According to Memorandum of Understanding, Vietnam has reduced tariff elimination of at least 85% of tariff lines in 2015, the remaining 5% of tariff lines—but not exceeding 250 tariff lines at the HS 6-digit level which will be eliminated tariffs in 2018.

—According to the Memorandum of Understanding between Vietnam and China signed on 18th July, 2005, the tax cut schedule of a number of specific items (under the common and sensitive track) is faster than the general provisions. The items on the list of sensitive tariff commitments have tariff rate earlier than the general provisions, mainly including:

The remaining items of import tariff is excluded items (not reduction) in accordance with WTO rules.

2. Commitments in Trade in Services

According to the Framework Agreement on Comprehensive Economic Cooperation ASEAN-China, the Trade in Services has regulated follow:

With a view to expediting the expansion of trade in services, the Parties agree to enter into negotiations to progressively liberalize trade in services with substantial sectoral coverage. Such negotiations shall be directed to:

a. progressive elimination of substantially all discrimination between or among the Parties and/or prohibition of new or more discriminatory measures with respect to trade in services between the Parties, except for measures permitted under Article V(1)(b) of the WTO General Agreement on Trade in Services (GATS);

b. expansion in the depth and scope of liberalization of trade in services beyond those undertaken by ASEAN Member States and China under the GATS;

c. enhanced co-operation in services between the Parties in order to improve efficiency and competitiveness, as well as to diversify the supply and distribution of services of the respective service suppliers of the Parties.

—Although there is no specific agreement on trade and economic cooperation, Vietnam has had legislations for specifying and enforcing the provisions of the Agreement signed between ASEAN and China, by Circulars on promulgation of the Vietnam's Special preferential import tariff for realization of the ASEAN-China Free trade area in the specific period.

C. Conclusion

Although it has no formal and specific Agreement on Trade and Economic Cooperation between Vietnam and China, but the Agreement on Trade in Goods of the Framework Agreement on ASEAN-China Comprehensive Economic Cooperation (hereinafter abbreviated to as the ASEAN-China Agreement on Trade in Goods) and the Memorandum of Understanding between Vietnam and China have partly created favorable conditions for building the 21st-Century Maritime Silk Road. With the benefits are brought by the 21st-Century Maritime Silk Road, hoping that the trade and economic cooperation between China and Vietnam will be grown strongly, enabling the "WIN-WIN" between the two countries.

关于越南建设 21 世纪海上丝绸之路：经济贸易合作的法律问题

Nguyen Thi Thao[*]
潘　静　译

习近平总书记提出关于重建古丝绸之路，即建设 21 世纪的海上丝绸之路，此举对促进各方经济发展、商品贸易和文化交流具有重大意义。中国建设海上丝绸之路，意义重大，机遇良多，同时也面临着许多困难，如中国与越南等国在经贸合作方面的法律问题。虽然目前中国与越南没有具体协议规范双边经济贸易合作问题，但中国和东盟达成了中国—东盟贸易自由协议等协议。作为东盟成员国，越南对框架协议有具体法律规定，并和中国达成了谅解备忘录，也有利于促进两国商品交易、经济发展与合作。下文笔者将浅析中越合作中越南法律的概况。

一、简介

2013 年习近平总书记提出建设"丝绸之路经济带"和"21 世纪海上丝绸之路"，即"一带一路"的战略构想。他强调"21 世纪海上丝绸之路"将为古丝绸之路沿途各地经济文化注入新的生命力，提供新的机会。这一战略构想的提出发扬了古丝绸之路互信互利、平等包容、互相学习、共赢合作的精神。同时也符合 21 世纪提倡和平、发展、合作和共赢的准则。

"海上丝绸之路"沿途的国家将会建设一个连接海陆空的三维多层次交通网，这将促进多国经济发展，为中国、东盟各国带来新的机遇，如促进各国旅游业发展。同时也将更好地连接水路运输，极大地促进基础设施建设。当然建

---

[*]　越南国家 5 号律师事务所法律顾问。

设这条连接多国的海上丝绸之路要求复杂,困难重重。

目前关于"21世纪海上丝绸之路"的经济贸易问题和建设问题中越没有双边协议,越南也没有法律调整这些经济贸易合作问题。中国和东盟已签署了一系列经济贸易协议,越南作为东盟成员国,也受到这些协议的规范。

二、主要内容

(一)中国—东盟经济合作

2001年,关于"促进21世纪中国—东盟经济关系"的报告作出承诺:十年内建立中国—东盟自由贸易协定,促进贸易投资;对东盟各成员国尤其是新东盟四国的技术帮助和技术能力建设;开展在金融、旅游、农业、人力资源发展、中小企业、产业合作、知识产权等方面的合作。双方计划在十年内建成中国—东盟自由贸易区。

具体内容如下:在十年内建立中国—东盟自由贸易区,东盟六国、中国和新东盟四国分别在2010年和2015年降低或消除关税。自贸区由发展中国家组成,符合WTO的授权条款,不用遵守更加严格的关税贸易总协定第二十四条规定。中国—东盟自由贸易协定基本覆盖了所有交易。降低关税有两种途径,一种是"早期收获计划",即三年内涉及的产品免交关税,在自贸协议生效前惠及成员国。另一种是根据拟定的时间表降低产品关税,东盟六国和中国在2010年底取消关税,新东盟四国在2015年底取消关税。框架协议同时覆盖了开放的服务、投资和经济合作事项。

(二)越南法律

2005年越南同意签署中国—东盟货物贸易协议并且达成谅解备忘录,并根据协议条款和备忘录发布了减免关税的法律规定;指导完善海关进出口管理统计工作。评估越南和中国东盟进出口宏观情况,并及时评估管理政策。相应地越南就中国—东盟自由贸易协议作出了一些承诺。

1.在货物贸易方面的承诺

2002年11月中国和东盟各国签署了中国—东盟全面经济合作框架协议,协议允许越南承诺在东盟自贸区内减免关税。越南在东盟自贸区降低关税和关税自由化的货物分为三种:早期收获计划、正常商品和敏感商品。

早期收获计划所指的货物主要是进口关税第一至八章列出的农渔产品。

减免关税情况如下：

表 1　早期收获计划货均关税减负表

最惠国关税	早期收获计划最惠国关税年限				
	2004	2005	2006	2007	2008
最惠国关税≥30%	20%	15%	10%	5%	0%
15≤最惠国关税<30%	10%	10%	5%	5%	0%
最惠国关税<15%	5%	5%	0～5%	0～5%	0%

越南的敏感货物是指谅解备忘录附件三的 388 种商品，主要是鸡蛋、糖料、烟草、机动车辆(汽车和摩托车)、石油、钢铁、建筑用材等等。这些敏感类货物关税减免如下：

1)敏感类货物：2015 年关税为 20%,2020 年降低至 0～5%；

2)高度敏感类货物：包括 HS 第六章的货物和 2018 年关税为 50%的货物。

普通类(必须减免关税的货物)

包括进口关税列表中90%的货物和 2006 年实施的关税减免货物。传统货物关税的减免如下表：

表 2　传统货物关税减免表

X＝2003 年 1 月 1 日东盟贸易自由协议最惠国关税率

X＝2003 年 1 月 1 日东盟贸易自由协议最惠国关税率	东盟贸易自由协议最惠国关税率							
	该年度 1 月 1 日截止							
	2005	2006	2007	2008	2009	2011	2013	2015
X≥60%	60	50	40	30	25	15	10	0
45%≤X<60%	40	35	35	30	25	15	10	0
35%≤X<45%	35	30	30	25	20	15	5	0
30%≤X<35%	30	25	25	20	17	10	5	0
25%≤X<30%	25	20	20	15	15	10	5	0
20%≤ X<25%	20	20	15	15	15	10	0～5	0
15%≤X<20%	15	15	10	10	10	5	0～5	0

续表

X＝2003年1月1日东盟贸易自由协议最惠国关税率	东盟贸易自由协议最惠国关税率							
	该年度1月1日截止							
	2005	2006	2007	2008	2009	2011	2013	2015
10%≤X＜15%	10	10	10	10	8	5	0～5	0
7%≤X＜10%	7	7	7	7	5	5	0～5	0
5%≤X＜7%	5	5	5	5	5	5	0～5	0
X＜5%	其他							0

除上表的关税减免分布外,越南还作出额外关税承诺:2009年1月1日前列表中50%的货物关税减免至0～5%;2013年1月1日以后不再征收列表中45%的货物关税。

表3　越南额外关税承诺表

货　　物	关税承诺	
	％	年限
大宗货物	30%	2012
小宗货物	45%	2014
摩托车	45%	2012
摩托车零件	13%	2013
钢铁建材	15%	2014
电器制冷设备	10%～15%	2012—2013
石油	20%	2009

2005年中越签署谅解备忘录指出根据WTO规则,剩余的进口关税货物是不用减免关税的货物。

2.服务贸易承诺

为加快服务贸易进程,根据中国—东盟全面经济合作框架协议,各方同意分区域逐步开放服务贸易,逐步消除贸易歧视;深化贸易自由;深化各方服务合作,提高效率和竞争力,使各方提供的服务和分配多元化。越南在自贸区实施的特殊关税优惠政策,细化了中国和东盟签署的协议。

三、结束语

虽然目前中国和越南没有正式的经济贸易合作协议，但中国—东盟全面经济合作框架协定中货物贸易协议和中越谅解备忘录为建设 21 世纪海上丝绸之路创造了有利条件。期待海上丝绸之路惠及中越，强化双方经贸合作，实现两国双赢。

Trade Facilitation—ASEAN and China

Nguyen Thi Thu Thuy[*]

1. Introduction

The Association of Southeast Asian Nations (ASEAN) was formed in 1967 by Indonesia, Malaysia, Philippines, Thailand and Singapore, joined by Brunei in the 1980s (known as ASEAN-6), and by Cambodia, Laos, Myanmar and Vietnam in the 1990s. The ASEAN-10 members are diverse in size, level of economic development, resource endowment, and industrial and technological capabilities. In 1992 ASEAN agreed to form the ASEAN Free Trade Area (AFTA) with tariffs reduced to the $0 \sim 5\%$ level by 2002 (brought forward from 2008) for ASEAN-6 and to the zero level by 2010 for ASEAN-6 and by 2015 for Cambodia, Laos, Myanmar and Vietnam. In addition, ASEAN has in place a services liberalization agreement and an investment liberalization agreement. ASEAN is also forging FTAs with China, Japan, South Korea and India, while individual ASEAN countries are forming bilateral FTAs with a growing number of countries in the Asia Pacific and beyond.

China has experienced rapid and sustained economic growth since its economic reforms and open door policy launched in 1978—1979. Its WTO accession in November 2001 marks another stage of economic reform and opening to outside world that is expected to make China even more efficient

---

* Legal Consultant, Hoang Dam and Global Partnership Law Firm.

and competitive. The size and speed of growth of China's economy and its WTO accession will impact significantly on economic relations and economic prospects in East Asia and beyond.

As an active member of Association of Southeast Asian Nations (ASEAN), Vietnam strives to promote cooperation between ASEAN and China. Expressing most vividly as Vietnam was completed as a dialogue partner of ASEAN-China in 2011. The consistent of Vietnam's view is to strengthen cooperation not only beneficial to the parties but also for common prosperity of the region. Vietnam is trying its best with ASEAN countries and China to promote strong growth strategic partnerships across all sectors, especially in the field of trade and investment. Deputy Foreign Minister Pham Quang Vinh said: "In recent years, Vietnam with its renewed momentum, we've been completed a long way in economic integration in general and the regional economy, in particularly. We have very good integration with ASEAN. At the present, Vietnam is also considered one of the best performing with the targets set for a member state of the integration of ASEAN economic community. This is the basis for better integration of Vietnam in the program of free trade agreement with ASEAN partners, including China."

2. Trade Facilitation

2.1. Definition of Trade Facilitation

There is no standard definition of the term "trade facilitation". Various definitions have been used by international organizations and in trade agreements. In the context of the WTO and the Organization for Economic Co-operation and Development (OECD), for instance, trade facilitation means: "the simplification and harmonization of international trade procedures including the activities, practices and formalities involved in collecting, presenting, communicating and processing data and other information required for the movement of goods in international trade".

By comparison, many bilateral and regional trade agreements have a broader understanding of trade facilitation, extending more generally to "any procedures, processes or policies capable of reducing transaction costs and facilitating the flow of goods in international trade". This paper adopts a broader definition than the one used in the context of WTO negotiations. The review of trade facilitation provisions in section 3 covers a number of behind-the-border issues affecting the free flow of goods, including non-tariff measures such as sanitary and measures, standards, technical regulations and conformity assessment procedures.

2. 2. Potential Benefits of Trade Facilitation

Inefficient trade procedures can produce harmful effects for a country's exports. Some experts have estimated that each additional day that a product is delayed prior to being shipped reduces trade volumes by at least 1 percent. The reduction in trade transaction costs through trade facilitation can bring significant welfare gains. Improved trade facilitation in a sample of 75 countries could increase trade by 10 percent or US $377 billion. For the Asia—Pacific region alone, improving trade facilitation along four dimensions, namely port efficiency, customs environment, regulatory environment and service sector infrastructure, could increase intra-APEC trade by around 10 percent or US $280 billion.

Some studies have focused on the potential gains from trade facilitation reforms in the areas covered in the WTO negotiations on trade facilitation. It would appear from these studies that compliance with GATT Article V (Freedom of transit) and Article Ⅷ (Fees and formalities connected with importation and exportation) could yield a US $107 billion and $33 billion increase in manufacturing trade, respectively. Furthermore, compliance with GATT Article X (Publication and administration of trade regulations) could yield a US $154 billion increase in trade.

Moreover, improving trade facilitation could produce greater benefits than tariff reductions. The world-wide gains from improved trade facilitation (US $110 billion) are of comparable magnitude to the results of full liberalization of goods and services trade (US $150 billion). Tariff costs account for a small portion of the overall international trade costs of Asian sub-regions—typically 10 percent or less. This confirms in their view the need for trade policy-makers and negotiators to sharpen their focus on reducing non-tariff barriers, including trade facilitation and improvement of trade logistics services.

Efforts by ASEAN trade policy-makers to reduce non-tariff barriers have paid off. The changes in trade costs of around 200 countries between 1990 and 2007 as measured by the difference in "free on board" (FOB) and "cost insurance freight" (CIF) values of imports by Australia, a third country market. ASEAN countries had reduced trade costs by more than the global average from the mid-1900s until 2003, corresponding to the period during which AFTA was being established and suggested that this might support at least in part the effectiveness of trade facilitation provisions in trade agreements.

However, while tariff reductions have played a significant role in reducing overall trade costs in APEC (Asia-Pacific Economic Cooperation) and ASEAN, progress on reducing non-tariff trade costs has been less impressive. Trade costs in APEC and ASEAN countries in the periods 1995—2008 and 2001—2007 respectively. There has been encouraging progress towards the reduction of trade costs (although there were some data limitations that made it difficult to assess in the case of ASEAN) but that performance varied markedly across countries.

For developing countries, implementing trade facilitation measures may be more challenging but they stand to gain the most from trade facilitation reforms. Unlike the elimination of tariff barriers which may affect a country's imports rather than its exports, the reduction of trade transaction costs can be beneficial to both importers and exporters, providing a win-win opportunity for developing countries.

3. Facilitation Trade between ASEAN and China

A proposal from Chinese Premier Zhu Rongji for ASEAN-China cooperation at the ASEAN and China Summit in November 2000 led to the formation of an ASEAN-China Expert Group and its 2001 report on *Forging Closer ASEAN-China Economic Relations in the Twenty-First Century*. The Report made the recommendations on establishment of an ASEAN-China

FTA within 10 years, including special and differential treatment and flexibility for CLMV countries, and an "early harvest" package of mutually agreed list of goods to be liberalized ahead of implementation of China's commitments to the WTO; wide range of trade and investment facilitation measures; technical assistance and capacity building to ASEAN members, particular CLMV; and expansion of cooperation in areas such as finance, tourism, agriculture, human resource development, small and medium enterprises, industrial cooperation, intellectual property rights, environment, forestry and forestry products, energy and sub-regional development. At the ASEAN and China Summit in November 2001, ASEAN and China agreed to launch negotiations for an ASEAN-China FTA (ACFTA) and to establish it within 10 years.

The ASEAN-China FTA as well as several regional and bilateral FTAs concluded or under negotiation and study have raised a number of issues concerning FTAs.

International trade theory is clear that customs unions and free trade areas are inferior and second-best positions to multilateralism. While they result in trade creation among members, they also cause trade diversion from lower-cost suppliers outside the membership. The term "FTA", however, has become increasingly inappropriate to describe the recent spate of economic cooperation arrangements in East Asia. These are no longer "regional" as they cut across geographical regions. They are also no longer "FTAs" as they extend beyond the traditional FTA focus on trade liberalization through removal of tariffs and NTBs on trade in goods to include liberalization of trade in services and investment, trade and investment facilitation, and economic and technical cooperation. These are "new age FTAs" and have adopted new terminology such as ASEAN-Japan Comprehensive Economic Partnership, ASEAN-China Comprehensive Economic Cooperation. Empirical studies to model the effects of such "FTAs", focusing only on results of tariff elimination, fail to capture their broader and dynamic effects.

The proliferating FTAs have given rise to some concerns in academic discussions that regionalism and bilateralism could undermine multilateralism and the WTO. It may be premature to conclude whether FTAs in East Asia are stumbling blocks or building blocks without careful examination of the motivations and designs of such FTAs. On motivations, East Asian economies active in RTAs appear to be also active in the WTO process. On design, in many FTAs the scope and pace of trade and investment liberalization are beyond those achievable in the WTO. Many e-conomies are using the FTAs to pressure and consolidate domestic economic reforms. And to the extent that FTAs normally cover sectors, areas, and issues beyond the current scope of the WTO, they are a WTO-plus in trade and investment liberalization and facilitation and enhances technical and economic cooperation between countries.

Increasingly, countries are simultaneously participating in several and often overlapping FTAs, giving rise to the "spaghetti bowl effect" and the "hub and spokes" effect. The spaghetti bowl effect arises from different and divergent rules of origin, technical standards and conformance requirements, and schedules for tariff and NTB reductions. Producers and exporters have to observe all these varied requirements, which mitigates against economies of scale in production and distribution and adds to business transaction costs. The hub and spokes effect arises when a country signs onto several FTAs and becomes a hub with its market shared among many spokes. Hence a hub gains more from an FTA than a spoke. However, with a proliferation of o-verlapping FTAs, many countries end up as hubs.

China's motivations in offering ACFTA are both political and economic. Politically, China wishes to remain on friendly terms with itsneighbors on its southern front. ACFTA is part of confidence building that includes China's participation in the ASEAN Regional Forum and China's accession to the ASEAN Treaty of Amity. ACFTA is to allay ASEAN concerns that China poses a threat with its economic ascendency by providing preferential access to its rapidly growing domestic market. China is also eyeing the ASEAN region for its various natural resources, especially oil and its market of 560 million consumers. Closer economic relations with ASEAN will enable China to build its geopolitical clout in Southeast Asia and counterbalance the influences of Japan and US. The swift progress of ACFTA has hastened

Japan as well as the US, South Korea and India to propose economic cooperation arrangements with ASEAN as well.

ASEAN governments welcomed the China initiative for a number of reasons. First, China is a huge and dynamic economy and its growing demand for ASEAN goods and services could serve as a new engine of growth. Chinese tourists are already a key factor in the growth of tourism in the region. ASEAN also looks to more Chinese investments as well. China's WTO entry will also mean a trading partnership based on international rules and discipline. Closer ASEAN-China economic ties will also enable ASEAN to reduce dependence on the US, EU and Japan. Second, China's offer of special treatment and development assistance for the CLMV group as well as the extension of WTO most-favored-nation benefits to the non-WTO members of ASEAN have helped them to accept the China initiative more readily. Third, China and ASEAN will be able to go further than the WTO in liberalizing agricultural trade, as China's temperate agriculture and ASEAN's tropical agriculture are complementary in many product areas. Thailand, in particular, looks to accelerating agricultural exports to China. Nonetheless there are continuing concerns over the impact of preferential opening of ASEAN markets, as many ASEAN labor intensive manufactures will not be able to compete with China on price.

Economic Ministers of the Member countries in ASEAN-China signed an important protocol in the scope of the 17th ASEAN Summit in Hanoi on 29th October 2010 to facilitate of trade between ASEAN and China. Earlier, mid-term meeting of the Group Rules of Origin of ASEAN-China Trade Negotiations Committee (ACTNC) held in August 2009 in Jakarta, Indonesia, completed a revise of procedure and monitor Regulations the origin of the goods on trade agreements in the framework of the ASEAN-China Free Trade Area (ACFTA).

This is the result of negotiationsfor over the last 2 years of the Vietnam's Ministry of Trade and other ASEAN members with China in order to amend and supplement the provisions of the Rules of Procedure and monitor the origin of Trade Agreement commercial goods under the ACFTA to suitable the practice and the development of free trade in the region. The amendment of those regulations will help facilitate trade between ASEAN and China, to remove difficulties and shortcomings often encountered before such as regulations do not accept C / O with bills issued by third countries, and so on.

Regulation amendments also contribute to promoting the exchange of two-way trade turnover, to improve the efficiency of Goods Trade Agreement under ACFTA. This amendment opens an opportunity for production and business to business for Enterprises of the member countries participating in the Agreement. Some ASEAN countries such as Vietnam, Singapore, Malaysia, Brunei and Laos together with China started implementing this regulation amendment from 1st May, 2011.

On 23rd November, 2013, in Shenzhen, Guangdong Province (China), there was an "Enter ASEAN Forum and Workshop of legal Free Trade" 7th with the participation of experts, academics, representatives of the Enterprises and Traders of China. Discussions at the Forum focused on the theme of enhancing economic development between China and the ASEAN, promotion strategies Fee Trade Area (FTA) China-ASEAN.

Opening speech forum, Ms. Former Vice President Assembly of China, Chairman of China-ASEAN Association, said that precede the opportunities and challenges in building the FTA, China should actively participate in the process of negotiating multilateral trade partners in the region, involved in the development of global trade rules have higher standards to gradually gain greater spokesman of the global economic institutions. To cope with the serious challenges of the international economic situation today, China must maintain balance, structural adjustment, steady growth, especially right through implementing strategies to build the FTA to expand foreign relations, promote institutional reform domestic economy, improving the quality of economic development.

Up to 2013, China has signed a total of nine agreements on building up FTA with 17 countries in Asia,Latin America, Oceania and Europe. These countries now account for 12% of total foreign trade of China, including ASEAN-China trade reached 493 billion US dollars in 2012, up 50 times since the two sides established dialogue relations in 1991. Cumulative bilateral investment between China and ASEAN reached $ 100 billion, becoming an important factor in the economic growth of both parties.

4. Conclusion

Trade facilitation is considered to be an important enabler in the growth of regional value chains and an important driver of economic integration. With the gradual elimination of tariffs, a number of new barriers to trade have been erected. These barriers are increasingly targeted in negotiations at the bilateral, regional and multilateral levels. Despite many ongoing initiativesin trade facilitation, there is evidence that the ASEAN region remains fragmented, partly due to difficulties of moving goods across borders. Inefficient border administration affects the competitiveness of ASEAN exports by raising costs and shipping times. While the overall performance of ASEAN may have improved in recent years, there is considerable room for improvement of trade processes and procedures in individual countries.

The implementation of trade facilitation measures can effectively complement efforts at the multilateral level. The identification of best practices or model trade facilitation principles could assist in this regard. In addition, individual countries should strive to identify priority areas for actions.

贸易便利化—中国和东盟

Nguyen Thi Thu Thuy[*]
潘　静　译

一、简介

东南亚国家联盟成立于 1967 年,成员国有印度尼西亚、马来西亚、菲律宾、泰国和新加坡,20 世纪 80 年代文莱加入,即东盟六国,20 世纪 90 年代柬埔寨、老挝、缅甸和越南相继加入。1992 年东盟组成东盟自由贸易区,决定实施服务自由化协议和投资自由化协议。随后东盟和中国、日本、韩国和印度等亚洲国家和其他地区实现了贸易自由。

自 1978 开始实行改革开放以来,中国经济持续高速增长。2001 年 11 月中国加入世界贸易组织,标志着中国改革开放步入新的阶段,增强了中国的竞争力。中国的发展影响着东亚乃至世界经济关系和经济前景。

越南积极促进中国和东盟的合作,2011 年越南成为中国东盟自由贸易对话伙伴。越南表示近几年越南发展势头强劲,越南完成了整体经济和区域经济整合,为越南和东盟,和中国开展更好的经济整合奠定了基础。

二、贸易便利化

不同的国际组织和贸易协议对"贸易便利化"有不同的解释。本文采用的解释比 WTO 协议的解释更为广泛。第三章对贸易便利的规定包括了货物自由转移的境内壁垒,如零关税政策中的卫生标准、政策规定、技术规定和合格评估程序等等。

---

[*]　越南黄丹国际法律事务所法律顾问。

由于低效率的贸易程序会对一国出口产生不利影响。货物装运时间延长一天，贸易量至少减少 1%。通过实现贸易便利化降低贸易成本效果显著。在亚太地区，提高贸易便利的四元素，即港口效率、海关环境、政策环境和服务区基础设施就可提高亚太经合组织成员国 10% 的贸易量，即增加 2800 亿美元的贸易收入。

研究发现在 WTO 协议规定的区域实现贸易便利化的改革极具潜力。实现贸易便利化带来的好处远大于降低关税。贸易政策制定者和谈判者需要关注怎样减少非关税壁垒，包括实现贸易便利化和提高贸易流通服务。从 20 世纪中叶到 2003 年东盟各国减少的贸易成本幅度远大于全球平均水平，同时这一时期东盟自由贸易区成立，至少证明贸易协议中贸易便利规定是有效的。

发展中国家实行贸易便利化措施可能面临更多的挑战，同时成果也是最显著的。减少贸易成本对进口方和出口方均有利，对发展中国家而言是一个双赢的机会。

三、中国和东盟的贸易便利

2000 年 11 月中国作出了一份经济报告，评价了中国—东盟自由贸易区成立十年来的成果，包括对柬埔寨、老挝、缅甸和越南（新东盟四国）的特殊差别待遇和灵活机制；对东盟成员国的技术帮助和能力建设；开展金融、旅游、农业、人力资源发展等各方面的合作。此外中国和东盟各国一致同意在十年内建成自由贸易区。

国际贸易理论证明建立多边贸易是主要选择，建立关税同盟和自由贸易区是次要选择。传统的自由贸易区通过免除货物关税和消除非关税障碍实现贸易自由，包括服务和投资贸易自由、贸易投资便利、经济技术合作。许多经济体以自贸协议促进国内经济改革。从某种程度上来说自贸协议通常覆盖了世贸协议的内容。这些协议都是比世贸组织的贸易投资更加自由化、便利化，有利于促进两国经济技术合作。

当一国加入几个贸易自由协议形成一个中心市场，辐射多个市场时就形成了"中心辐射"效应。在自由贸易协议中中心市场获得的利益远大于辐射市场，不过随着贸易自由协议的重叠部分增多，许多国家最终都成为了中心市场。中国加入《东盟全面经济合作自由贸易协议》有政治和经济因素，加入该协议旨在维持中国和东南亚各国友好关系。东盟各国认为中国经济对本国经济构成了威胁,中国—东盟自贸区的形成是为了减少东盟各国的忧虑。中国看重东南亚地区丰富的自然资源和巨大的消费者市场。和东盟建立友好关系有利于扩大中国在东南亚地区的影响力,打破日本、美国在这一地区的影响平衡。中国—东盟自贸区的形成促使日本、美国、韩国和印度加强和东盟各国经济合作,东盟各国政府也欢迎中国的加入。

作为一个活跃的经济体,中国对东盟商品和服务的需求是东盟经济增长的引擎。中国游客已经成为了东南亚地区旅游业增长的关键。东盟期待引进更多的中国投资。和中国建立密切的联系有利于东盟减少对美国、欧盟和日本的依赖。其次,中国给予新东盟四国的特别待遇和发展帮助,以及给予东盟非世贸成员的成员国待遇都促使了这些国家主动接纳中国。

中国和东盟农产品的相互补充使得中国和东盟在农业方面的开放程度比世贸组织的更高。由于东盟各国劳动密集型产品没有中国产品的价格优势,许多人仍然担心开放东盟市场带来的不利影响。

2010年10月中国和东盟各国签署了了一项重要协议,促进中国东盟贸易便利。早在2009年双方已修改了商品原产地监管程序,旨在促进双边贸易,提高中国和东盟货物贸易效率,也为成员国的企业生产贸易和电子贸易带来了机遇。

2013年11月东盟会议提出开放中国—东盟自贸区,促进双方经济发展,开放双方自贸区。中国提到建立自贸区面临机遇和挑战,需积极参与区域多边贸易伙伴关系,制定更高标准的全球贸易规则,在全球经济机制问题上有更多的发言权。为应对当今世界经济危机,中国必须保持经济平衡、调整结构、稳步增长,调整自贸区战略,开拓国际关系,促进国内经济机制改革,提高经济发展的质量。

截止到2013年,中国和多个国家达成自贸协议,中国—东盟从建立自由贸易以来,贸易对话已超过50次。双边投资累计已达1000万美元,成为双方经济增长的重要因素。

四、结束语

实现贸易便利是区域价值链增长和经济整合的动力。随着关税的逐渐降低,新的贸易壁垒不断出现。这些壁垒也是双边、区域和多边对话的关注点。尽管有许多推动贸易便利化的积极因素,但东盟地区的货物进出口仍有困难。低效率的边境管理增加了贸易成本和装运时间,影响了东盟出口的竞争力。

近年来东盟总体表现良好,但贸易进程和贸易程序仍然有待提高。修改贸易便利化措施有利于提高多边贸易,良好的贸易便利实践模式可以推进贸易便利。

亚洲基础设施银行(AIIB)

相关法律问题研究

THE STUDY OF LEGAL ISSUES IN AIIB

Legal Issues on Infrastructure Construction and Connectivity

Dy Molany*

Abstract   Infrastructure is the basic physical and organizational structure needed for the operation of a society or enterprise, or the services and facilities necessary for an economy to function. Connectivity has improved across most parts of the Asia-Pacific region, but still needs to be done. In particular, enhancing transportation and energy infrastructure in developing countries remain a challenge. Developing infrastructure networks and connectivity are essential to integrating core and wider economic activities and basic service in the region. After years of tremendous demand for infrastructure projects and construction services, infrastructure companies now face overcapacity pressures, as well as problems related to a shrinking construction market that many developed economics have experienced. The Asian Infrastructure Investment Bank (AIIB) recently established by China is very timely and will be beneficial to the nations of the Association of Southeast Asian Nations (ASEAN). In conclusion, infrastructure is at the core of regional connectivity and integration by boosting productivity and growth, and facilitating trade and investment.

I. Introduction

The development of infrastructure is gaining increased attention as a means to support regional integration and cooperation in East Asia. The as-

---

* Legal Official, Ministry of Justice, Cambodia.

sociation of Southeast Asian Nations (ASEAN), which has been leading efforts for economic integration in the region, unveiled the Master Plan on ASEAN Connectivity (MPAC) in October 2010 to enhance connectivity among ASEAN members. They also launched the ASEAN infrastructure Fund (AIF) in April 2012, which draws upon the foreign reserves of member-states. In particular, the 21st ASEAN Summit, held in Cambodia in November 2012, produced a consensus on launching the ASEAN Economic Community (AEC) by 2015, with the APT countries seeking to join the Regional Comprehensive Economic Partnership (RCEP) until the completion of the AEC. It means that ASEAN will continue to maintain its centrality and remain proactive by being the driving force in the evolving regional architecture.

Infrastructure is the basic physical and organizational structure needed for the operation of a society or enterprise, or the services and facilities necessary for an economy to function. It can be generally defined as the set of interconnected structural elements that provide a framework supporting an entire structure of development. It is an important term for judging a country or region's development.

The term typically refers to the technical structures that support a society, such as roads, bridges, tunnels, water supply, sewers, electrical grids, telecommunications, and so forth, and can be defined as the physical components of interrelated systems providing commodities and services essential to enable, sustain, or enhance societal living conditions.

Viewed functionally, infrastructure facilitates the production of goods and services, and also the distribution of finished products to markets, as well as basic social services such as schools and hospitals; for instance, roads enable the transport of raw materials to a factory. In military parlance, the term refers to the buildings and permanent installations necessary for the support, redeployment, and operation of military forces. Research by anthropologists and geographers shows the social importance and multiple ways that infrastructures shape human society and vice versa.

II. Definition

Infrastructure is the basic physical systems of a business or nation. Transportation, communication, sewage, water, and electric systems are all examples of infrastructure. These systems tend to be high-cost investments, however, they are vital to a country's economic development and prosperity.

Infrastructure generally refers to the most basic level of organizational structure in a complex body or system, upon which the rest of the structure is based. In economic terms, it often refers to basic public services, such as power and water supplies, public transportation, telecommunications, roads, and schools.

The term typically refers to the technical structures that support a society, such as roads, bridges, tunnels, water supply, sewers, electrical grids, telecommunications, and so forth, and can be defined as the physical components of interrelated systems providing commodities and services essential to enable, sustain, or enhance societal living conditions.

Viewed functionally, infrastructure facilities the production of goods and services, and also the distribution of finished products to markets, as well as basic social services such as schools and hospitals; for instance, roads enable the transport of raw materials to a factory. In military parlance, the term refers to the buildings and permanent installations necessary for the support, redeployment, and operation of military forces. Research by anthropologists and geographers shows the social importance and multiple ways that infrastructures shape human society and vice versa.

III. Hardversus Soft Infrastructure

"Hard infrastructure" refers to the large physical networks necessary for the functioning of a modern industrial nation, whereas "soft infrastructure" refers to all the institutions which are required to maintain the economic, health, and cultural and social standards of a country, such as the financial system, the education system, the health care system, the system of government, and law enforcement, as well as emergency services.

Hard infrastructure consists of transportation infrastructure, energy infrastructure, water management infrastructure, communications infrastructure, solid waste management, earth monitoring and measurement networks whereas Soft infrastructure includes Governance infrastructure, Economic infrastructure, Social infrastructure, Cultural, Sports and recreational infrastructure.

Ⅳ. Infrastructure Debt

Infrastructure debt is a complex investment category reserved for highly sophisticated institutional investors who can gauge jurisdiction-specific risk parameters, assess a project's long-term vitality, understand transaction risks, conduct due diligence, negotiate (multi)creditor's agreements, make timely decisions on consents and waivers, and analyze loan performance over time.

Ⅴ. Infrastructure Connectivity and Competitiveness

Developing infrastructure networks and connectivity are essential to integrating core and wider economic activities and basic service in the region. The latest world Economic Forum (2010) Global Competitiveness Report, and the Infrastructure Quality assessment included within, illustrates the importance of infrastructure quality in global competitiveness. Moreover, various studies have also shown that the quality and extensiveness of infrastructure networks greatly impact economic growth and reduce income inequalities and poverty (ADB/ADBI 2009).

To date, connectivity has improved across most parts of the Asia-Pacific region, but still needs to be done. In particular, enhancing transportation and energy infrastructure in developing countries remain a challenge. Asian economies exhibit a wide variation in road and rail densities as well as in rates of electrification. Even though marked improvements in road and electrification have been seen over the last two decades, there is still a long way to go before basic infrastructure needs are fulfilled.

The concept of connectivity through the development of regional infrastructure projects or infrastructure that links one country to another is not really new to Asia. History shows that transport connectivity in Asia started with the Silk Road used to be the most important cross-border artery and was an extensive, interconnected network of pan-Asian trade routes linking East, South, Central, and Western Asia. In 1992, the concept of pan-Asian transport connectivity was revived by the United Nations Economic and Social Commission for Asia and the Pacific (UNESCAP). The Asian Land Transport Infrastructure Development (ALTID) initiative is comprised of three pillars, the Asian Highway (AH), the Trans-Asian Railway (TAR), and the facilitation of land transport projects through intermodal transport terminals.

Regional infrastructure projects are usually more complicated and expensive than typical national infrastructure projects. In this context, it is also a complex, yet necessary, exercise to estimate the financing demand for regional projects and national projects with regional implications. It is hoped that by providing estimates of the need regional infrastructure financing, it will help to clearly define the issues and challenges at hand and facilitate the planning and development of solutions for identifying appropriate investment strategies and financial resources, as well prioritizing projects for utilization of limited resources.

VI. Critical Issues in the Next Decade of China's Infrastructure Effort

Over the past 30 years, China has become the world's largest infrastructure market, thanks to its economic reforms and burgeoning urbanization effort. As positive and dramatic as this evolution has been, it is now possible to identify several critical issues that will bear heavily on the direction and shape of China's infrastructure planning and its construction sector. In brief, the single-source financing model that underpins government-ledinfrastructure development is not sustainable, the quality of urban infrastructure is poor, and despite the vigor of China's infrastructure-building efforts, infrastructure companies now face overcapacity challenges similar to those in developed economies. To understand where China's remarkable infrastructure story goes next, it is valuable to explore these developments and anticipate ways to address these critical issues.

Ⅶ. Building A New Finance Model upon Private Infrastructure Investment

Government-led infrastructure development's heavy dependence on a single source of financing has increased government debt significantly. The model is not sustainable. For a long time, China's infrastructure financing mainly came from government lending and land-transfer revenues. As revenues have diminished, solvency pressures and risks for local governments have risen to high levels. To address to the issue, the central government has made it an economic priority to control and reduce local-government debt risk this year by reducing the amount of credit banks provide to local governments and by increasing the level of audit and transparency of local-government accounts. In light of these circumstances, a better infrastructure-development model would shift away from dependence on government to greater reliance on market finance. The central government is advocating the idea of diversified ownership by encouraging social investment in infrastructure operations through franchises, equity investment, and public-private partnerships (PPP).

China Ministry of Finance is working to promote the PPP model in infrastructure projects by identifying the respective rights, obligations, risks, and revenues of both public-and private-sector partners. In this way, the government hopes to build complementary and mutually beneficial partnerships with the private sector on public projects. Private investment in joint ownership of projects helps reduce government debt, solve financing issues, and improve operational efficiency and revenues at the same time.

Ⅷ. Improving the Quality of New Urban Infrastructure

The quality and operational efficiency of urban infrastructure, especially of new urban projects is poor. Recently, the Chinese government issued a national urbanization plan that extends to 2020, this sets the tone for its "new urbanization" effort, which calls for significant Infrastructure creation. At the same time, however, more and more attention is focused on the fact that so much new infrastructure is of low quality. Moreover, inadequate urbaninfrastructure, low standards for construction practices, and operational management of projects contribute to a failure to meet the infrastructure needs in China's cities.

To solve the issue, the central government is determined to improve urban infrastructure in four areas:

—urban transit, including subway, light rail, and bus rapid transit;

—City pipe networks, including water supply, rainwater, fuel gas, heat supply, telecommunication, power grid, drainage and water logging prevention, flood control, and utility tunnels;

—Sewage treatment and garbage disposal;

—eco-gardens.

Ⅸ. Globalizing Made in China

After years of tremendous demand for infrastructure projects and construction services, infrastructure companies now face overcapacity pressures, as well as problems related to a shrinking construction market that many developed economics have experienced. China's urbanization and infrastructure development has transitioned from rapid growth to stable development. Therefore, initiatives to boost domestic demand, such as the "new urbanization" effort, will have limited impact on domestic infrastructure-market expansion. Within ten years, significant demand will fade for the construction of highways, high-speed rail systems, ports, and airports, bringing the overcapacity issue in construction to the fore.

145

In the meantime, however, China's construction industry still enjoys comparative cost advantages globally. That makes tapping overseas infrastructure demand a strategic priority. At present, developing countries in Asia, Africa, and Latin America are still in the early stages of industrialization and urbanization, which is driving substantial demand for infrastructure. Simultaneously, developed economies including the United States and European nations are renovating and upgrading infrastructure on a large scale, which will also provide overseas opportunities for Chinese construction companies.

China's government is pushing construction companies to go global. For example, on his recent visit to Southeast Asia and Central and Eastern Europe, Chinese Premier Li Keqiang promoted Chinese transportation-equipment manufacturing in sectors including high-speed trains. The Chinese government has also put forward plans for a "Silk Road Economic Belt" with Asia and Europe and a "Maritime Silk Road" with Southeast Asian neighbors to encourage cooperation in trade. As these connections would rely oninterconnecting highways, railways, air routes and other networks, the government anticipates that they will provide significant strategic opportunities for Chinese construction companies to go global and strengthen international cooperation.

X. China's Creation of AIIB to Facilitate Trade

The Asian Infrastructure Investment Bank (AIIB) recently established by China is very timely and will be beneficial to the nations of the Association of Southeast Asian Nations (ASEAN), Thailand's former deputy prime minister, Korn Dabbaransi said Saturday. It is very good international financial institution whose financial facilities land-linked ASEAN countries such as Vietnam, Myanmar, Cambodia, Laos and Malaysia could make use of. He believed that after the ASEAN Economic Community (AEC) is accomplish in 2015, the trade volume between the land-linked ASEAN nations will increase substantially as countries such as Vietnam, Myanmar, Cambodia, Laos, Malaysia and Singapore will be able to utilize the financial facilities provided by the bank to improve the road connection among them. The challenge for ASEAN is how the AEC could extend beyond its borders to connect with countries including China, India, Japan and South Korea, he said. We should not stop at AEC, we should also go beyond our borders.

XI. Conclusion

In conclusion, infrastructure is at the core of regional connectivity and integration by boosting productivity and growth, and facilitating trade and investment. Traditional sources of financing through public budgets are already overstretched, which highlights the need for innovative, pragmatic infrastructure financing solutions. The key challenge is to ensure systematic channeling of private capital into bankable infrastructure projects on the basis of robust market-based policies and institutions.

关于基础设施建设和互联互通的法律问题

Dy Molany *

王垚丹 译

摘要 基础设施是一个社会或企业经营所需的最基本的物质和组织结构,也是经济运转所必需的服务和设施。亚太地区大部分已经实现连通,但仍然需要大力促进,尤其在促进发展中国家的交通运输和能源基础设施方面,仍然是一个巨大挑战。发展基础设施网络覆盖和互联互通,对于区域核心广泛的经济活动和基础服务的一体化至关重要。多年来,基础设施项目建设都有巨大的(市场)需求,但基础设施公司现在面临着产能过剩的压力,以及发达地区经济曾经经历过的建筑市场萎缩问题。最近中国创设的亚洲基础设施投资银行如久旱甘霖,对东南亚国家联盟(东盟)的国家来说十分有利。总结来说,基础设施是区域互联互通和一体化的核心,推动生产力和经济增长,促进贸易和投资。

一、简介

基础设施的发展支撑东亚的区域一体化和合作,引发了多方关注。东盟一直致力于区域经济一体化,于2010年10月公布了东盟互联互通总体规划,来加强东盟成员间的互联互通。同时在2012年4月创立了东盟基础设施基金,用来吸引成员国的外汇储备。特别是2012年11月在柬埔寨举行的第21届东盟峰会,对于将在2015年建立东盟经济联合体方面达成共识,在该联合体建成之前APT(Austral Asia-Pacific Trust 澳洲—亚太互信)国家积极寻求加入区域全面经济伙伴关系。这意味着东盟将继续保持中心地位,在促进区

---

* 柬埔寨司法部国际关系部官员。

域基建方面起主要推动作用。

二、概念

　　基础设施是一个企业或国家最基本的物质系统。运输，通讯，排水，水供应和电力系统均属于基础设施。这些系统都趋向于高成本投资，但也对一个国家的经济发展和繁荣具有重要作用。基础设施通常被定义为互联互通结构性要素，为发展的整体结构提供了一个框架，也是评判一个国家或区域发展状况的重要指标。

　　基础设施通常表示支撑一个社会的技术结构，例如道路、桥梁、隧道、用水供应、污水处理、输电网络/电力网络、（电信）通讯等，也可以是提供商品和服务的互联互通系统的物理组成，这些商品和服务能够维持或者改善社会生存条件。

　　从功能上来说，基础设施不仅促进商品和服务的生产，同时也促进了成品流向市场（商品（成品）市场的流通）以及便利了基本的社会服务，例如学校、医院以及从原材料到加工工厂的道路交通运输。而在军事领域，基础设施系指为军事部署和军事行动提供必要支持的军事设施和常备设施。此外，人类学家和地理学家的研究也表明了基础设施对于塑造人类社会的社会重要性和多样性（反之亦然）。

　　"硬基础设施"指一个现代工业国家正常运转所必需的大型物质网，而"软基础设施"指所有需要用来维持一国的经济、健康、文化和社会标准的制度，例如金融系统、教育系统、健康保护系统、政府系统和法律执行，以及急救服务。

　　硬基础设施由交通运输基础设施、能源基础设施、水管理设施、通讯交流设施、固体废物管理、地表检测和测量网组成，而软基础设施包括政府设施、经济设施、社会基础设施、文化、运动和休闲基础设施。

　　基础设施债务是一个复杂的投资种类，往往适用于那些经营机构的投资者，这些投资者可以估计出特定司法风险，评估一个项目的长期生命力，了解交易风险，进行尽职调查，与债权人进行协议商谈，做出及时的赞同或放弃的决定，并且分析不良贷款绩效。

三、基础设施互联互通和竞争

　　发展基础设施网状和互联互通对区域核心广泛的经济活动和基础服务的

一体化至关重要。2010年世界经济论坛全球竞争报告,包括其中的基础设施质量评估,说明了全球竞争中基础设施竞争力的重要性。同时,不同的研究也证明基础设施网的质量和数量极大影响着经济增长,减少收入不公平和贫困。

时至今日,亚太区域绝大部分地区已经大力促进了互联互通,但仍然需要努力。尤其是促进发展中国家的交通运输和能源基础设施仍然是一个巨大挑战。在公路和铁路密集度以及电力化方面,亚洲经济展现出巨大的改变,但依然道阻且长。通过区域基础设施建设(来连接亚洲各国)以实现互联互通对于整个亚洲来说早已不再新鲜。历史表明亚洲的交通连通始于丝绸之路。1992年,联合国亚太经社委再次提起泛亚交通互联互通。亚洲陆地交通基础设施发展最初创立时由三部分组成,即亚洲公路、泛亚铁路,以及道路运输项目。

四、中国基础设施建设的关键问题和改善

过去30年,由于经济改革和迅速发展的城市化,中国已经成长了世界最大的基础设施市场。目前有一些对中国基础设施的批判性问题,政府主导的基础设施发展的这种单一财政模式并不是可持续的,城市基础设施质量较差,并且企业也面临着产能过剩的问题。探讨中国这种异常的基础设施问题的走向,探索其发展和参与方式对于解决这些关键问题来说意义重大。

政府主导的财政模式增加了政府债务。长期以来中国的基础设施都依靠政府支持,使得财政收入减少,偿付压力和风险达到很高程度。为了解决这一问题,中央政府开始放松对经济的控制,通过减少银行贷款和增加政府债务透明度来减少当地政府的债务风险,就此形成一个更好的基础设施发展模式,不再单纯依赖政府而更多地依赖市场。中央政府正倡导多元化所有权,即通过特许权、公平投资和公私合伙关系鼓励社会投资基础设施。

中国中央政府在以下四个领域改善城市基础设施:

1. 城市交通运输,包括铁路、轻轨和公交快速运输;

2. 城市管道网络,包括水供应、雨水、燃料气体、热供应、通信、输电网、排水或水涝预防、洪水控制和公用隧道;

3. 污水处理和废弃物处置;

4. 生态园。

中国的城市化和基础设施建设已经由快速增长转型为稳固发展,中国的建筑行业在全球依然具有相对成本优势。目前,亚非拉美州的发展中国家依然处于工业和全球化的前期阶段。同时,包括美国和欧盟在内的发达国家也

在对基础设施进行大规模更新和升级,这也给中国的建设公司提供了大量海外机会。

最近由中国创设的亚洲基础设施投资银行是一个全球化的金融组织,财政扶持可以为很多东盟国家,例如越南、缅甸、柬埔寨、老挝、马来西亚和新加坡提供便利。

Legal Challenges and Solutions on the Establishment of ASIAN Infrastructure Investment Bank

Hun Sopheap[*]

Abstract   The Asian Infrastructure Investment Bank (AIIB) is an international financial institution proposed by China. The purpose of the multilateral development bank is to provide finance to infrastructure projects in the Asia Pacific region. Although infrastructure investment are also considered important in order to facilitate the flow of investment and trade in all sector, but the most important goal is the infrastructure investment itself and how to create a broader financial market for the private sector to absorb state money and public finance in a broader scale in order to enter the infrastructure market. In order to be successful as a political institution, the AIIB will need to be successful as a development institution. This is where the subject gets really interesting. Because in order for to the AIIB to be successful, the leader of the bank, i. e. China, will need to be as advocate for something that it is not particularly known for, it needs to be stressing good governance.

Ⅰ. Introduction

The Asian Infrastructure Investment Bank (AIIB) is an international financial institution proposed by China. The purpose of the multilateral development bank is to provide finance to infrastructure projects in the Asia

---

[*]   Secretary of the Minister of Justice of Cambodia.

Pacific region. AIIB is regarded by some as a rival for the International
Monetary Fund (IMF), the World Bank and the Asian Development Bank
(ADB), which the AIIB says are dominated by developed countries like the
United States and Japan.

II. History

The first news reports about the AIIB appeared in October 2013. China
has been established institutions like the IMF, World Bank and Asian Development Bank which are dominated by American, European and Japanese interests. It has been identified the region requires $8 trillion to be invested
from 2010 to 2012 in infrastructure for the region to continue economic development. It is hoped that the new bank will allow China which has
enormous capital to finance these projects and allow it a greater role to play
in the economic development of the region consummate with its growing
economic and political clout.

In June 2014 China proposed doubling the registered capital of the bank
from $50 billion to $100 billion and invited India to participate in the
founding the bank. On October 24, 2014, a signing ceremony held in
Beijing, formally recognized the establishment of the bank. 21 countries
signed the bill, which included: China, India, Thailand, Malaysia,
Singapore, the Philippines, Pakistan, Bangladesh, Brunei, Cambodia, Kazakhstan, Kuwait, Laos, Myanmar, Mongolia, Nepal, Oman, Qatar, Sri
Lanka, Uzbekistan, and Vietnam. U. S. pressure led Australia, Indonesia
and South Korea from signing up as founding members, despite the fact that
they had formerly expressed an interest in it.

The next step is to negotiate the bank's articles of agreement, which is
expected to be completed by the end of 2015.

III. Invited Countries

The initial $50 billion was mostly provided by China, but Pakistan,
India, Singapore and Vietnam were also signatories. However, there are a

total of 21 signatories. Japan, South Korea, Indonesia, and Australia were not in attendance, but China's Ministry of Finance said "any country that signs and ratified the articles can still officially become a 'founding' member" though they must first be accepted by the existing members.

Ⅳ. Literature Review

Infrastructure funding scheme: Infrastructure is the most basic public infrastructure to support economic activity of a country. Availability of infrastructure determines the level of efficiency and effectiveness of economic activity. Given the vital infrastructure for economic development, it is the duty of government infrastructure development entirely. Empirical datashows that there is a strong relationship between the availability of basic infrastructure in the economy.

The study by Aschauer (1989) concluded that the availability of infrastructure services is an important production factor. The study also found that decline in productivity may be caused by the deterioration of the availability of infrastructure services. Meanwhile, Berndt and Hansson (1991) suggest that the increase in infrastructure services proven to reduce the cost of production factors. Norton (1992) showed that the infrastructure in the telecommunications sector has a significant positive impact on economic growth. Briefly, the studies above show that investment in infrastructure have a positive impact on the economic.

Various studies to measure impact of infrastructure in the economic, among others, conducted by the World Bank (1994) which states that the economic growth of percent turned out to be closely related to the growth in the availability of infrastructure services by one percent anyway. Further studies measuring the elasticity of the availability of infrastructure to be economy performed by Roller and Waverman (1996), canning (1999), Marianne Fay (1999), Calderon and Serven (2002). Various studies show that it has a significant infrastructure investment and positive impact on the economy.

The problem is the increase in demand is not matched by the ability of

the Government to provide funding for infrastructure development, even
from year to year decrease government's financial capability. To bridge the
decreased ability of the government to fund infrastructure, then it needs to
develop a range of funding schemes such as the Public-Private Partnership,
business to business and SPV scheme.

V. InternationalFinancing Scheme

Issues on infrastructure Crisis have strong linkages with the financial crisis
and trade that hit the global economy. Infrastructure market liberalization is a key
strategy in order to restore financial market. Same with the invasion in food
markets, agriculture, climate market, social insurance market, all of which are
encouraged to be a crutch for the stability of financial market.

Although infrastructure investment are also considered important in
order to facilitate the flow of investment and trade in all sector, but the most
important goal is the infrastructure investment itself and how to create a
broader financial market for the private sector to absorb state money and
public finance in a broader scale in order to enter the infrastructure market.
There are at least three international financial institution that can be a source
of infrastructure funding namely:

Multilateral Development Banks, including the World Bank, the Asian
Development Bank (ADB), and other financial that become affiliates such as
the multilateral investment Guarantee Association (MIGA), under certain
circumstances, these agencies can offer credit enhancements such as partial
risk guarantees to the project company and the lenders.

Foreign & Domestic Commercial Banks providing debt financing for the
project. It may be possible to secure all domestic debt financing for project
that are smaller, but larger projects may require merging with government
financing.

ASEAN infrastructure Fund (AIF). AIF is an ASEAN infrastructure
financing institution established to provide financial support for infrastructure
development in ASEAN by utilizing the excess liquidity in the region.

The World Bank was established to promote long-term foreign

investment loans on reasonable terms. The purpose of the Bank, as set forth in the "Articles of Agreement" are as follows: (I) to assist in the reconstruction and development of members by facilitating the investment of capital for productive purpose, (II) to promote private investment by means of participation in loans and other investments made by private investors, (III) when private capital is not available on reasonable terms, to supplement private investment by providing on suitable finance for productive purpose out of its own capital funds raised by it and its other resource, (IV) to promote the long-range balanced growth of international trade and the development trade and the maintenance of equilibrium in balance of payments by encouraging international investment of the productive resources of members, thereby in raising productivity, the standard of living, and conditions of labor in their territories, (V)to arrange the loans made or guaranteed by it in relation to international loans made or guaranteed by it in relation to international loads though other channels so that the more useful and urgent project large and small alike, will be dealt with first, and (VI) to conduct its operations with due regard to the effect of international investment on business conditions in the territories of member and in the immediate postwar years, to assist in bringing about a smooth transition from a wartime to peacetime economy.

The Asian development Bank (ADEB) is being one of the Multilateral Development Banks, was funded in 1996 by 31 member government to promote the social and economy progress of the Asian and Pacific region. Over the past 31years, the Bank's membership has grown to 57, of which 41 are from within the region and 16 from outside the region.

The Bank's principal function are (I) to extend loans and equity investment for the economic and social development of its developing member countries (DMCs), (II) to provide technical assistance for the preparation and execution of development programs, and for advisory services, (III) to promote and facilitate investment of public and private capital for development purposes, and (IV) to respond to requests for assistance in co-ordinating development policies and plans of its DMCs. The ASEAN infrastructure fund (AIF) is a join initiative of the Finance Minister of

ASEAN and the Asian development Bank (ADB) in an effort to provide
financial support for infrastructure development in the ASEAN region. This
initiative is motivated significant difference in the level of infrastructure development in the ASEAN countries (infrastructure development gap). In
addition, the presence of excess domestic liquidity (domestic resources)
must be absorbed and utilized for infrastructure development in ASEAN.
AIF, the implementation will be realized in a special vehicle (SPV) that will
be administered by ADB. Though the SPV, the capital that has been formed
will then leveraged. At a later stage, if the SPV has had top billing
infrastructure project that they fund, this bill can then be securitized to
increase liquidity so as to increase its lending capacity anyway. Thus, the
SPV will be able to mobilize funds at a higher level. At the same time, the
SPV is going to be build a good track record for AIF.

Ⅵ. AIIB May Get a Head Start on TPP

Although AIIB plan was initially set in motion as a reaction to the TPP,
the TPP negotiations currently have no clear direction. Other states
participating in the negotiations are standing by as they watch how the negotiations between Tokyo and Washington develop, while the process might
"drift along" depending on the outcome of the U. S. midterm elections.
However even if the TPP negotiation "drift along", the AIIB will likely
come in to being.

China will be the first to obtain an effective tool at strengthening
economic coordination within the Asia region. That will probably result in
alarm bells over "whether this is a good thing" ringing in Japan and the
United states, both of which tend to preoccupy themselves with domestic
politics. Competition is a good thing for an economy.

The AIIB's establishment outside the existing international financial
order will exert a complicated influence on international development
financing. However, when Tokyo and Washington lobby other countries
"not to join" in the AIIB, whose founding they cannot stop, they will only
deepen the fissures in the international financial community. Exclusion and

berries are bad for an economy.

One often hears from Japan and the United States that the right way to deal with a rising China is to "approach with a stance of both engagement and hedging is evident, the engagement is not.

Cooperating with China in issues such as global warming and anti-terrorism "for the entire world's sake "would also serve as engagement, but engagement is considerably difficult where succumbing to the zero-sum game of national interests comes easily. As exemplified by territorial disputers, this is all the more so in the realms of diplomacy and security.

And if that is the case, then we should think with more seriousness about the possibility of engagement on economic issues, even if what is on the table is an NIH (Not Invented Here) scenario, such as the AIIB.

Ⅶ. Will China's AIIB Succeed?

One of the hot topics in the Ministries of Finance across Asia of late is what to make of China's newly announced plans to create a new development institution to be named the Asian infrastructure investment Bank—the AIIB for short. What makes this fledgling institution so interesting is the political support it is receiving within China's leader Xi Jinping at the annual meeting of the Asia-pacific Economic Co-operation (APEC) forum in Bali last year.

Since then, there has been a great deal of speculation as to who will be joining, who was invite to join and who was not invited to join. At the same time, there has been considerable discussion about the true intent of the AIIB, with much speculation that the true purpose of the new bank to challenge Japan's primacy with the Asian Development Bank in Manila.

The challenge to Japan is undoubtedly true as the essence of such multi-nationals is political, they are at their heart political engines riding on the rails of development. As such, all of the countries that make up the ADB have been invite to join the AIIB including the United States, Japan, South Korea and India. Whether or not these countries join is getting a great deal political attention, right up to and including that of the Oval Office in the White House.

The popular perception seems to be that the US is trying to block the AIIB. But that seems most unlikely as the US does not, frankly, have the wherewith all to do so. How can they really object when someone is effect offering emerging countries cheap money, which they clearly need. If you cannot do something, then politically it makes no sense to even try.

The truth of the matter is more likely that the Obama Administration, or any Administration, could not persuade this Congress to pony up funds for another new multination organization, particularly one run by the Chinese. In fact, the US is once again in arrears on its capital contribution to be the ADB.

At the same time, if the US did support the creation of the AIIB, it would go a very way to upsetting their most important ally at a time when they very much need Japan as a natural geopolitical counterweight to China. Moreover, one of the most important roles of the ADB is to serve as a political bridge between Japan and the rest of Asia. Why upset that apple cart?

For the countries of Asia, the question of whether or not to join is a relatively easy one. It is hard to see anyone abstaining. Why snub their giant neighbor China on this issue, particularly when they are offering money and developmental aid? There is also no downside risk. At worst, they will be getting a few projects with much needed cheap capital without the nettlesome constraints of conditionality.

But in order to be successful as a political institution, the AIIB will need to be successful as a development institution. This is where the subject gets really interesting. Because in order for to the AIIB to be successful, the leader of the bank, i. e. China, will need to be as advocate for something that it is not particularly known for, it needs to be stressing good governance.

There has been a lot of talk of late about Asia's infrastructure needs and the amount of capital that will be required to address those needs. This is nothing new. Those number have been bounced around for decades without much progress. As such the numbers continue to grow year by year. The current ADB estimates suggest that Asia will need $8 trillion in national infrastructure and $290 billion in national infrastructure through 2020 to sustain the region's grow trajectory.

With this, comes the standard focus on how much each institution brings to the table. In AIIB's case the consensus seems to be that the initial target is around ＄100 billion of new capital. Everyone thus welcomes the idea of the AIIB and usually adds that the ADB can use some competition which is undoubtedly true.

But neither the ADB nor the AIIB can raise anywhere near the required sums. Indeed, the ADB finances less than 2 percent of Asia's needs. Something the AIIB can only hope to match in the next decade. As such, the only source of such funds can be the private sector. Public sector lending can only go so far. Of course, the development banks can, and do, support the private sector in their efforts to "catalyinctsze" private sector investment flows, albeit half-heartedly-a testament to their political and big government instincts.

Yet the real issue is not how much money there is on the table. At the ADB we never turned down an infrastructure transaction for lack of money. It was usually for the absence of good projects and because many countries were frankly not ready for series effort at infrastructure programs. Most of the infrastructure companies across a number of the difficulties they have faced in past years.

The real question is really who will now bring the really needed managerial and technical skills to the emerging countries which so clearly need the goods and services considered standard features of a modern economy. This element will only follow the presence of good governance. Where these elements in place, the money would rush in of its own accord.

In order to entice the private sector to step up its investments into long term infrastructure projects, the countries of Asia must first improve their governance regimes. The rule of law, independent regulators and judiciaries, predictability, clean politics, political stability, etc. are all essential elements in the highly competitive race for private capital. Singapore and Hong Kong are good demonstrations of this reality.

Absent these elements, all the money in the world be of little use as it will not venture into the emerging economies.

Indeed, the world is awash with money as it is, it just chooses to sit idle for the time being for lack of attractive investment opportunities.

To a limited degree the ADB understands is and this has been as important element in the success of their private sector operations over the last dozen years. The real question is can China credibly press these governance issues when their own governance is hardly the model of transparency and predictability.

If China can bring itself to stress governance as an essential requirement of development, the AIIB will have the ability to be a success. They say they are committed to doing so. And who knows, maybe some of this will rub off on China's own administration. But if not, the AIIB will become merely an embarrassing shill for China's own commercial interests. Indeed, China has made a habit of the safeguard that the international community has come to regard as the norm. without these in place, the AIIB's efforts could be counterproductive in the long run as the host governments treat the Chinese project managers with the same passive aggressive indifference they have treated everyone else.

With the visibility of Xi Jinping's personal endorsement and credibility on the line, this will be most interesting to watch.

Ⅷ. Conclusion

In conclusion, AIIB is regarded by some as a rival for the IMF, the World Bank and the Asian Development Bank (ADB), which the AIIB says are dominated by developed countries like the United States and Japan.

亚洲基础设施投资银行成立的相关法律问题和解决办法

Hun Sopheap[*]

王垚丹　汪智芳　译

摘要　亚洲基础设施投资银行（亚投行）是由中国发起成立的一个国际性金融机构。其宗旨是为亚太地区的基础设施项目提供财力支持。虽然基础设施投资是促进投资和贸易流动的重要一环，但最重要的目标是基础设施投资本身以及如何创建一个更广阔的金融市场，使私营企业吸纳国有资金和公共资金进入基础设施市场。欲形成一套有效的管理体系，以中国为首的亚投行，将需要作为一个不断学习善政的倡导者。

一、简介

亚洲基础设施投资银行（亚投行）是由中国发起成立的一个国际性金融机构。该多边开发银行的宗旨是为亚太地区的基础设施项目提供财力支持。亚投行被视为是国际货币基金组织、世界银行和亚洲开发银行的竞争对手，而国际货币基金组织、世界银行和亚洲开发银行是由美国和日本等发达国家利益主导。

有关亚投行的新闻报道最早见于 2013 年 10 月。2010 年到 2012 年间，区域经济发展需要对基础设施投资 8 万亿美元。人们都希望亚投行将允许拥有庞大资本的中国财政扶持这些项目，允许其在经济发展中占据一个更重要的地位。

在 2014 年 6 月，中国提出将亚投行的注册资本由 500 亿美元增加至 1000 亿美元，并邀请印度共同建立银行。2014 年 10 月于北京举行签约仪式，

---

[*]　柬埔寨司法部部长秘书。

正式建立亚投行,21 个国家加入。下一阶段将对银行协议的条文进行协商,预计于 2015 年底完成。

最初的 500 亿美元大部分由中国提供,但巴基斯坦、印度、新加坡和越南也同样签约,总共有 21 个签约国。日本、韩国、印度尼西亚和澳大利亚并未出席,但中国财政部部长表示"只要签订并认可成立亚投行的相关协定,任何国家都可正式成为创始成员国"。

基础设施基金方案:基础设施是支持一个国家经济活动最基本的公共设施。基础设施的可用性决定了经济活动的效率和效益水平。作为经济发展的重要设施,政府有责任全面发展基础设施。实验数据表明基本设施的可用性和经济之间存在重要的联系。

Aschauer(1989)的研究表明基础设施服务的有效性是一个重要的生产因素。该研究也表明生产力下降可能是由基础设施服务的可用性降低造成的。同时,Berndt 和 Hansson(1991)也认为基础设施服务的增加减少了生产成本。Norton(1992)表明通讯领域的基础设施随经济增长具有重要的积极作用。以上的这些研究都表明基础设施投资对经济具有积极影响。

二、国际融资方案

基础设施风险问题已经与金融危机和贸易紧紧联系。基础设施市场自由化是重建金融市场的关键。所有的食品市场、农业市场、社会保险市场都是金融市场稳定性的强大支柱。至少有三个国际金融机构属于基础设施基金的来源,即:

1.多边开发银行,包括世界银行,亚洲开发银行和其他金融附属机构,例如多边投资担保机构。在特定情形下,这些机构可以提供信用担保,例如为项目公司和借款者提供特定的风险担保。

2.国内外商业银行也会为项目提供债务融资。

3.东盟基础设施基金。

三、亚投行可能对 TPP 形成领先优势

虽然亚投行计划最初是对 TPP 的一个回应,但最近 TPP 协商并没有明确的方向。其他参与协商的国家都在关注东京和华盛顿之间的协商将如何发展,然而这个过程却依赖于美国中期选举的结果。即使 TPP 协商随波逐流,

但是亚投行会继续进行。

中国首先采用有效的方法增强亚洲区域的经济协调。这将会对日本和美国的怀疑"是否这是一个良好的事情"敲响警钟。竞争对经济来说是良好的事情。在现有国际金融秩序之外建立的亚投行将会对国际金融发展发挥一个十分复杂的影响。我们经常听到来自日本和美国的论断，即对应中国崛起的正确方式是"参与与对立明显并存，但并不参与"。中国面对全球变暖和反恐"为了全世界的安全"积极参与，但是参与是相当困难的，屈从于零国家利益的游戏规则就简单多了。以领土争论为例，所有的都是关于外交和安全领域的。

四、中国的亚投行能否成功

近期亚洲财政部门的一个热门话题是什么促使中国创设一个全新发展机制亚投行。这样一个毫无经验的机构广受欢迎的原因是中国国家主席习近平去年在巴厘岛举办的亚太经合论坛年度会议上的大力支持。

自此，人们开始猜测谁将参与，谁被邀请参与和谁不会被邀请。同时，人们也在热烈讨论亚投行的真正目的，很多人推测亚投行的真正目的是挑战日本在亚洲开发银行中的地位。对日本的挑战无疑是正确的，因为这样一个银行的实质是政治。就这点而言，亚洲开发银行的所有国家都被邀请加入亚投行，包括美国、日本、韩国和印度。这些国家是否加入将会引起广泛的政治关注。

普遍的看法是美国试图阻止亚投行。但美国不可能这么做，他们真正反对的是有人为新兴国家提供便宜的资金，当然这也正是这些国家所需要的。如果你没有办法做一些事情，政治因素也没有需要去尝试。事实的真相更可能是奥巴马政府或者是任何政府都无法说服议会为其他的新型多国组织提供资金，特别是由中国主导的。同时，如果美国确实支持亚投行的运行，这将打乱美国与日本的盟友关系，而美国十分需要日本作为一个天然的地理政治因素来制衡中国。亚开行最重要的角色之一就是作为日本和亚洲其他地区之间的政治桥梁。

对亚洲其他国家来说是否加入亚投行的问题就很简单。很少会有国家放弃。首先他们都不会在这个问题上冷落强大的邻居中国，更何况中国提供了资金和发展帮助，同时也不存在下降的风险。即便在最糟糕的情况下，他们也会得到一些项目资金支持。

　　如果中国能将强化治理作为发展的必要条件，那么亚投行具有成功的可能。由于习近平个人言行的知名度和信誉度，未来中国对亚投行的管理值得期待。

Frontier Issues on Islamic Finance System and Banking Capital Operation

Teh Tai Yong[*]

Abstract　　In recent years, much has been discussed about the momentum that Islamic Finance System has achieved on the international financial world. Islamic Finance is a financial system that is carried out in line with the principles of Shariah. This paper discusses the Legal Frontier Issues on Islamic Finance System & Banking Capital Operation and link the issues to China's 21st-Century Maritime Silk Road initiatives. The paper delves into the issues relating to (i) Legal Concept of Islamic Finance System; (ii) Regulatory Framework; (iii) Financial Instruments of the Islamic Finance system; and (iv) Hub of Islamic finance system. It is proposed that countries within the 21st-Century Maritime Silk Road initiatives should establish a finance institution, in line with the Asian Infrastructure Investment Bank (AIIB), to achieve its objective to promote peace, development, cooperation and adopting a win-win strategy for all.

Introduction

In recent years, much has been discussed about the momentum that Islamic Finance System has achieved on the international financial world. More and more countries are adopting Islamic Finance, alongside with the existing Conventional Finance System.

---

[*]　Partner, Teh Kim Teh, Salina & Co.

Islamic Finance is a financial system that is carried out in line with the principles of Shariah. It is a vital development in many countries now. According to Global Islamic Financial Report 2014, the actual size of the global Islamic financial services industry grow from US $ 1. 036 Trillion in 2009 to US $ 1. 813 Trillion in 2013. We also see steady growth of Islamic Finance products, including Sukuk (which is Islamic Bond), Islamic Banking, and fund management.

The aim of this paper is to discuss few legal issues on Islamic System and Banking Capital Operation. The views expressed in this paper are driven by the understanding of the topic from the Malaysian's perspective.

Legal Concept of Islamic Finance System

The First Legal issue is the "Legal Concept of Islamic Finance System". It is extremely important to highlight what is allowed and what is prohibited in the Islamic finance system. We refer to these as the "DO's and DON'T's".

Regarding the DO's—under such system, parties who intend to enter into a legal transaction must observe few things. (i) There must be clear and specific contracting parties, (ii) There must be clear and specific expression of contract, and (iii) There must be clear and specific subject matter.

Regarding the DON'T's—Islamic finance system prohibits the following matters:

(1)(i)Interest (which is called as Riba or Ursury). In the olden times, Ursury is seen as a tool of oppression by the rich against the poor. It is a practice of charging unreasonable high interest rates to unfairly enrich the lender. This is known as the "loan shark" in recent times. If the lender is not allowed to charge "Interest", what would the lender earn from the transaction? In Islamic Finance system, the portion earned by the lender is called as "Profit". For example, a customer borrows RMB1,000,000 from a bank. He has to repay the bank for 10 years and the total repayments is RMB1,200,000. The RMB200,000 that bank earns is called as the "Profit".

(2)(ii)(which is called as Gharar). In the financial term, the Maximum Rate has to be stated in the contract. It is called as the "Ceiling Rate". Unlike the practice in conventional banking, the interest rate floats with the market condition, customers of Islamic finance system know their maximum exposure; and (iii) Prohibited products/ activities (such as gambling, consumption of alcohol or pork). These activities are prohibited in the religion. Hence one must not obtain Islamic finance to carry out these types of activities.

The above DOs and DON'Ts are strictly adhered to in the Islamic finance system. Parties must observe all of the conditions to comply with Shariah principles.

The challenge for many countries is that—Islamic finance system is still at the early stage of development. Although there are transactions being carried out under the Islamic finance system, this concept is still relatively new to the common people.

In the world where Conventional Finance System is so entrenched in our daily life, many would then make comparison between Conventional Finance System and Islamic finance system. It is opined that Islamic finance system should not be compared in such manner. Islamic finance system should be viewed from its own lens.

In Islam, the God is the owner of all wealth in the world, and humans are merely his trustees. Therefore, humans need to manage wealth according to God's commands, which promote justice and prohibit certain activities. However, the people have the right to enjoy whatever wealth they acquire and spend in sharia-compliant ways, as long as their behavior aligns with the religion.

The Islamic economics is based on core concepts of balance. It is a balancing between (i) material pursuits and spiritual needs; and also balancing between (ii) individual and social needs. This balancing exercise will ensure that the motives and objectives are beneficial to society at large.

We may also link this to the purpose of the concept "One Belt and One Road"—that is to promote peace, development, cooperation and adopting a win-win strategy for all.

Regulatory Framework

The Second issue is about the "Regulatory Framework". A good and comprehensive legal or regulatory framework is the key element for implementing Islamic Finance System. One of the key challenges facing this industry now is that there is a limited number of country that has enacted specific law to recognise and govern Islamic Finance System. In order to have an effective finance system, these countries have to enact the laws relating to Islamic Finance System.

Generally, a good legal regulatory structure is vital for an "enabling environment" for development of a financial system. This is especially relevant to this industry because of the complex nature of Shariah-compliant investments and continual innovation of financial products. Further to that, a good legal regulatory framework for the Islamic finance system can nurture an environment that supports its growth, strengthens its stability, and safeguards the interests of all parties.

Take Malaysia as an example, we have enacted the *Islamic Financial Services Act* 2013 (IFSA 2013) and *Central Bank of Malaysia Act* 2009 (CBMA 2009) to recognise and regulate the Islamic finance system. The Central Bank of Malaysia has issued many guidelines to regulate finance system. The Malaysian Courts have decided on many cases involving Islamic finance system.

The Regulatory Framework forms the basis for development of Islamic finance system in Malaysia—from the enactment of laws, to Shariah governance, as well as the dispute resolution aspects.

It should be pointed out that Malaysia did not have this Framework right from the start. Malaysia has adopted Islamic finance system for few decades but some of these laws are enacted quite recently. In another words, we do not have to wait for a "perfect framework" in place to kick-start the system. We may improve the system along the way. Of course, we can always learn from the experiences from other jurisdictions on how to make it a successful system in shortest possible time.

The 21st-Century Maritime Silk Road is an initiative that involves many countries in the world. Some of these countries already have Islamic finance system in place right now. For starting point, we can consider to sign a bilateral Memorandum of Understanding (MoU) to establish such Islamic finance system for countries within "21st-Century Maritime Silk Road".

For this purpose, we may refer to the establishment of Asian Infrastructure Investment Bank (AIIB) signed by 20 countries in October 2014 in Beijing. This will then serve as the Regional Legal Framework between the nations within "21st-Century Maritime Silk Road".

The next phase is to establish the National Legal Framework in each of the countries torecognise the Islamic finance system.

Financial Instruments of the IFS

The Third issue is about the "Financial Instruments of the IFS". To facilitate trades and cooperation, the Islamic finance innovated many financial instruments to cater for different transactions. Generally, Islamic finance contracts are divided into few categories:

(1) Sale Based Financing (which includes Murabahah; Bay Bithaman Ajil, Bay al-Inah, Tawarruq, Istisna);

(2) Lease Based Financing (which includes Ijarah);

(3) Participatory Based Financing (which includes Musharakah Mutanaqisah);

(4) Fee Based Financing (which includes Wakalah, Kafalah).

Each of the above instruments serves different purpose. It is possible to have a combination of different instruments in a financing transaction.

On Islamic capital market, the Islamic Bond—known as Sukuk is very popular now. Sukuk is issued and traded in accordance with the terms and conditions of Shariah. It is based on the principle of participation in profit and loss.

In the meantime, Islamic finance system must also address the banking issues of collateral, management of contracts, asset recovery and etc.

Islamic finance system has a comprehensive framework, which covers

Islamic capital market, Islamic financial market, Islamic financial institutions. We may adopt this system to complement the existing conventional finance system. The finance market is huge, hence it should be viewed as complimentary, rather than competition to each other.

Hub of Islamic Finance System

The fourth issue relates to the "Hub of Islamic Finance System". To develop the Islamic Finance System well for "21st-Century Maritime Silk Road", we need to establish an effective and suitable Hub. It is proposed that Malaysia could play an important role for this mission. There are few reasons for this proposal.

First, Malaysia has mature Islamic banking and finance industry. There are now 14 Islamic banks consisting 4 foreign Islamic banks and 2 domestic Islamic banks with foreigners' participation. It is proven that even non-Muslims like me, can accept Islamic banking. Malaysia is the main centre for globalSukuk issuance for Malaysian, Asian, and Middle Eastern companies.

Secondly, Malaysian government is very supportive on the initiative of Islamic finance system. It has put in place a strong and robust regulatory framework. It has created business-friendly policies for businesses to encourage growth of Islamic finance system.

Thirdly, there are many investment opportunities. Malaysian government has initiated series of economic transformation plans to spur the economies. If we were to link such initiatives to all countries within "21st-Century Maritime Silk Road", the investment opportunities are massive.

Fourthly, the Global connectivity of Malaysia to the world is good. We have matured maritime, air and road systems that connect us to the world. The Straits of Melaka serves as the connection between maritime route between China and Asian counties.

Many are aware of the air tragedies of the Malaysian Airlines this year. However, this is a threat affecting global issues, and not to any particular country. Despite the fact that air traffic for passengers is affected, trades for other goods and services continue to use Malaysia as the connection point.

Due to the favourable environment, Islamic banking has captured 20% of the market share in Malaysia. The statistics show that the assets growth, financing growth and deposits growth are all on the upward trend.

Conclusion

It is pertinent to clearly distinguish this beautiful finance system from the act of terrorism committed by the Islamic State—"IS". Islam is a religion that promotes peace and harmony. Many Muslim countries have stood up to condemn the extremists' acts, which is not consistent with the teachings

To conclude, Islamic finance has gained more popularity in many countries in recent years. The "21st-Century Maritime Silk Road" may also consider adopting such finance system to realize its objective to promote peace, development, cooperation and adopting a win-win strategy for all.

伊斯兰金融体系与银行资本运作的前沿问题

Teh Tai Yong*

赵　以　译

摘要　近年来,有关伊斯兰金融体系在国际金融领域所呈现的势头的讨论之声不绝于耳。伊斯兰金融体系奉行的是伊斯兰教法规范。本文所讨论的是伊斯兰金融体系与银行资本运作之间的法律边界问题,然后将其与中国发起的"21世纪海上丝绸之路"联系起来,从四个方面进行讨论:其一,伊斯兰金融体系之法律概念;其二,伊斯兰金融体系之监管框架;其三,伊斯兰金融体系之金融工具;其四,伊斯兰金融体系之核心。本文认为21世纪海上丝绸之路计划的相关国家应建立一套金融制度,并与亚洲基础设施投资银行(简称AIIB)共同实现其促进和平、发展、合作共赢的战略目标。

一、简介

目前,除了传统金融体系,越来越多的国家正在采用伊斯兰金融体系。据2014年全球伊斯兰金融报告显示,全球伊斯兰金融服务业的实际规模已从2009年的1.036万亿美元增长至2013年的1.813万亿美元。我们见证了伊斯兰金融产品的稳定增长,包括Sukuk(即伊斯兰债券)、伊斯兰银行业务以及基金管理。本文将主要从马来西亚的视角来探讨伊斯兰金融体系与银行资本运作之间的几个法律问题。

二、法律概念

首先,伊斯兰金融体系中有些行为是允许的,有些是禁止的。在这里,我

---

*　马来西亚郑今智及莎丽娜律师馆合伙人。

们把允许的称作"可为行为",禁止的称作"勿为行为"。其中"可为行为"系指根据意思自治而形成法律行为的当事人必须遵守的事项:(1)须有清晰明确的缔约方;(2)契约的表述须明确具体;(3)须有清晰明确的标的。

而"勿为行为"则指伊斯兰金融体系所禁止的事项:(1)暴利(伊斯兰金融体系中称作"Riba"或"Ursury")。古时候,"Ursury"被视为富人压迫穷人的一种工具。即富人取财无道——通过发放贷款,规定畸高利率,收取高额利息。也即现代人们所熟知的"高利贷"。(2)不确定性(伊斯兰金融体系中称作"Gharar")。伊斯兰金融法规规定,合同必须规定最高利率,即"利率上限"。这与实践中银行利率随着市场行情而上下浮动的传统银行借贷业务不同,伊斯兰金融体系中的借贷方了解自己的最高风险;(3)违禁产品或禁止行为(譬如赌博、喝酒或吃猪肉)。上述"可为"和"勿为"模式均在伊斯兰金融体系中受到严格限制,当事人必须奉行上述所有规定,遵守伊斯兰律法规范。

伊斯兰世界中,上帝掌管世间所有财富,人类只不过是上帝的托管人罢了。人类需要按照上帝的意志去管理财富,并恪守正义,谨言慎行。此外,只要人类的行为不违背教法,他们就有权享有自己取得财富并以符合伊斯兰教法的方式支配这些财富。

伊斯兰经济的核心概念是平衡:(1)平衡物质追求与精神需要;(2)平衡个人需求与社会需求。这种平衡机制将保证金融活动参与者的动机和目的可以最大限度地造福社会。我们也可以将此与"一带一路"的目标联系起来,那就是促进和平、发展、合作共赢的战略目标。

三、监管框架

一个良好的综合性法律体系或者监管框架是伊斯兰金融体系运行的关键。由于伊斯兰教法下的投资项目以及不断革新的各种金融产品的复杂特性,在良好的金融监管框架下所形成的"有利环境"不仅可以促进其行业增长、增强其行业稳定,同时还能维护各方利益。

以马来西亚为例,为维护和管控伊斯兰金融体系,马方已分别于2013年和2009年颁布了《2013伊斯兰金融服务法案》(简称"IFSA 2013")和《2009马来西亚中央银行法案》(简称"CBMA 2009")。此外,马来西亚中央银行也已出台许多指导条例,许多涉及伊斯兰金融体系的案例,马来西亚相关法院也做出了判决。在马来西亚,监管框架已成为伊斯兰金融体系发展的基础——从法律的制定到伊斯兰教法的管辖以及争议解决的方方面面。

应该指出马来西亚并非从一开始就有这种监管框架,但是其采用伊斯兰金融体系已有几十年之久,只不过那些法律是新近才制定颁布的。此举表明,我们不必等到有了一个"完美的监管框架"才可以开始这个体系,而是可以在实施的过程中不断完善这个体系。同时,还可以不断从其他司法管辖区汲取经验,学习怎样才能在尽可能最短的时间内把它变成一个成功的体系。

21世纪海上丝绸之路方兴未艾,亚洲基础设施投资银行也刚刚在2014年10月由20个国家在北京签订成立。假以时日,这将成为"21世纪海上丝绸之路"相关国家之间的一个区域性法律框架。而接下来就是在这每一个国家里建立其各自的国家法律框架,以此来维护伊斯兰金融体系。

四、金融工具

为促进贸易与合作,满足不同的业务需要,伊斯兰金融创新了许多金融工具,大致有以下几个类别:(1)基于销售的金融业务;(2)基于租赁的金融业务;(3)基于参与合伙的金融业务;(4)基于收费的金融业务。每一种金融工具都发挥着不同的作用,但一项金融交易中可能结合有几种不同的工具。在目前伊斯兰金融市场上,根据伊斯兰教法规范,按照自负盈亏的原则而发行并交易的伊斯兰金融债券非常流行。

同时,伊斯兰金融体系也必须解决担保物的银行业务问题、合同管理问题、财产恢复问题等。伊斯兰金融体系是一个全方位的巨大构架,涵盖了伊斯兰资本市场、金融市场以及各种金融机构。因此可以采用这一体系,将其作为传统体系的补充从而弥补当前传统金融体系的不足。

五、核心

为"21世纪海上丝绸之路"更好地发展伊斯兰金融体系,我们需要建立一个与之相匹配的有效核心。有人认为马来西亚就可担此重任,理由是:一,马来西亚拥有成熟的伊斯兰银行和金融产业。目前,他们有14家伊斯兰银行,包括4家外资伊斯兰银行和2家马外合资银行。马来西亚还是亚洲地区伊斯兰债券的主要发行中心。二,马来西亚政府极力支持伊斯兰金融体系的创设,现已建立起一套强大而又稳固的监管框架,还出台许多优惠政策。三,大量投资机会。为刺激经济发展,马方政府已经实施一系列经济转型计划。倘若把这些转型计划与"21世纪海上丝绸之路"上所有相关国家联系起来,将会出现极其丰富的投资机会。四，马来西亚与全球有着良好的连通性。这里有成熟的海洋、空中、陆地交通系统可与全世界链接起来。位于马来西亚的马六甲海峡正是中国与亚洲之间的海路链接点。此外，由于良好的投资环境，伊斯兰银行业务已经占到马来西亚市场份额的 20％。并且，有数据显示，伊斯兰资产、金融、储蓄的增长全都处于上升趋势。

六、结语

伊斯兰教是一种倡导平静与和谐的宗教。因此，必须明确地把这个出色的金融体系从那些伊斯兰国家所犯下的恐怖罪行中区别开来。而且多数穆斯林国家也已公开谴责那些与伊斯兰教义相悖的极端分子的暴行。我们不应让这些暴行成为伊斯兰金融体系的绊脚石。况且，近年来，伊斯兰金融体系在许多国家已经变得越来越普及。因此，"21 世纪海上丝绸之路"也可以考虑采用这种金融体系以实现其促进和平、发展、合作共赢的战略目标。

Issues on Infrastructure Construction and Connectivity

Tan Poh Hui[*]

In October 2013, President Xi Jinping, during a speech in the Indonesia Parliament, put forward the idea that China is willing to establish the 21st-Century "Maritime Silk Road" together with the ASEAN countries. This proposal was strongly welcomed and received by the ASEAN countries. Quote Professor Yang Baoyun of South-East Asian studies at Peking University, "the new route carried both economic and diplomatic implications. Like the historical route centuries ago, the new maritime silk road will bring tangible benefits to neighbours along the route and will be a new driving force for the prosperity of the entire East Asian region".

This proposal excites the neighbouring countries especially the ASEAN countries very much. While most of the parties are giving positive comments and support towards this proposal, it should be mindful that this is a cross-countries multi-connectivity proposal that would require the cooperation, understanding, communication and high diplomatic wisdom for each party in order to make this proposal a success at the fastest pace.

China as a fastest-moving developing large country in the world has taken the initiative to rebrand and restructure this ancient maritime route. Looking back at the history, this maritime route reached its pinnacle during the Ming Dynasty. The well known history about Cheng Ho and its contribution to the trade and economy has been recorded in history of many countries including Malaysia. The close relationship and trust between China

---

[*]   Legal Associate, Jeff Leong, Poon & Wong.

and the ASEAN countries is important in making this proposal a success. However, Rome was not built in a day, in order to accomplish this mega proposal, in my humble opinion, there are a few issues that would require the careful consideration of the relevant parties in order to achieve the best result that expected by everyone.

First of all, besides China, the main beneficiaries of this proposal would be the ASEAN countries. ASEAN countries comprise of ten countries, they are Vietnam, Cambodia, Malaysia, Singapore, Philippines, Indonesia, Brunei, Laos, Myanmar and Thailand. There is one important point that we need to recognize is that all the ASEAN countries are developing countries except for Singapore. Moreover, the developing pace and standard is different for each ASEAN country and thus frankly speaking the concerns, necessities, abilities and desires would be different for each ASEAN country as well. I believe that all ASEAN countries are very positive and supportive towards this proposal due to its huge economic benefit and the development that would be brought to their countries, therefore all the ASEAN countries would try their best to cooperate and communicate in order to make this proposal a success as soon as possible. However as mentioned above, the developing pace of each country is different therefore the ability to accommodate this proposal will be different for each country as well.

I understand that an Asian Infrastructure Investment Bank ("AIIB") and a Silk Road Fund ("Fund") will be established for the purpose of funding and support the connectivity, infrastructure and development of the ASEAN countries and other countries in the Silk Road region. China as the proposer for this mega project, has taken the initiative to inject a huge amount of money into the Funds to show its determination and optimistic view towards this proposal. This initiative has also injected confidence and trust onto the relationship and cooperation between China and ASEAN countries in this proposal.

In May 2014, Asean-Five, the original members of Asean, agreed to become the founding members of AIIB as a unit. Asean-Five agreed to set the minimum amount of contribution to AIIB with their contribution to the Asia Development Bank as the benchmark. At the bilateral meeting between

President Xi and President Joko "Jokowi" Widodo on November 9 during the APEC forum in Beijing, both discussed Indonesia's participation in the AIIB, in which Jokowi reemphasized Indonesian's intention to sign the memorandum of understanding (MOU) on the AIIB. It was followed by Indonesia's signing of the MOU on November 25 in Jakarta. Indonesia's signing of the MOU is expected to strengthen cooperation between the two countries, to make AIIB a new source of funding for its infrastructure build-up and increase Indonesia's role in international fora as well as playing a strategic role in the AIIB. Indonesia also intends to play a significant part in deciding the policy and work program of the AIIB for its own national interests.

As mentioned above, the ability and capability of each country is at different level with special regard to finance ability. With regard to financing matter, there are a few potential issues that would arise in my humble opinion. Firstly, I understand that the details and requirements regarding to the application for the financing aid from the AIIB and the Fund are still not announced and cleared yet. This may due to the large amount of issues that need to be determined and discussed before the exact details can be announced to the countries. The management and operation of the AIIB and the Fund is not sure yet, although China has taken the initiative to announce its contribution, other countries will also participate in the contribution onto the Fund and the AIIB, for example Indonesia. Therefore, I believe that each of the participating country will want to participate in the management and decision making of the AIIB and the Fund in order to safeguard the interest of their own country. With regard thereto, while China has been positive towards the establishment of the AIIB and the Fund, various discussions and negotiations will need to be carried out to ensure that every participating country is satisfied with the management and operation.

As most of the ASEAN countries will need the financing aid from the AIIB and the Fund in order to build the necessary infrastructures and to import experts and technologies, the countries will be eager to know about the application procedure, requirements, restrictions and so on. The application requirements will need to be carefully determined to ensure fairness but to balance off with the economical consideration and repayment ability of such countries before granting the financing aid. Various aspects will need to be taken into consideration to avoid any dissatisfaction arise from granting such loan as every country will be observing, evaluating and comparing the financing aid requirements. Also, various economical and diplomacy complications may arise in the event that some countries are unsatisfied with the financing aid system or in the event where some countries are unable to repay the loan according to repayment schedule, or due to economic crisis, political instability and so on. The methods and approaches that will be adopted by the AIIB and the Fund in dealing with the various situations should be stated clearly as well in order to avoid any potential dispute.

Following the discussion on the financing aid, the second step would be on the planning and construction of necessary infrastructure for the ports and the connecting infrastructures for the ports. Along the maritime silk road, there are many important ports which are serving the heavy traffic of maritime activities to accommodate the increasing demand of transportation by ships. However, with the 21st-Century Maritime Silk Road's proposal, the existing ports may not be sufficient to accommodate the shipping traffic which we foresee will be increased tremendously from year to year. Many of the ASEAN countries have expressed their will in building more ports and infrastructure to accommodate the rising traffic and demand of maritime services. However, the ASEAN countries have also expressly raised up their concern on the financing issue.

Therefore, it is very important now to plan and discuss for the building of infrastructures and additional ports along the Maritime Silk Road. On top of the financing aid issues, the next issues would be the process, quality, timeframe to be given for building such infrastructures and additional ports by each country. The China and ASEAN countries as the cooperating parties for this proposal, would have to consider carefully on the possible outcome for failing to complete the infrastructure and ports buildings in a specified timeline and the implications that it would bring to each country.

Besides, most of the ASEAN countries may need external experts to aid for the design, supervision and construction of the infrastructure buildings which also involves a lot of advanced technologies support. The assistance from the experts may cause a lot of money as well, and would this be included in the scope of financing aid is also an important consideration to be taken into account. Also not to forget that this mega project will encite the infrastructure construction related companies to try to participate in this mega project and to be benefited form it. The similar issue will be: Will the AIIB and the Fund have a say in deciding the experts and also the infrastructure construction company? This is an issue that needs to be clearly stated, although it seems like the building of infrastructure and ports are internal issue of the country, however as the construction is financed by the Fund and the AIID of which the money is injected by various countries, the investing countries may want to have a control on the quality of the con-struction companies and experts or to recommend the construction companies of their own countries.

In the event that the infrastructure project will go through a bidding process, the bidding process and selection process will need to be transparent and systematic as well, otherwise it will raise a lot of doubts and challenges from the participating countries in the event that the bidding process is not impartial. The quality of the experts and construction companies will need to be carefully and diligently evaluated in order to meet the requirements as set out by the AIIB and the Fund, if any. Otherwise, various negative implications may arise due to the low quality work produced by the experts or construction companies, in a worst case scenario, it may involve international issues and disputes.

The next major issue will be on the international shipping law and the dispute resolution methods. All the relevant countries involved in this Maritime Silk Road shall enter into an agreement stipulating the consensus on the dispute resolution methods. As different country has different maritime law, the relevant countries shall work together to determine and discuss on the possible disputes that may arise during the course of the transportation or the problems at the ports. Then, every party shall reach a consensus on the dispute resolution methods and subject themselves to such resolution.

As the maritime activities will be more and more active in future, the issues on territories and territorial water have to be faced squarely by every country. We have to admit that the issues on territories and territorial water have been raised from time to time due to the sovereignty that every country is holding on. Some of the territorial water issues have not been resolved as of today. Therefore it is undeniably that these issues may be brought up again in future due to the active maritime activities. As this Maritime Silk Road's proposal mainly brings advantages and benefits to all the relevant countries, it is important for every country to note that the cooperation and toleration is very important while dealing in this proposal.

In addition, as a member of the mother earth, one issue that we cannot forget is the sea pollution. Strict regulation and laws have to be abide by all countries to preserve the environment and eco balance of the sea. We shall not forget to protect the most important medium of this proposal—the sea. While every party is trying to maximize the benefit gained from this proposal, the rules and laws in relation to sea protection have to be discussed utmost as well. Without protecting this medium properly, the Maritime Silk Road shall be rendered as a selfish project by the human beings.

Another issue that will require the cooperation from all ports and countries is the issue of human trafficking and illegal shipping of goods. The immigration department of each country will have to cooperate closely to combat the potential illegal activities following with the increase of maritime activities.

Lastly, I would like to give a suggestion that the experts in legal industry, finance industry and all other relevant industries to have more communication and discussion from time to time. More legal forums should be carried out as much as possible. This Maritime Silk Road proposal has successfully caught the eyeballs of the world. It is a very important event to show the power and ability of the China and ASEAN countries. Therefore, for this bigger vision, all relevant countries should work together hand in hand to achieve the win-win situation for every country. Besides, diplomatic communication has to be carried out between the governments in order to build and strengthen trust and confidence in each other.

As this proposal involves multi-connectivity and various countries, constant and close communication has to be carried out between the countries at this preliminary stage in order to achieve mutual understanding and objective. China as the main proposer of this proposal has to take initiative to communicate with the relevant countries from time to time and will need to serve as a central communication hub for all the countries. All countries will need to cooperate and communicate with each other closely in order to achieve a mighty outcome for this rebranded Maritime Silk Road.

基础设施建设及互联互通的若干法律问题

Tan Poh Hui[*]
金 鑫 译

2013 年十月,中国国家主席习近平在印度尼西亚国会的一次演说中提出中国将与亚洲国家一道共同构建"21 世纪海上丝绸之路"的构想。这一构想受到亚洲国家的热烈欢迎和支持,尤其是东盟国家受到极大的鼓舞。北京大学东南亚研究中心的杨保云教授认为:"新丝路带来的影响不仅有经济上的还有外交上的。正如那次历史性的大航海一样,新的海上丝绸之路也将为沿途国家带去切实利益,而且还将成为整个东亚地区繁荣发展的新的驱动力。"

中国作为当今世界发展最快的发展中大国正在积极地重塑、重建这条古老的海上丝绸之路。回看历史,这条海路在明朝时期达到了历史最顶峰。史上著名的航海家郑和以及他对贸易和经济所做的贡献已经被许多国家(包括马来西亚)载入史册。中国与东盟国家衣襟相连、彼此信任对于这一构想的成功实现意义非凡。但是,伟业非一日之功,就笔者的浅见,要想实现这一宏大构想,需要各方合作一致、相互理解、相互沟通,以高超的外交智慧用最快的速度致力于这一构想的成功实现,所有关乎各方切身利益的问题都需要认真考虑。

首先,除中国外,这一构想的受益方主要就是那些东盟国家——越南、柬埔寨、马来西亚、新加坡、菲律宾、印度尼西亚、文莱、老挝、缅甸、泰国。但是除新加坡外所有这些东盟国家都是发展中国家。而且各国的发展速度、水平各不相同,其关注、需要、能力、愿望自然也各不相同。而亚洲基础设施投资银行(AIIB)和丝路基金(Fund)的建立恰逢其时——正是为了东盟国家和其他丝路国家的互联互通、基础设施建设和发展提供资金和支持。作为这一宏大构

---

* 马来西亚梁潘及黄律师事务所法务助理。

想的首创者,中国已率先为丝路基金注入大量资金以显示其决心和态度,同时也为中国和东盟国家之间的合作关系注入了信心和信任。

2014年5月五个东盟原始成员国一起同意作为创始成员国加入AIIB,而且同意以对亚洲发展银行的贡献为最小基准点向AIIB竭尽绵薄之力。2014年11月9日,在北京举行APEC峰会期间,国家主席习近平和印度尼西亚总统佐科·维多多进行了双边会晤,共同讨论了印度尼西亚加入AIIB的问题,印度尼西亚总统维多多再次强调印度尼西亚希望就AIIB签订一份理解备忘录。其目的是希望加强中印双方的合作,使AIIB成为印方基础设施建设的新的资金来源,提高印方在国际舞台上的地位从而可以在AIIB中扮演一个战略性的角色。此外,印方还希望可以在关乎其国家利益的AIIB政策和工程项目决定中发挥重要作用。

如前文所述,各个国家的能力尤其是经济能力参差有别。就笔者浅见,一些与经济相关的潜在问题应给予足够关注。第一,向AIIB和Fund申请经济援助的相关细节和要求仍不清楚。在具体细节出台之前可能会有大量的问题需要讨论决定。而且AIIB和Fund的管理和运作也不明朗。为维护各自的国家利益,每一个成员国都希望可以参与AIIB和Fund的管理和政策制定。因此,虽然中国积极推动AIIB和Fund的建立,但为保证满足各成员国对AIIB和Fund的管理和运作,仍需进行大量的讨论协商。由于大多数东盟国家都需要来自AIIB和Fund的经济援助以便其必要的基础设施建设和专家技术的引进,这些国家迫切想要知道申请经济援助的程序、要求、限制等等。在给予经济援助之前,为确保公平不仅需要详细列明申请条件,还应平衡考虑这些国家的经济能力和偿付能力。而且要对每一个申请国进行观察、评估,对比其经济援助的条件。但是,贷款期间可能会引发各种经济和外交并发症,从而导致有些国家对这个经济援助系统不满,或者由于经济危机、政治动乱等问题致使有些国家不能按期还款。因此为避免各种可能发生的纠纷,AIIB和Fund在处理各种情形时所采取的方式和手段应当事先清楚地确定下来。

第二,必要的港口建设和援助计划。为满足日益增长的船舶转运需求,海上丝绸之路沿岸有许多重要的港口承担着繁重的海上交通压力。而且,随着"21世纪海上丝绸之路"的建设,航运交通压力将会越来越大,目前这些港口可能已不能满足航运需求。许多东盟国家表示,他们希望建设更多的港口和基础设施以调整日益增长的海运需求。但是,这些东盟国家也清楚地表达了他们就援助问题的关切。

大多数东盟国家可能都需要外部专家来帮助其进行基础设施的设计、监督和建设,其中也包括大量先进的技术支撑。邀请专家援助需要大量的资金,而这类资金也在经济援助范围之内。但是不要忘了,这么一个宏大的建设工程自然会吸引相关建筑公司前来分一杯羹。那么问题来了,在决定哪些专家和哪些建筑公司的时候 AIIB 和 Fund 是否有发言权？尽管基础设施和港口建设似乎都只是这些国家的内部问题,但这些建设工程是由 Fund 和 AIIB 提供的资金,而资金来源则是各个参与国,因此这些投资国可能希望控制这些建筑公司和专家或者指定他们自己国家的建筑公司。如果这些建设工程要进行公开竞标,那么竞标程序和遴选过程透明,专家和建筑公司的品质和条件也必须进行评估,而且要有计划有步骤,否则一旦出现不公,必将会引来成员国的大量质疑甚至国际争端。

接下来所讨论的主要问题就是国际航运法和争议解决办法。不同国家有不同的海商法,海运兴起就不可避免地会发生许多海事纠纷,为满足各方的共同关切,海上丝绸之路的所有相关国家应共同设计一套各方一致同意的争议解决办法。此外,领土领水问题也是未来海洋活动无法避免的一项羁绊,但在海上丝绸之路所带来的各种机遇和利益面前,各方在解决这类问题时都应保持克制,须知合作才能共赢。

另一个不容忽视的问题则是海洋污染。为保护海洋环境和生态平衡,各成员国都应严格遵守相关海洋法律法规。倘若不能很好地保护海洋,那么想从海上丝绸之路中获取最大利益便只是一个空想,海上丝绸之路也会变成一个为人类谋取私利的恶性工程。再有就是所有港口国家应相互协作共同应对贩卖人口、非法货物走私等各种海洋不法活动。

最后,笔者建议法律界、金融界以及所有其他相关产业界内的专家应经常进行不定期的交流和讨论,为海上丝绸之路献计献策。海上丝绸之路已经成功地吸引了全世界的关注,向世界展示中国和东盟国家的力量和能力是一件积极重要的事情。因此,为实现这一世纪伟业,让这条海上丝绸之路重新焕发光辉,所有相关国家都应加强彼此信任、携手一致、紧密协作、互通有无、共创互利共赢的新局面。

The Asian Infrastructure Investment Bank: Investing into the Future of Asia

Everlene O. Lee[*]

Abstract   Infrastructures are important in the economic development of any country and indeed, the formation of the Asian Infrastructure Investment Bank (the "AIIB") is a welcome development to many developing Asian nations. There is no question that multilateral institutions have played a significant role in financing and supporting infrastructure activities in the developing world and the establishment of the AIIB will indeed contribute to badly needed capital to address the growing infrastructure needs of Asia. However, the signing of the memorandum of a-greement between the 22 countries headed by China in late 2014 is just the beginning for the AIIB, as there are challenges and issues which the AIIB member-countries need to address even before it commences operation. The good news is that the AIIB can tap on the wealth of information and experience of existing multilateral agencies which had come before it to resolve these issues and challenges and find the best solution to ensure that all stakeholders benefit from this worthy endeavor.

Introduction

A regular office worker in Manilawould usually take the Metro Rail Transit ("MRT") or the Light Railway Transit ("LRT") going to and from

---

* Senior Associate, Angara Abello Concepcion Regala &. Cruz Law Offices.

work, if one is available within his/her route. At present, there are several railway stations in Metro Manila crisscrossing the metro and, during the rush hour, you will see them jam-packed with workers rushing to get to work or go home. Waiting in line, some for one to two hours, to be able to take a 20 to 30 minute ride to get to their destinations. However, despite the difficulties of taking the MRT or LRT, most Filipinos still prefers to take this mode of transportation as the traffic problems in Metro Manila have reached serious proportions. [1] During weekdays, vehicles traversing Epifanio de los Santos Avenue ("EDSA"), one of Philippines' major thoroughfare, will go no faster than 15 kph[2], on the average.

A study conducted by the Japan International Cooperation Agency ("JICA") in 1999 showed that the Philippines was losing some P140 billion (approximately US $ 3. 11 billion) annually to traffic congestion. It said that the national economy was directly losing ₱ 40 billion (approximately US $ 0. 88 billion) in the forms of gasoline and diesel fuel, man-hours, electricity, salaries of traffic aides and increased expenses for mobile phones, and indirectly, ₱ 100 billion (approximately US $ 2. 22 billion) in the forms of lost business opportunities, depreciated value of real property and increased cause of health care due to air pollution. [3] Today, the cost of traffic congestion is ₱ 2. 4 billion per day and is expected to increase to ₱ 6

① "Improving Traffic Problems in the Philippines" http://web. worldbank. org/ WBSITE/EXTERNAL/COUNTRIES/EASTASIAPACIFICEXT/EXTEAPREG-TOPTRANSPORT/0,, contentMDK: 20018096-menuPK: 574025-pagePK: 2865114-piPK2865167-theSitePK:574066,00. html.

② "Improving Traffic Problems in the Philippines" http://web. worldbank. org/ WBSITE/EXTERNAL/COUNTRIES/EASTASIAPACIFICEXT/EXTEAPREG-TOPTRANSPORT/0,, contentMDK: 20018096-menuPK: 574025-pagePK: 2865114-piPK2865167-theSitePK:574066,00. html.

③ "Metro Manila traffic costs P140B a year" Manila Bulletin, 13 December 2014, https://ph. news. yahoo. com/metro-manila-traffic-costs-p140b-000556493. html; "Social Issues in the Philippines. http://www. txtmania. com/trivia/social. php.

billion per day if adequate solutions to ease congestions are not implemented by 2030. [1]

JICA projects that for the short term plan between 2014 to 2016, the Philippines will need approximately ₱ 520 billion (approximately US $ 11. 5 billion) to build sufficient infrastructure to alleviate the traffic congestion. [2]

The traffic situation has even affected the Philippines' main seaport when a daily truck ban from 5am to 9pm was implemented to address monstrous traffic. Import growth fell for two straight months in May and June of 2014 as a result of the same. [3] Ports being linked in the supply chain, a congestion in one major port leads to increasing problems for other ports as the congestion problems arising from accumulating Manila-bound cargo in ports such as Hong Kong, Shenzhen, Busan and Kaoshiung. [4]

Another infrastructure facility which is greatly in need of repair and re-habilitation for the Philippines is the country's airport. Another JICA study has concluded that "unless adequate air transport infrastructure is developed as soon as possible, the Ninoy Aquino International Airport('NAIA') and the Philippine national could lose its competitive edge further ... the runway capacity at NAIA is already almost saturated and the development of a new gateway airport in the Greater Capital Region ('GCR') is an urgent need. "[5]

---

① "Traffic to cost P6B a day—JICA Study" Manila Bulletin, Roy Mabasa, 5 September 2014, http://www. mb. com. ph/traffic-to-cost-p6b-a-day-jica-study/.

② "Roadmap for Transport Infrastructure Development for Metro Manila andIts Surrounding Areas (Region III and Region IV-A—Main Points of the Roadmap" National Economic and Development Authority and the Japan International Cooperation Agency, August 2014.

③ "Port congestion blamed for import decline in June", Rappler. com, 26 August 2014. http://www. rapller. com/business/economy-watch/67294-port-congestion-import-decline-june2014, 15 December 2014.

④ Kritz, Ben D. Port Congestion is a Global Problem" *The Manila Times*, 27 October 2014, http://www. manilatimes. net/port-congestion-global-problems/137468/. 14 December 2014.

⑤ Chanco, Boo"JICA study cites urgency of NAIA situation"*Demand and Supply*, 15 August 2011.

The JICA report further states that "as far as the international passenger and cargo movements are concerned, the gateway airports in Asia is twice or more than the traffic levels than NAIA is in 2009. The numbers of operating airlines for international routes as well as number of cities connected by international flights at NAIA are also very small when compared to the comparison gateway airports in Asia. " [1]

This is just the tip of the iceberg, so to speak.

Importance of Infrastructure

According to the Philippines' Economic Planning Secretary, Arsenio Balisacan, "It's a no-brainer that we have to boost infrastructure. We have a huge backlog in almost all types of infrastructure ... " [2]

Infrastructures are important in the economic development of any country. The disparity in the development of infrastructure in developed countries as opposed to developing or less developed countries are stark. Infrastructure is encompassing from the basic: paved roads, railroads, seaports, to the more complex: communication networks, financial systems, and energy supplies, all of which support production and marketing for industries within the country. [3] Furthermore, the quality of an infrastructure directly affects a country's economic growth potential and the ability of an enterprise to engage effectively. [4]

---

[1] Chanco, Boo "JICA study cites urgency of NAIA situation" *Demand and Supply*, 15 August 2011.

[2] Bondo, Joan, "P2. 4 Billion Traffic" The Philippine Daily Inquirer, http:// business. inquirer. net/130649/traffuc0cists-p2-p4-daily. 15 December 2014.

[3] Tanwi, "The Infrastructure is Important to the Economic Development of an Economy, 27 February 2008, http://wwww. studymode. com/essays/The-infrastructure-is-important-To-The-132698. html. 14 December 2014.

[4] Tanwi, "The Infrastructure is Important to the Economic Development of an Economy, 27 February 2008, http://wwww. studymode. com/essays/The-infrastructure-is-important-To-The-132698. html. 14 December 2014.

The importance of quality infrastructure for sustained economic development is well recognized[1] and cannot be emphasized enough. "Infrastructure provides services that support economic growth by increasing the productivity of labor and capital thereby reducing the costs of production and raising profitability, production, income and employment. Infrastructure investment and consumption of infrastructure services have significant implications for achievement of sustainable development objectives."[2] On the other hand "high transaction costs arising from inadequate and inefficient infrastructure can prevent the economy from realising its full growth potential regardless of the progress on other fronts."[3]

Of late, there has been increasing discussions about the infrastructure needs of Asia and the amount of capital that will be required to address those needs. According to the Asian Development Bank (the "ADB"), this is nothing new. Those numbers, according to the ADB, have been bounced around for decades without much progress. [4] As such, the numbers continue to grow year by year. The current ADB estimates suggest that Asia will need US $ 8 trillion in national infrastructure and US $ 290 billion in regional infrastructure through 2020 to sustain the region's growth trajectory. [5]

---

[1] Singh, Shailender, Batra, G. S. , Singh, Gajendra, "Role of Infrastrucute Services on the Economic Development of India", *Management and Labor Studies*, August 1997 Vol 32 No. 3 347-359.

[2] Tanwi, "The Infrastructure is Important to the Economic Development of an Economy, 27 February 2008, http://wwww. studymode. com/essays/The-infrastructure-is-important-To-The-132698. html. 14 December 2014.

[3] Singh, Shailender, Batra, G. S. , Singh, Gajendra, "Role of Infrastrucute Services on the Economic Development of India", *Management and Labor Studies*, August 1997 Vol 32 No. 3 347-359.

[4] "Will China's Asian Infrastructure Investment Bank suceed?" *Businessspectator. com. au*, 8 December 2014. http://www. sino-us. com/12/Will-China-s-Asian—Infrastructure-Investment-Bank-suceed-. html. 13 December 2014.

[5] "Will China's Asian Infrastructure Investment Bank succeed?" *Businessspectator. com. au*, 8 December 2014. http://www. sino-us. com/12/Will-China-s-Asian—Infrastructure-Investment-Bank-suceed-. html. 13 December 2014.

Significant Role of Multilateral Agencies

There is no doubt that the role of multilateral institutions in financing and supporting infrastructure activities in the developing world is extremely important. [1] The contribution of multilateral agencies like the World Bank, ADB, African Development Bank, Inter-American Development Bank, and the European Bank for Reconstruction and Development in infrastructure development and its subsequent enhancement of economic growth and alleviating poverty are significant. [2] More so now than ever, given the growing demand for infrastructure in Asia—that multilateral agencies assistance is expected to play an even greater role in bridging the infrastructure deficit and sustaining economic growth in the region." [3]

Thus, the establishment of the Asian Infrastructure Investment Bank (the "AIIB") is a welcome development for Asian countries. The memorandum of understanding (the "MOU") inked between China, Bangladesh, Brunei, Cambodia, India, Indonesia, Kazakhstan, Kuwait, Laos, Malaysia, Mongolia, Myanmar, Nepal, Oman, Pakistan, Philippines, Qatar, Singapore, Sri Lanka, Thailand,

----

[1] "Role of Multilateral Institutions in Supporting Infrastructure Development in the Region and Alternative Forms of Financing Infrastructure". ADB Institute. http://www.adbi. ord/discussion-paper/2007/09/27/2364. infrastructure. challenges. sout. asia/role. of. multilateral. institutions. in. supporting. infrastructure. development. in. the. region. and. alternative. forms. of. financing. infrastructure/ 13 December 2014.

[2] "Role of Multilateral Institutions in Supporting Infrastructure Development in the Region and Alternative Forms of Financing Infrastructure". ADB Institute. http://www.adbi. ord/discussion-paper/2007/09/27/2364. infrastructure. challenges. sout. asia/role. of. multilateral. institutions. in. supporting. infrastructure. development. in. the. region. and. alternative. forms. of. financing. infrastructure/ 13 December 2014.

[3] "Role of Multilateral Institutions in Supporting Infrastructure Development in the Region and Alternative Forms of Financing Infrastructure". ADB Institute. http://www.adbi. ord/discussion-paper/2007/09/27/2364. infrastructure. challenges. sout. asia/role. of. multilateral. institutions. in. supporting. infrastructure. development. in. the. region. and. alternative. forms. of. financing. infrastructure/ 13 December 2014.

Uzbekistan, and Vietnam in the latter part of 2014 is indeed a momentous one. However, the signing of the MOU is just the beginning, as much work still needs to be done to get the AIIB going. Certainly, there will be issues and challenges for such a large undertaking as the AIIB which signatories to the AIIB must address through cooperation and mutual understanding.

Some of these issues and challenges may be gleaned from those already being encountered.

Issues and Challenges

Cooperative regulations. It has been the experience of other multilateral agencies that despite a machinery of cooperation, building critical agreement often proves impossible. When states perceive a conflict with their immediate national interest, they repeatedly disagree on fundamental issues, hindering the prospects for cooperative regulations to truly reform the international system. [1]

Voice and Participation. Policy disagreements may also emerge between developed and developing country members of the AIIB, which may have distinctive interest and outlooks. [2] This may result to underdeveloped and developing countries having distinct disadvantages based on their contribution to the fund. Based on the World Bank's experience, several concerns were raised regarding the allocation of voting power and decision-making arrangement within its different arms, which has affected the voice and participation of the World Bank's smallest and poorest members. [3]

Sufficient scrutiny on how funds are spent; Accountability. Based on the experience of Dr. Claire Curtis-Thomas, an engineer and former Member of

---

[1]　"Global Finance Issue Brief: Scope of the Challenge" The Global Governance Monitor.

[2]　"Global Finance Issue Brief: Scope of the Challenge" The Global Governance Monitor.

[3]　Zedillo, Ernesto, Chair"Repowering the World Bank for the 21st-Century" Report of the High-Level Commission on Modernization of the World Bank Group Governance, October 2009.

Parliament of the United Kingdom, "I have spent many years trying to track the funds coming out of [Development for International Development] DFID and into [multilateral] budgets. Where does the money end up? Who is left within the United Kingdom, within DFID, to ensure that the money is being spent on that particular project, and it is being spent well. "[①] Further, it was noted in the same DFID report that Adam Smith International was "concerned that the World Bank spending on infrastructure, in particular, might need to be kept under close eye, saying 'sometimes it seems that the WB priority is to 'get money out the door', when in fact the enabling environment is still so problematic that little will be achieved. "[②]

Procurement systems for the large infrastructureprojects funded through the multilateral agency does not advantage local people. According to Professor Antonio Estache of the Universite Libre de Brussels, "Procurement of goods and services for infrastructure projects, where building materials, labour or expert advice, provides an opportunity to reduce poverty by providing small and medium-sized firms with much-needed contracts and employment for local people. But the current system used for large infrastructure project tends to disadvantage local firms. " [③] Dr. Estache further comments that "It is not only whether a road has been built that matters. It also matters whether it was built at the agreed quality, at the agreed cost, at the agreed speed. It is also whether competition for the

---

[①] "DFID's Role in Building Infrastructure in Developing Countries—International Development Committee: 3: Where the challenges remain". http://www. publicatoins. parliament. uk/pa. cm201012/comselect/cmintdev/848/84606. htm. 15 December 2014.

[②] "DFID's Role in Building Infrastructure in Developing Countries—International Development Committee: 3: Where the challenges remain". http://www. publicatoins. parliament. uk/pa. cm201012/comselect/cmintdev/848/84606. htm. 15 December 2014.

[③] "DFID's Role in Building Infrastructure in Developing Countries—International Development Committee: 3: Where the challenges remain". http://www. publicatoins. parliament. uk/pa. cm201012/comselect/cmintdev/848/84606. htm. 15 December 2014.

contract was fair and contributed to the development of local firms. "[1] In addition, the potential for corruption is also present in the procurement process. [2]

Absence of good project. The ADB has noted that the real issue is not usually how much money is on the table but rather because many countries were not ready for serious efforts at infrastructure programs. [3]

Governanceand Transparency. In today's age, where "good governance" is the focal point of many debates, the challenge for AIIB is to ensure that it puts into place a set of formal and informal structures, conventions, and rules that will determine how it is steered and how its decision making processes[4] will work in a transparent way. It must ensure that it possess adaptability, accountability, legitimacy and a strong focus on results[5] to ensure its effectivity.

Conclusion

Although there are many challenges ahead for the AIIB, it can avoid many of the pitfalls experienced by many other multilateral agencies which had come before it. Having been forewarned of the potential issues and

---

[1] "DFID's Role in Building Infrastructure in Developing Countries—International Development Committee: 3: Where the challenges remain". http://www. publicatoins. parliament. uk/pa. cm201012/comselect/cmintdev/848/84606. htm. 15 December 2014.

[2] "DFID's Role in Building Infrastructure in Developing Countries—International Development Committee: 3: Where the challenges remain". http://www. publicatoins. parliament. uk/pa. cm201012/comselect/cmintdev/848/84606. htm. 15 December 2014.

[3] "Will China's Asian Infrastructure Investment Bank suceed?"Businessspectator. com. au, 8 December 2014. http://www. sino-us. com/12/Will-China-s-Asian—Infrastructure-Investment-Bank-suceed-. html. 13 December 2014.

[4] Zedillo, Ernesto, Chair"Repowering the World Bank for the 21st-Century" Report of the High-Lvel Commission on Modernization of the World Bank Group Governance, October 2009.

[5] Zedillo, Ernesto, Chair"Repowering the World Bank for the 21st-Century" Report of the High-Lvel Commission on Modernization of the World Bank Group Governance, October 2009.

challenges，the member countries of the AIIB are now forearmed，and can hopefully tackle these issues even before they start major infrastructure support and activities to ensure that the best interest of all concerned are taken into consideration and all stakeholders benefit from this worthy endeavor.

亚洲基础设施投资银行：面向亚洲未来的投资

Everlene O. Lee[*]

孙晓丹 译

　　摘要　基础设施对于国家的经济发展举足轻重,亚洲基础设施投资银行(下文简称 AIIB),在亚洲许多发展中国家广受欢迎。毋庸置疑,在融资与支援上,多边机构对发展中国家的基础设施建设意义重大,在亚洲国家要求进一步扩建基础设施的现在,AIIB 将能够提供亚洲国家建设基础设施亟需的资金。在中国的带领下,亚洲 22 国于 2014 年末签署了建立 AIIB 的协议备忘录,但考虑到参与建立亚洲基础设施投资银行的成员国在计划实施之初即已面临的诸多挑战和问题,备忘录的签署只是开端。AIIB 可以利用现有多边机构丰富的信息资源,以及其解决此类问题,应对此类挑战的经验教训,寻找最佳方案,保证所有相关国家都能从这一建设项目中有所收益。

一、简介

　　在马尼拉工作的白领通常乘坐地铁或轻轨上下班,逢到上下班高峰,马尼拉的地铁和轻轨站就会陷入拥堵。人们会排队 1 至 2 个小时,然后坐 20 到 30 分钟的地铁到达目的地。但尽管如此不便,多数菲律宾人仍会选择乘坐地铁或轻轨,因为马尼拉市区的交通问题已经相当严重,工作日里,EDSA,菲律宾的一条主干道上,车辆前行的平均速度不会超过 15kph。

　　日本国际协力机构(JICA)1999 年的一项研究表明,菲律宾每年会因交通拥挤损失 1400 亿比索(约合 31.1 亿美元),国民经济总值因石油柴油消耗、工时支出、用电、交通津贴和增加的通信费直接损失 400 亿比索(约合 8.8 亿美

---

　　[*]　菲律宾安加拉·阿贝罗·雷加拉·克鲁斯律师事务所高级法务助理。

元），因错失交易机会和空气污染导致的不动产贬值和医保投入的增加而间接损失 1000 亿比索（约合 22.2 亿美元）。现在，每天因交通拥挤造成的损失是 24 比索，据估计，如果 2030 年时仍缺乏缓解交通拥挤的有效举措，这一损失会增至 60 亿比索。

JICA 预计，2014 至 2016 在这一较短时期，菲律宾需投资 5200 亿比索（约合 115 亿美元）建设基础设施，缓解交通拥堵。

而且，为缓解交通问题，每天 5 点至 21 点禁行卡车的措施，也影响到菲律宾主海港的运营。这也是菲律宾 2014 年 5 月和 6 月进口增长率连续两个月下降的原因。由于海港处于一条供应链上，马尼拉一个主海港的拥堵，会进而影响到与之有关的其他海港的运营，如香港、深圳、釜山、高雄等港口。

机场是菲律宾另一亟待修建的基础设施。JICA 的另一项研究认为，"马尼拉国际机场（NAIA）和菲律宾国内机场会进一步丧失竞争优势……NAIA 的跑道承载力已接近饱和，急需在大首都区（GCR）建成一座新的门户机场"。JICA 报告还认为，"考虑到国际人员和货物流动，亚洲门户机场的交通承载力至少要比 2009 年 NAIA 的提高两倍。与亚洲其他门户机场相比，NAIA 国际航班的运行航线，以及所连接的城市也还太少。"

上述需求还只是冰山一角。

二、基础设施的重要性

菲律宾经济规划部部长阿塞尼奥·巴利萨坎认为，"毫无疑问，我们需要大力建设基础设施，几乎所有类型的基础设施，我们都需要完善"。

发展中国家或落后国家的基础设施和发达国家相比，差距相当明显。基础设施包括：道路、轨道和海港，复杂基本基础设施有：通信网络、金融体系和能源供应，这些设施是一个国家国内工业生产和销售的支撑力量。而且，基础设施的力量会直接影响到国家的经济增长潜力和企业有效参与经济建设的能力。

经济要实现可持续发展，理应建设高质量的基础设施。"基础设施能够提高劳动力和资本的生产效能，减少生产成本，提高利润，增加产量，促进收益，保障就业，促进经济增长。投资建设基础设施，利用基础设施，对于实现可持续发展目标意义重大。"相反，"不充分和低效率的基础设施导致高额交易成本，不考虑其他方面因素下，会成为经济潜力充分发挥的障碍"。

近期关于亚洲基础设施建设需求，以及满足需求所需资本数额的讨论有所增加。而亚洲开发银行(ADB)关于这些事项也早有记载。ADB记录显示，关于资本数额的讨论已进行数十年，进展甚小，所需资金则逐年递增。ADB预计，亚洲现在需要8万亿美元用于国内基础设施建设，到2020年之前，需要2900亿美元用于建设区域基础设施，维持区域经济增长。

三、多边机构的重要性

毫无疑问，多边机构在融资和支援上，对发展中国家的基础设施建设至关重要。世界银行、亚洲开发银行、非洲开发银行、美洲开发银行、欧洲复兴开发银行等多边机构在建设基础设施，促进经济增长，减少贫困上发挥着重要作用。在亚洲基础设施建设需求日益增长的现在，多边机构的重要性显得更加重要——期望多边机构在弥补基础设施短缺，实现区域经济可持续发展上提供更多帮助。

因此，亚洲诸国支持建立 AIIB。中国、孟加拉国、文莱、柬埔寨、印度、印度尼西亚、哈萨克斯坦、科威特、老挝、马拉西亚、蒙古国、缅甸、尼泊尔、阿曼、巴基斯坦、菲律宾、卡塔尔、新加坡、斯里兰卡、泰国、乌兹别克斯坦和越南在2014年末签署的谅解备忘录(MOU)有着重要意义。但 MOU 的签署只是个开始，要让 AIIB 正式运作，仍需大量工作。AIIB 这样的大型项目难免会遇到问题和挑战，这就需要各个成员国精诚合作、相互理解，争取解决。

通过已经出现的，或可一窥将会遇到的问题和挑战。

四、问题与挑战

1.合作规则

其他多边机构的经验表明，就算有合作机制，订立合作协议往往无效。各州存在与国家冲突的切身利益时，常常会在基本问题上产生歧义，妨碍合作规则的适用，影响国际体系的实际变革。

2.话语权与参与度

AIIB 的发达国家和发展中国家成员之间，可能存在利益和目标分歧，就可能导致政策冲突，而因为所出资金差别，结果可能是落后国家和发展中国家承受明显劣势。世界银行经验证明，要考虑不同国家间投票权和决策权的分配，保证小国家和穷国家成员国的话语权和参与度。

3. 资金利用的适度监管:可信度

英国前议员、工程师,Claire Curtis-Thomas 博士说过:"我用很多年追查英国国际发展部(DFID)投入多边机构的资金取向。这些钱花到了哪里？英国,或者国际发展部内,是谁在监督这笔钱的使用,确保它用在了特定项目,确保它得到了很好的利用。"而且,这份 DFID 报告也载明,亚当斯密国际"认为世界银行用于基础设施建设的资金尤其应该严密监管,有时,世界银行的任务像是'把钱花出去',结果是该改善的环境还是问题百出,收效甚微"。

4. 多边机构所投资的大型基础设施项目,其采购系统没有惠及当地人民

布鲁塞尔自由大学的 Antonio Estache 教授认为,"采购基础设施建设所需商品和服务,如建材、劳动力或专家建议,为中小型企业提供了订立合同的机会,为当地人民提供了就业岗位,能够减轻贫困。但是大型基础设施工程的现有系统却在倾轧当地企业。"Estache 教授评论道:"要紧的不只是修没修路,路的质量达不达标,有没有超出预算,有没有按期完成,这些都很重要,竞标是否公平,工程是否造福于当地企业,这也不容忽视。"另外,采购系统还有产生腐败的可能。

5. 缺乏优良工程

ADB 注意到,真正的问题通常不是可供使用的资金有多少,而是许多国家还没有为建设基础设施做好准备。

6. 管理与透明度

当今时代,"管理得当"成为讨论热点,AIIB 的挑战之一,就是确保落实一套正式和非正式体系、习惯和规则,决定 AIIB 的目标,保证决策过程透明化,还要兼顾灵活性、可靠性、合法性、合目标性,确保银行高效运行。

五、结论

AIIB 的建立,虽然会面临诸多挑战,但能够规避许多其他多边机构经历过的问题。AIIB 各个成员国意识到这些潜在挑战和问题,就能够未雨绸缪,在大型基础设施项目建设之前就把问题处理好,确保实现所有相关方利益最大化,所有参与方从中获益。

东盟国家国别网络空间

立法与制度问题研究

RESEARCH ON THE LEGISLATION AND SYSTEM OF RESPECTIVE A CYBER SPACES IN ASEAN COUNTRIES

On Cyber Law of the Kingdom of Cambodia

Dy Molany*

Abstract　Cyber law is also known as Cyber Law or Internet Law. The increase in Internet traffic has led to a higher proportion of legal issues worldwide. Common types of Cybercrime include online bank information theft, identity theft, online predatory crimes and unauthorized computer access. More serious crimes like cyber terrorism are also of significant concern.

Cambodia is drafting the Cyber law todetermine education, prevention measures and combat all kinds of offense commit by computer system, ensure the implementation of law anti-cybercrime and combating all kinds of offense commit by computer system and also ensure safety and prevent all legitimate interest in using and developing technology. By the way, the Cyber law itself has its own advantages and disadvantages so the government should study in depth on this law before it was ratified so that the law can be used beneficially and effectively for the Kingdom of Cambodia.

I. Introduction

Cambodia also has much lower internet penetration than other countries. It is said to be only about 5 percent of the country's population. Few people in Cambodia, relative to the, had internet access. It is a poor

---

* Legal Official, Ministry of Justice of Cambodia.

country, and 80 percent of the population lives in the countryside. Many are not even on the national electricity grid. But things have begun to change rapidly. With the presence of the cheapersmart phones, better 3G mobile coverage and Facebook, Cambodians have been getting online, especially the younger generation. In 2011, according to Kounila Keo, probably the country's best known blogger, People started sharing information online-news and video of traffic accidents, land grabbing incidents, protests, etc. "These were the kind of things they would not see in the media." Then in 2013, the country's most popular social media site, Facebook, "blew up with information, videos and texts about events. Some people even joke that TV, radio, newspaper belong to the government or companies while Facebook belongs to the people."

This spooked the government, especially since the social media crowd tends to support the political opposition, which was enjoying unprecedented popularity. Teenagers used online tools to mobilize, campaign and openly express criticism that would have been only discussed in private just a few years earlier.

Ⅱ. Definition

Cyber law is the area of law that deals with the Internet's relationship to technological and electronic elements, including computers, software, hardware and information systems (IS).

Cyber law is also known as Cyber Law or Internet Law. Cyber Laws prevent or reduce large scale damage from cybercriminal activities by protecting information access, privacy, communications, intellectual property (IP) and freedom of speech related to use of the internet, websites, email, computers, cell phones, software and hardware, such as data storage devices.

The increase in Internet traffic has led to a higher proportion of legal issues worldwide. Because cyber laws vary by jurisdiction and country, enforcement is challenging, and restitution ranges from fines to imprisonment.

Cyber law is a rapidly evolving area of civil and criminal law as applicable to the use of computers, and activities performed and transactions conducted over internet and other networks. This area of law also deals with the exchange of communications and information thereon, including issues concerning such communications and information as the protection of intellectual property rights, freedom of speech, and public access to information.

Cyber crime is defined as a crime in which a computer is the object of the crime (hacking, spamming···etc.) or is used as a tool, hate to commit an offense (child pornography, hate crimes). Cyber criminals may use computer technology to access personal information, business trade secrets, or use the internet for exploitative or malicious purposes. Criminals can also use computers for communication and document or data storage. Criminals who perform those illegal activities are often referred to as hackers. Cybercrime may also be referred to as computer crime.

Common types of Cybercrime include online bank information theft, identity theft, online predatory crimes and unauthorized computer access. More serious crimes like cyber terrorism are also of significant concern.

Cybercrime includes a wide range of activities, but these can generally be broken into two categories:

—3-Crimes that target computer networks or devices. These types of crimes include viruses and denial-of -service (DoS) attacks.

—4-Crimes that use computer networks to advance other criminal activities. These types of crimes include cyber stalking, fraud or identity theft.

Ⅲ. Threats to Internet Security

The expansion of the internet and cyberspace over the last few years has seen this sphere become important to society and has changed the way people live and communicate on a global scale. The internet now serves as primary source of information, a means of conducting business and a way of communicating with others. However, the expansion of cyberspace has come the increase of cyber-crime. Although definitions of "Cyber-crime" can differ based on the sources and the range of acts included within any one definition can vary, a broad definition can include anything from state-sponsored attacks to gain intelligence—a form of modern-day espionage—to hacking websites in acts of dissidence and political protests to copyright offenses to the online dissemination of child pornography to crime such as identify and information theft—e-scams, raids of bank accounts and more.

More than one million people worldwide are victims of cybercrime every day, at a cost to the global economy of around USD 300 billion a year. A February 2013 report by the United Nations (UN) office on Drugs and Crime (UNODC) notes that upward of 80 percent of cybercrime acts are estimated to originate in some of form of organized activity, with cybercrime black markets established on a cycle of mal ware creation, computer infection, harvesting of personal and financial data, data sale, and "cashing out" of financial information.

With such high expansion rates of threats, there is a need for a level of protection for internet users so that they can feel safe in the cyber sphere. The borderless nature of the internet, which connects people and business regardless of geographical limitations, makes it difficult to pin criminal activity down to one legal jurisdiction. This system of communication has enabled the easy conduct of transactions and interactions across the world, but has brought into question the jurisdiction of and responsibility for cyber security and cyber criminals. Many nations seek to afford a certain level of protection to their citizens accessing the cyber space, for example by ensuring safe passage of personal data and protecting young children from indecent images. Cyber-crimes often replicate crimes that are traditionally committed offline, such as identity theft, and fraud, and in most jurisdictions existing legislation covering these crimes can be applied online. However, the perpetuation of some crimes is considerably easier under the guise of internet anonymity. There is a danger of cyber threats to not just individuals, but to business and governments as well.

Thus far, cyber-crime in Cambodia has most noticeable manifested in the form of Anonymous Cambodia, a branch of the worldwide hacking group Anonymous that aims to unwell government's secrets. In July 2013, ahead of elections, they claimed to have hacked into the Cambodian National Election Committee's ("NEC") database in protest against perceived attempt to register ineligible voters to vote in the National Assembly Elections. In September 2013, Anonymous Cambodia also hacked into the websites of the Press and Quick Reaction Unit of the Council of Ministers, the Council of legal and Judicial Reform and CPP-aligned TV Station TVK. In additional to Anonymous, a political attacks on websites of those of Legend Cinemas, Sabay News, Lao Airlines and Sorya Transport have also take place, allegedly to "draw attention to faulty security protocols." Finally, there are also growing concerns that as online credit card transactions and other forms of e-banking-thus far limited-increase in frequency in Cambodia, cyber-crime will increase correspondingly, especially give Cambodia's weak Internet infrastructure.

Ⅳ. TheDraft of Cyber Law in Cambodia

The Ministry of Information of Cambodia is currently drafting a law that will extend current print media rules to other media platform, including the internet. This law will be used to formalize content management rules so that they can be easily applied by future information ministers, "and we are drafting the legislation in order to have a proper law to manage radio, television and other platforms," says Khieu Kanharith, Information Minister of Cambodia. The Minister says the recent explosion of media outlets has made the law necessary.

1. Purpose
This Law has a purpose to determine education, prevention measures and combat all kinds of offense commit by computer system.

2. Objective
This law has objectives:

—5-Ensure the implementation of law anti-cybercrime and combating all kinds of offense commit by computer system

—6-Ensure safety and prevent all legitimate interest in using and developing technology

3. Scope

This law is applicable to all offenses in this law in the following situation：

—7-Offense committed inside the Kingdom of Cambodia. or

—8-Offense committed inside or outside the Kingdom of Cambodia and effect to legal and natural person or interest of the Kingdom of Cambodia.

4. Term and Definition

The technical terms in this law are as follow：

a. "Computer system" means any device or assembly of interconnected devices or that are in an operational relation，out of which one or more provide the automatic data processing by means of a computer program.

b. "Automatic data processing" is the process by means of which the data in a computer system are processed by means of a computer program.

c. "Computer program" means a sum of instructions expressed in letters，or codes，or illustrations，or in any other possible forms，once incorporated in a computer，which has its aim to accomplish a task or particular result by means of a computer or through an electronic procedure capable of information processing.

d. "Computer data" are any representation of facts，information or concepts in a form that can be processed by a computer system. This category includes any computer program that can cause a computer system to perform a function.

e. "Content" refers to electronic form including text，images，graphics，animation，symbols，voices，and videos.

f. Service providers refer to：

1. Any natural or legal person offering the users the possibility to communicate by means of a computer system；

2. Any other natural or legal person processing or storing computer data for the persons mentioned in paragraph 1 and for the users of the services offered by these.

g. "Traffic data" are any computer data related to a communication by means of a computer system and generated by this，which represent a part in the chain of communication，indicating the communication's origin， destination, route, time, date, size, volume and duration, as well as the type of service used for communication.

h. "Security measures" refers to the use of certain procedures, devices or specialized computer programs by means of which the access to a computer system is restricted or forbidden for certain categories of users;

i. "Competent authority" refers to the Secretariat of National Committee on Anti-Cybercrime or any competent authority in other countries.

j. "Website" refers to place on the Internet, which you can find any information.

k. A person acts without right in the following situations:

1. is not authorized, in terms of the law or a contract;

2. exceeds the limits of the authorization;

3. has no permission from the competent natural or legal person to give it, according to the law, to use, administer or control a computer system or to carry out scientific research in a computer system.

V. Offences in the Drafted Cyber Law of Cambodia

A. Illegal Access

1. The access without right to a computer system in an offence shall be sentenced from six (6) months to three (3) years and fined from one million Riel (1,000,000) to six million Riel (6,000,000).

2. It is an offence where the act provide in paragraph (1) is committed with the intent of obtaining computer data, shall be sentenced from six (6) months to five (5) years and fined from one (1) million Riel (1,000,000) to ten million Riel (10,000,000).

3. It is an offence where the act provided in paragraph 1-2 is committed by infringing the security measures, shall be sentenced from three (3) years to twelve (12) years and fined from six million Riel (6,000,000) to twenty four million Riel (24,000,000).

B. Data Espionage

1. Any person who obtains without authorization, for himself or for another, data which are not meant for him and which are specially protected

against unauthorized access, shall be sentenced from 1 year to 3 years and fined from two million Riel (2,000,000) to six million Riel (6,000,000).

2. Data within the meaning of subsection 1 are only such as are stored or transmitted electrically or magnetically or in any form not directly visible.

C. Illegal Interception

The interception without right, made by technical means, of non-public transmissions of computer data to, from or within a computer system, including electronic magnetic, emissions from a computer system carrying such computer data, shall be sentenced from 2 years to 7 years and fined from four million Riel (4,000,000) to fourteen million Riel (14,000,000).

D. Data Interference

The alteration, deletion or deterioration of computer data or restriction to such data without right is an offence, shall be sentenced from 2 years to 7 years and fined from four million Riel (4,000,000) to fourteen million Riel (14,000,000).

E. Unauthorized Data Transfer

The unauthorized data transfer from a computer system or by means of a computer data storage medium is an offence shall be sentenced from 3 years to 12 years and fined from six million Riel to twenty four million Riel (24,000,000).

F. System Interference

The act of causing serious hindering, without right, of the functioning of a computer system, by inputting, transmitting, altering, deleting or deteriorating computer data or by restricting the access to such data, shall be sentenced from 3 years to 15 years and fined from six million Riel (6,000,000) to thirty million Riel (30,000,000).

G. Child Pornography

1. Any person when committed intentionally and without right, the following conduct:

a. Producing child pornography for the purpose of its distributing through a computer system;

b. Offering or making available child pornography through a computer system;

c. distributing or transmitting child pornography through a computer system;

d. procuring child pornography through a computer system for oneself or for another person;

e. possessing child pornography in a computer system or on a computer-data storage medium.

shall be sentenced from 1 year to 3 years and fined from two million Riel (2,000,000) to ten million Riel (10,000,000).

2. For the purpose of paragraph 1 above, the term "Child pornography" shall include pornography material that visually depicts:

a. a minor engaged in sexually explicit conduct;

b. a person appearing to be a minor engaged in sexually explicit conduct;

c. realistic images representing a minor engaged in sexually explicit conduct.

H. Contents and Websites

Any persons who engage in activities set forth in the followings:

1. Establishing contents that deemed to hinder the sovereignty and integrity of the Kingdom of Cambodia is a punishable offense ofincarceration from one to three years and fined of two million Riel (2,000,000) up to six million Riel (6,000,000).

2. Publications that deemed to incite or instigate the general population that could cause one or many to generate anarchism is punishable of incarceration from one to three years and fined from two million Riel (2,000,000) and up to six million years (6,000,000).

3. Publications or continuation of publication that deemed to generate insecurity, instability, and political cohesiveness is a punishable office of incarceration from one to three years and fined of two million Riel (2,000,000) and up to six million Riel (6,000,000).

4. Publications or continuation of publication that deemed to be non-factual which slanders or undermined the integrity of any governmental agencies, ministries, not limited to departments, federal or local levels, is a punishable offense of incarceration from one to three years and fined of two

million Riel (2,000,000) and up to six million Riel (6,000,000).

5. Publications that deemed damaging to the moral and cultural values of the society as stated herein：

a. Information that incites or instigates prejudice on race or clan, color, gender, language, religion, beliefs or political views, origin of race or nationality, and not limited to levels or class in society；

b. Writings or pixilation that deemed to display inappropriate activities of persons, copulations between humans or animals, or devalue the moral of family values and pixilation that deemed to display domestic violence；

c. Manipulation, defamation, and slanders；

d. Drawings, pictorials, or pixilation that deemed to slander or defame human beings or commoners of the state performing activities unbecoming, with animals of any species is punishable of incarceration from one to three years and finedfrom two million Riel(2,000,000) up to six million Riel (6,000,000).

Publicizing with the intent to threatened and commit a crime not limited to one form of felonies or other felonies with the intent to interrupt a person or persons well-beings is punishable of incarceration from one to three years and fined from two million Riel (2,000,000) up to six million Riel (6,000,000). In the case of with the intent to threaten shall be treated as such law that is currently being enforced.

Ⅰ. Intellectual Property Right and Related Rights

Offences related to Intellectual Property Right and Related Rights need to implement it base on the existing Copyright and Related Right Law of the Kingdom of Cambodia.

J. Computer Related Fraud

The causing of a loss of property to another person by inputting, altering or deleting of computer data, by restricting the access to such data or by any interference with the functioning of a computer system with the intent of procuring an economic benefit for oneself or for another shall be sentenced from 3 years to 12 years and fined from six million Riel (6,000,000) to twenty four million Riel (24,000,000).

K. Computer Related Forgery

The input, alteration or deletion, without right of computer data or the restriction without right, of the access to such data, resulting in inauthentic data, with the intent to be used for legal purpose, is a criminal offence and shall be punished with imprisonment from two to seven years.

L. Misuses of Device

1. Any person when committed intentionally and without right:

a. the production, sale, procurement for use, import, distribution or otherwise making available of:

i. a device, including a computer program, designed or adapted primarily for the purpose of committing any of the offenses established in accordance with the Illegal Access and the Misuses of Device;

ii. a computer password, access code, or similar data by which the whole or any part of a computer system is capable of being accessed, with intent that it be used for the purpose of committing any of the offenses established in Illegal Access and Misuses of Device. A party may require by law that a number of such items be possessed before criminal liability attaches.

Shall be sentenced from 1 year to 6 years and fined from two million Riel (2,000,000) to twelve million Riel (12,000,000).

2. The Misuse of Device shall not be interpreted as imposing criminal liability where the production, sale, procurement for use, import, distribution or otherwise making available or possession referred to in paragraph 1 of this article is not for the purpose of committing an offence established in accordance with the Illegal Access and Misuses of Device, such as for authorized testing or protection of a computer system.

M. Attempt

Attempt to commit a misdemeanor as stated in Article 427 (Accessing or Maintaining Access to Automated Data Processing System), Article 428 (Act of obstructing the Operations of Automated Data Processing System), Article 429 (Fraudulent Introduction, Deletion or Modification of Data), Article 430 (Participation in Group or an Agreement to prepare for the commission of offences) of Criminal Code and Article 21 (Illegal Access),

Article 22 (Data Espionage), Article 23 (Illegal Interception), Article 24 (Data Interference), Article 25 (Unauthorized Data transfer), Article 26 (System Interference), Article 27 (Child Pornography), Article 28 (Contents and Websites), Article 29 (Intellectual Property Rights and Related Rights), Article 30 (Computer Related Fraud), Article 31 (Computer Related Forgery) and Article 32 (Misuse of Device) of this law shall face the same punishment as misdemeanor.

N. Accessory Penalty applicable to certain Cybercrime Offences

For the felonies and the misdemeanors described in this present chapter, the following additional penalties may be pronounced:

1. the deprivation of civil rights;

2. the prohibition against pursuing a profession during which time the crime was committed in course of or during the occasion of pursuing of this profession;

3. the confiscation of any instruments, materials or any objects which have been used to commit the offense or were intended to commit the offense;

4. the seizure of the objects or funds with which the offense was funded and/or carried out;

5. the confiscation of incomes or properties earned/generated by the offense;

6. the seizure of the utensils, materials and the furniture garnishing a premise in which the offense was committed;

7. the confiscation of one or several vehicles belonging to the convicted person;

8. the posting of the decision of the sentence for two (2) months maximum;

9. the publication of the decision of the sentence in the newspapers;

10. broadcasting of the decision of the sentence by all means of audio-visual communications for eight (8) days maximum.

O. Accessory Penalty Applicable to Certain Legal Entities

The legal entity that commits offences as stated from article 21 to 32 in this law shall be subjected to fine of ⋯ to ⋯ and face accessory penalties as follows:

1. Dissolution;

2. Placement under the court watch;

3. Baring of operation of an activity or activities;

4. Expulsion from public procurement;

5. Prohibition on public saving appeal;

6. Prohibition of the business establishment open to the public or used by the public;

7. Confiscation of instrument, material or any objects which are used by the public;

8. Confiscation of objects or funds which are subject of committing offence;

9. Confiscation of proceeds, materials and furniture in building where an offence is committed;

10. Posting of conviction judgment;

11. Publication of the conviction judgment on print media or the announcement on non-print media outlets.

VI. Criminal Code of Cambodia-Offense Related to Information Technology

1. Article 427—Unauthorized access to or remaining in automated data processing system

Fraudulently accessing or remaining within an automated data processing system shall be punishable by imprisonment from one month to one year and a fine from one hundred thousand Riels (100,000) to two million Riels (2,000,000).

Where the act causes the destruction of modification of data contained in that system or any alteration of the functioning of that system the sentence is imprisonment from one to two years and a fine from two million Riels (2,000,000) to four million Riels (4,000,000).

2. Article 428—Obstructing the functioning of automated data processing system

Obstructing the functioning of an automated data processing system shall be punishable by imprisonment from one to two years and a fine from two million Riels (2,000,000) to four million Riels.

3. Article 429—Fraudulent introduction, deletion or modification of data

The fraudulent introduction of data into an automated data processing system or the fraudulent deletion or modification of the data that it contains shall be punishable by imprisonment from one to two years and a fine from two million Riels (2,000,000) to four million Riels (4,000,000).

4. Article 430—Participation in a group or conspiracy to commit offences

Participating in a group or a conspiracy established with a view to the planning of one or more offences defined in this section shall be punishable by imprisonment from one to two years and a fine from two million Riels (2,000,000) to four million Riels (4,000,000).

5. Article 431—Attempt

An attempt to commit the misdemeanors defined in this section shall be punishable by the same penalties.

6. Article 432—Additional penalties (nature and duration)

The following additional penalties may be imposed in respect of the misdemeanor defined in this section:

(1) forfeiture of certain rights, either permanently or for a period not exceeding five years;

(2) prohibition from practicing a profession in the practice of or in connection with which the offence was committed, either permanently or for a period not exceeding five years;

(3) confiscation of any instruments, materials, or items which were used or intended to be used to commit the offence;

(4) confiscation of the items or funds which were the subject of the offence;

(5) confiscation of the proceeds or property arising out the offence;

(6) confiscation of the utensils, materials and furnishings in the premises in which the offence was committed;

(7) confiscation of one or more vehicles belonging to the convicted persons;

(8) publication of sentencing decision for a period not exceeding two month;

(9) publication of sentencing decision in the print media;

(10) broadcasting of sentencing decision by any audio-visual communication for a period not exceeding eight days.

Ⅶ. Advantages of Cyber Law

-Improved security of cyberspace
-Increase in cyber defense
-Increase in cyber speed
-Allows more options to save data
-Better response time to national crisis
-Protection against child pornography.

Ⅷ. Disadvantages of Cyber Law

-Improved hacker speed and ability
-Interconnected computers
-Improved viruses, mal ware and worms
-Increase in "cyber warfare" possibly
-More anonymity between hackers
-Freedom of speech is compromised
-Intrusion of privacy
-Only positive things must be posted
-Liking, sharing, tweeting or re-tweeting posts are libelous
-Ability to take down websites without warning.

Ⅸ. Conclusion

In conclusion, the government of the Kingdom of Cambodia is making its way to establish the cyber law due to the increase of internet usage as well as cybercrimes occurring at the meantime. In my opinion, I think that there still strengths and weakness on the drafted cyber law so the government should study in depth on this law before it was ratified so that the law can be used beneficially and effectively for the Kingdom of Cambodia.

柬埔寨王国网络法研究

Dy Molany[*]

刘俊杰　译

摘要　网络通讯的普及带来了网络犯罪的增加。柬埔寨正在起草网络法以确立教育、预防措施来应对各类的计算机犯罪,保障人们在使用和发展技术中的安全和合法利益。由于网络法草案本身存在一定的优势和劣势,政府在批准此部法律前应当对其进行深入研究,以使网络法能够更好地适用于柬埔寨王国。

一、柬埔寨网络使用现状及存在问题

柬埔寨是一个贫穷的国家,80％的人口都居住在乡村,甚至很多地方都没有连上国家电网,网络普及率仅有 5％。但是,随着智能手机的降价,3G 移动信号的覆盖范围的扩大,越来越多的柬埔寨人能够使用网络。

网络的普及影响了人类生活和通讯的方式,网络已经成为了主要的信息来源、交易方式以及通讯手段。然而,这也导致了网络犯罪的增加。网络犯罪主要分为两个种类:一是将计算机网络或设备作为对象的犯罪,包括病毒植入和黑客行为。二是使用计算机网络来从事其他犯罪活动,包括网络跟踪、欺诈、身份信息盗窃等。

无论是政府还是一般的商业和个人,都受到网络犯罪的威胁。2013 年,名为"柬埔寨匿名者"的黑客组织入侵柬埔寨国家选举委员会的数据库,抗议那些无资格的选民在国民议会选举中进行投票,又入侵部长理事会的新闻与快速反应处、法律与司法改革委员会的网站以及柬埔寨电视台,同时也对

---

[*]　柬埔寨司法部国际关系部官员。

Legend 电影、Sabay 新闻、老挝航空以及 Sorya 运输的网站进行了政治攻击。随着线上信用卡交易以及其他形式的电子银行业务的增多,人们的资金安全也日益堪忧。而且由于互联网用户以及交易不受地域限制,重复线下的如身份信息盗窃、欺诈等传统犯罪,在匿名互联网的掩护下变得更加容易。随着网络犯罪威胁的增加,保护网络使用者的安全迫在眉睫,网络相关法律的规制势在必行。

二、柬埔寨网络相关的法律规定

(一)柬埔寨网络法草案

网络法是调整带有例如计算机、软件、硬件、信息系统等技术和电子元素的网络关系的法律,又称为互联网法。网络法通过保护与互联网、网站、电子邮件、计算机、手机、软件、硬件的使用相关的信息获取、隐私、通信、知识产权、言论自由等的安全,来阻止和减少网络犯罪活动。

柬埔寨的网络法草案旨在确立教育和预防措施以应对各类计算机犯罪,保障用户在使用和发展技术中的安全和合法权益,适用于在柬埔寨王国领域内进行的犯罪以及不在王国领域内但对柬埔寨王国的法人或自然人的利益产生影响的犯罪。草案对"计算机系统"、"计算机程序"、"计算机数据"、"自动数据处理"、"服务提供者"、"主管部门"等专业术语进行了明确定义。

网络法草案规定了包括非法访问、刺探数据、非法截取、数据干扰、未经授权的数据传输、系统干扰、儿童色情、非法内容、知识产权相关犯罪、计算机欺诈、计算机伪造、滥用设备共 12 种计算机犯罪,并定义了上述犯罪的构成要件,所处刑期和罚金。同时,草案还规定了未遂犯罪的处罚,自然人和法人网络犯罪的附加刑的适用条件的具体内容。

(二)柬埔寨刑法典中网络犯罪相关规定

柬埔寨刑法典中有六个条文涉及与计算机相关的犯罪,包括第 427 条——未经授权的访问或留存自动化数据处理系统,第 428 条——阻碍自动化数据处理系统功能的实现,第 429 条——欺诈性的录入、删除或修改数据,第 430 条——参与团体或共谋犯罪,第 431 条——未遂犯罪,第 432 条——附加刑的性质和周期。

三、对柬埔寨网络法草案的评析及建议

柬埔寨正在起草的网络法本身存在一定的优势和劣势。优势在于:提升网络空间的安全、提高网络防御、提升网络速度、允许多方式储存数据、加快国家危机反应速度、抵制儿童色情。劣势在于:黑客的速度和能力也会提高、黑客间匿名性的加强、黑客网站攻击能力增强、侵犯隐私、病毒、恶意软件和蠕虫的复杂化、增加"网络战"的可能性。鉴于网络法自身的特点,政府在批准前应当对其进行充分研究,以使该法能够更好地适用于柬埔寨王国。

Indonesian National Cyber Security

Dwi Rezki Sri Astarini[*]

Introduction

Usage of information technology, media and communications has globally changed both public behavior and human civilization. The development of information technology and communications has also contributed to the borderless of world connection and has significantly made social, economic and cultural changes rapidly. A rapid development in the Information and Communication Technology (ICT) sector gives a positive impact on economic growth but also give a big threat for the cyber security.

Telecommunication in Indonesia entered new phase since Telecommunication Law adopted in 1999. The telecommunication industry growing rapidly. Currently, there are 10 telecommunication operators with 180 million mobile phone users. High number of mobile phones subscribes also following by the internet. The growth of the internet penetration in Indonesia is 12.5 % or by 30 million users in 2010. This growth rate was lower among other Asian countries, but in the term of number, that number ranked the top in Southeast Asia Region, or the highest ranked five in Asian region. The Indonesian government need to work harder increase internet users due to the World Summit for Information Society (WSIS) in 2003 had declared that

---

[*] Judge, Bangli District Court, Indonesia.

at least half of the world population has internet access in 2015.

Indonesia as one of the develop country, trying to develop their economic by increasing investment in ICT. For Indonesia internet important for civilization development. Therefore, every country including Indonesia needs to develop their national cyber security strategies to anticipate the cyber threat. Indonesia population reaches 255 million in 2015. In 2011 Internet user in Indonesia reached 55 million. It means government should be able to provide internet access to 70 million people. So Indonesian government should be more aware because the high number of the internet and internet utilization for life will increase the frequency of cybercrime.

Nowadays, new regime of new law is born. Known as Cyber Law. Cyber law formatted against cyber crime. Cybercrime was defined by the 2001 Budapest Convention (formally known as the Council of Europe's Convention of Cyber Crimes). Cybercrimes include identity theft or data (information resources), piracy accounts (email, IM, social networks), the spread of malware and malicious code, fraud, industrial espionage, hostage critical information resources and cyber welfare or war in cyber space. Convention of cybercrimes, has been split into several section, such as:

1. Offences against confidentiality, integrity and availability of computer data and system;

2. Computer related offences;

3. Content related offences;

4. Offences related to infringements of copyright and relative right;

5. Ancillary liability.

Explanation of national cyber security condition is consist of five pillars, which is legal measures, technical and procedural measures, organizational structures, capacity building and international cooperation. This paper only focusing on legal measures.

I. Legal Measures

The globalization of information has placed Indonesia as part of the world information community, therefore the making of regulation concerning organization of electronic information and transaction at national level is requiredin order that the development of information technology can be carried out in an optimal, distributive, and widespread manner throughout all level of society to advance the intellectual life of the people. Concerning about the cybercrimes, Indonesian government provide a series of legal instrument in protecting the security of the cyberspace by publishing the policies and regulations. Law Number 36 Year 1999 concerning Telecommunication and Law Number 11 Year 2008 concerning Electronic Transaction and Communication are two act that directly related to ICT security. Generally, Law Number 11 Year 2008 concerning Electronic Transaction and Communication divide by two, regulating about Information and Electronic Transaction , and regulating about Prohibited Act. There are:

1. Chapter I: General Provision, article 1-2

Definition of: electronic information, electronic transactions, information technology, electronic record, electronic system, electronic agent, electronic certificate, trustworthiness certification body, electronic signature, access, electronic contract, domain name, business entity and government.

2. Chapter II: Principles and Objectives, article 3-4

—The IT and Electronic Transaction usage being implemented under the principles of legal certainty, benefit, prudence, good faith, and freedom to choose technology or technology neutrality;

—The usage of IT and Electronic Transaction implemented with the objectives to:

a. Advance the intellectual life of the people as part of the world information community;

b. Develop the national trade and economy in order to improve public welfare;

c. Improve the effectiveness and efficiency of public services;

d. Give as wide opportunities as possible to any person to cultivate his/her insight and capability in the optimal and responsible use and usage of IT;

e. Give senses security, justice, and legal certainty for IT users and providers.

3. Chapter III: Electronic Information, Records and Signature, article 5-12

—The print out of the electronic information are lawful means of proof;

—Business actor that offer product through Electronic System must make available, full and true information about contractual conditions, producers and offered product.

4. Chapter IV : Provision of Electronic Certification and Electronic System, article 13-16

—Electronic Certification Service Providers include:

a. Indonesian electronic certification service providers;

b. Foreign electronic certification service providers.

—The Electronic Certification Service must make available to any service user accurate, clear and define information that includes:

a. Method that are adopted to identify the Signatures/Signers;

b. Things that can be used to recognize Electronic Signature creation personal data;

c. Things that can demonstrate the validity and security of Electronic Signatures.

—Any Electronic System Provider must provide Electronic System in reliable and secure manner and shall be responsible for the proper operation of the Electronic System.

5. Chapter V: Electronic Transaction, article 17-22

—Provision of Electronic Transaction maybe carried out within a public or private scope;

—It allows opportunities of information technology usage to state administrators, persons, business entities, and or the public, and must be implemented in a proper, responsible, effective, and efficient manner in order that the public can reapas much as benefits as possible;

—Electronic Transaction that are stated in Electronic Contracts shall bind on parties;

—The Parties have power to choose Law applicable to international electronic transactions they enter;

—If parties do not make choice of Law in international electronic transaction, the applicable law shall be under the principles of the Private International Law;

—Parties also have power to determine forums of court, arbitration or other alternatives dispute resolution institutions with jurisdiction to handle disputes that may arise from international Electronic Transaction they enter;

—Parties responsible for any legal effect in the conduct of Electronic Transaction shall be regulated as follow:

a. If conducted by person, any legal effect in the conduct of Electronic Transaction shall become the responsibility of parties to a transaction;

b. If conducted by proxy, any legal effect in the conduct of Electronic Transaction shall become the responsibility of the grantors of the proxy;

c. If conducted by electronic agents any legal effect in the conduct of E-lectronic Transaction shall become the responsibility of Electronic Agents providers.

—If damage of Electronic Transaction is occasioned by failure of the operation of Electronic Agents due to third parties direct measures against Electronic System, any legal effectshall become the responsibility of Electronic Agents.

6. Chapter Ⅵ: Domain Names, Intellectual Property Rights and Protection of Privacy Rights, article 23-26

—Domain names entitled on the first applicant principle basis (first come first serve). The usage of Information Technology, personal data shall be part of the privacy rights to be protected;

—Holding and use of domain names must be on the basis of good faith, non violation of fair business competition, and non infringements of the right of other person;

—Domain name administrators shall be the government and or public;

—Electronic Information or records that are created into Intellectual works, internet sites and intellectual works contained therein shall be protected as individual property rights under provision laws and regulation.

7. Chapter Ⅶ: Prohibited Acts, article 27-37

—Any person who knowingly and without authority distributes, transmits, causes to be accessible electronic information and electronic records with contents against propriety, gambling, affronts or defamation, extortion or treats, misleading information, hatred, violence or scares aimed personally are prohibited;

—Any person who knowingly and without authority or unlawfully accesses computers and or electronic system in any manner whatsoever with the intent to:

1. Obtain Electronic Information or Electronic Records;

2. Breaching hacking info, trespassing into or breaking through security system;

3. Interception or wiretapping of Electronic Information;

4. Interception of transmission of nonpublic Electronic Information.

Are prohibited;

—Any person who knowingly and without authority or unlawfully in any manner whatsoever:

1. Alters, adds, reduces, transmits, tampers with deletes, moves, hide electronic information or electronic record of other person or of the public;

2. Moves or transfers electronic information or electronic record to electronic system of unauthorized persons.

—Any person who knowingly and without authority or unlawfully manipulates, creates, alters, deletes, tampers with electronic information or electronic record with the intent that such electronic information or electronic record would seem to be authentic data.

8. Chapter Ⅷ : Dispute Resolution, article 38-39

—Any person can filling law suits against parties that provide electronic system or using information technology to their detriment. Any civil actions may resolve through court or other alternative dispute resolution in accordance with provisions of Law and Regulation.

9. Chapter IX : Role of the Government and Role of the Public, article 40-41

—The Government protect the public interest from any type of threat as the result of misusing electronic information and electronic transaction that offend public order in accordance with provisions of Law and Regulation.

10. Chapter X : Investigation, article 42-44

—The Criminal Investigation intended by this law shall made under the provisions of the Criminal Law Procedure and Provision of this law;

—In addition to investigators of the State Police of the Republic Indonesia, certain civil service officials within the government whose scope of duties and responsibilities is in the field Information technology and electronic transaction shall be granted special authority as investigators as intended by the law of criminal procedure to make investigation of criminal acts of information technology and electronic transaction;

—To make arrest of detention, investigators through public prosecutors are required to seek order of the local chief justice of the district court within a period of twenty four hours;

11. Chapter XI : Penal Provisions, article 45-52

—In this chapter, every person who doing prohibit acts will sentences to imprisonment and fine.

12. Chapter XII: Transitional Provisions, article 53

13. Chapter XIII : Concluding Provisions, article 54

Besides what written above, there's also several laws related to the cybercrimes prevails among others, which is Criminal Procedure Law (KUHP), the Law Number 44 Year 2008 concerning Pornography provide provision related to child pornography. The provision expressly among other prohibit every person to produce, make, reproduce, broadcast, distribute, duplicate, import, export, offer, trade, rent, hear, watch, own, keep or provide child pornography. Law Number 19 Year 2002 concerning copyright provide provisions concerning infringements of copy right and the peal code that regulated general criminal activities, and also Law Number 15 Year 2003 concerning Against Terrorism.

Ⅱ. Technical and Procedural Measures

Applying standard is an important step to protect of information in cyberspace. Those standard will become reference for each sector to enhance the capabilities in the field of information security. Indonesian government has been aware of it by adopting international standard on security management (ISO 27001).

1. Organizational Structure

In Indonesia，the cyber security are handled by this institution：

Regulator：

1. Directorate Information Security (KOMINFO)

In order to protect young generation，KOMINFO closed all porn web-sites；

2. Indonesia Security Incident Response Team on Internet Infrastructure (IDSIRTII)—KOMINFO

3. National Crypto Agency

Defense/Military：

1. Ministry of Defense (KEMENHAN)

2. Indonesian National Armed Forces (TNI)

3. Indonesian National Board for Terrorism (BNPT)

The cybercrimes that is attack national assets and disrupt national interest its called cyber terrorism or cyber welfare. In Indonesia，Indonesian National Board for Terrorism (BNPT) actively monitoring the potential infringement on cyber terrorism.

Law Enforcement：

1. Police

Indonesian National Police received at least 800. 000 reports linked to cybercrimes annually；

2. Prosecutor

3. Judge

Intelligence：

1. National Intelligence Agency (BIN)

2. Indonesian Military's Strategic Intelligence Agency (BAIS TNI)

2. Capacity Building

Capacity building capabilities contribute in creating the information security components. The capacity can be gained through：

1. Workshop and Trading

2. Public Private Partnership

3. Certification

4. Awareness Education

III. International Cooperation

Politically, Indonesia has free and active principle, it is stated in the preamble of the constitution. Indonesia has collaborated with International parties on the issue of cyber security. Indonesia has become a member of:

1. Member of ASEAN Network Security Action Council Working Group;

2. Member of International Telecommunication Union (ITU);

3. Bilateral Cooperation in Cyber Security;

4. Steering Committee Asia Pacific Computer Emergency Response Team (APCERT);

5. Member of FIRST (Forum of Incident Response and Security Teams).

IV. Conclusion

ICT growth in Indonesia gives the impacton a high cyber threat. Indonesian government has tried to address that problem by issued policies and regulation, develop technical and procedures, established organization security, improved capacity building and conducted international cooperation. Indonesian National Police and Indonesian Board for Terrorism had many effort and anticipate the cyberspace. Therefore future work is to determine the ideal conditions for cyber security in Indonesia, furthermore by understanding the current condition and ideal condition we can view the gap to make improvement.

印度尼西亚国家网络安全

Dwi Rezki Sri Astarini*

赵韦翰　译

一、导论

信息化技术、媒体以及通信的应用对人类文明和公众行为产生了普遍影响。随着信息技术和通信的发展,一个无国界的世界网络已经形成,并在社会、经济以及文化事务方面带来了显著变化转变。但是信息通信技术(ICT)在给经济带来积极影响的同时也给网络安全带来了巨大的威胁。

自电信法于 1999 年施行以来,印度尼西亚的电信产业迈入了一个新的阶段。目前,印尼拥有 10 家电信运营商和 1 亿八千万位手机用户。电信业的高速发展的背后缘由是网络的高普及率,在 2010 年印度尼西亚的网络用户就增加了 3 千万,互联网普及率增长了 12.5%。该增长率水平虽屈于其他亚洲国家,但其用户数量却为东南亚地区之最,甚至达到了全亚洲前五名。鉴于信息社会世界峰会(WSIS)于 2003 年就已经宣称"在 2015 年,全球至少一半的人口将能够接入网络",印度尼西亚仍需要加大对增加网络用户工作的投入。

印尼作为一个发展中国家,正通过增加 ICT 的投资来发展经济,而网络发展对于国家文明建设也有着重要作用。同时,包括印尼在内的所有国家都应当发展其国家网络安全战略以应对网络安全威胁。印尼人口在 2015 年已经达到了 2.55 亿,而在 2011 年印尼互联网用户就达到了 5500 万。这意味着政府需能够向 7 千万人提供的网络接入服务。在大量的网络和网络应用进入生活的情况下,印尼政府需对更为频繁的网络犯罪产生警觉。

---

* 印度尼西亚巴厘省班戈利地区法院法官。

现在,被用以规制网络犯罪的《网络法》诞生,在 2001 年的布达佩斯公约(正式名为欧洲网络犯罪协议理事会)中就已经对网络犯罪作出了定义,其包括对身份、数据(信息)、私人账户(邮件、实时通信、社交网络)的窃取,以及传播恶意软件和恶意代码,欺诈,商业谍报,挟持重要信息或网络福利,和发动网络空间战。根据公约,网络犯罪被分为以下几个部分:

1.侵犯电脑数据和系统的机密性、完整性以及可获取性;

2.计算机相关犯罪;

3.涉及内容的犯罪;

4.涉及违反版权及相关权益的犯罪;

5.附带责任。

国家网络安全状况由 5 项指标构成,分别为法律措施、技术和程序措施、组织结构、能力建设以及国际合作。本文仅重点关注法律措施方面。

二、法律措施

信息全球化进程使得印尼成为了世界信息化社区的一部分。因此,为了信息化技术的发展能造福于社会各个层面并提升人民生活水平,必须在国家层面构建一个针对电子信息管控的法规。印尼政府针对网络犯罪颁布了一系列政策和法规,并通过相关法律部门的运行来维护网络空间安全。1999 年 36 号法律是针对电子通信的,在 2008 年则颁布了针对电子事务处理和通信的 11 号法律,这两个是直接与 ICT 安全相关的法案。一般而言,针对电子事务和通信的 2008 年法律编号 11 被分为两大部分,关于信息和电子交易以及禁止行为的法律规定。如下:

1.第一章:总论,第 1 条至第 2 条

对以下概念进行定义:电子信息,电子交易,信息技术,电子记录,电子系统,电子代理,电子认证,权威认证机构,电子签名,访问,电子合同,域名,企业法人以及政府。

2.第二章:原则和目的,第 3 条至第 4 条

—IT 和电子事务的应用要遵从以下原则,司法确定性,有益性,审慎,诚信原则以及技术手段自由选择(科技中立性)。

—IT 和电子事务的应用要以以下目的作为目标:

a.推进人民生活的智能化;

b.促进贸易和经济发展以提高公共福利;

c.提升公共服务的效率；

d.发展并保障 IT 技术教育和培养；

e.为 IT 用户和供应者提供安全、公正、法治的环境。

3.第三章：电子信息，纪录和签名，第 5 条至第 12 条

—电子信息打印版具备法律效力；

—使用电子系统提供产品的商家需给出其合同、生产者以及产品的有效、完整、真实信息。

4.第四章：电子认证和电子系统，第 13 条至第 16 条

—电子认证的服务提供者包括：

a.印尼电子认证服务提供者；

b.外国电子认证服务提供者；

—电子认证服务需向用户提供准确清晰的信息：

a.确认签名或签名者的方法；

b.分辨电子签名的私人信息的手段；

c.证明电子签名有效性和安全性的手段；

—任何电子系统提供者应当提供安全可靠的电子服务，并需对其负责。

5.第五章：电子交易，第 17 条至第 22 条

—电子事务相关条文可适用于公共或私人领域；

—信息技术可向以下主体提供：政府官员，个人，企业法人和公众。为达到公共利益最大化，服务应当尽可能地合理、负责、有效和高效；

—电子合同中的电子交易对当事方有约束力；

—合同双方国际电子交易中可选择适用法；

—若合同双方在国际电子交易未就适用法律作出选择，其适应法律依照国际私法相应原则来确定；

—国际电子交易出现争端时，合同双方有权选择符合管辖权的诉讼，仲裁或其他争端解决方式；

—电子交易合同当事方应承担相应法律后果，具体如下：

a.如果行为人是自然人，其电子交易法律责任应由缔约双方承担；

b.如果行为人是代理人，其电子交易法律责任应由被代理权授予人承担；

c.如果行为人是电子代理商，其电子交易法律责任应由电子代理提供者承担；

—如果在电子交易中，因为第三方操控电子系统而导致电子代理失误产

生损失的,应由电子代理方承担所有法律后果。

6.第六章:域名,知识产权和隐私权保护,第23条至第26条

——域名授权采取先注先得原则。信息技术、个人数据属于隐私权范畴,受到法律保护;

——域名的持有和使用需基于善意,不违反公平竞争,不侵犯他人权益;

——域名管理者应为政府或公共机构;

——利用电子信息、纪录加工形成的智力成果、网站及其包含的智力成果受到知识产权保护。

7.第七章:禁止行为,第27条至第37条

——未经授权故意利用电子信息或记录实施以下行为的:侵犯知识产权,赌博,侮辱中伤,敲诈勒索,传播虚假信息,传播仇恨,以及对个人的暴力或恐吓;

——未经授权故意或非法访问计算机或电子系统实施下列行为的:

1.获取电子信息或记录;

2.黑客行为,入侵或攻击安全系统;

3.截取或监听电子信息;

4.截取传播非公开电子信息。

——未经授权故意或非法实施下列行为的:

1.对他人或公共电子信息或记录的更改,添加,传播,篡改删除,移动或隐藏;

2.将电子信息或记录上传到无授权用户的电子系统中。

——未经授权故意或违法对电子信息或记录实施操作,创建,改变,删减,篡改,欲使其被看做可信数据的。

8.第八章:争端解决,第29条至第38条

——可向造成损失的电子系统或信息科技的提供者提起诉讼。民事争端可依法提请诉讼或其他争端解决方式。

9.第九章:政府职能,第40条至第41条

——出现电子信息技术和电子交易滥用时,政府应依法保护公共利益并维护公共秩序。

10.第十章:调查取证,第42条至第44条

——根据本法案进行的刑事调查须遵从刑事诉讼法和本法相关规定;

——若本国警察在调查中涉及电子信息技术犯罪,可以依刑事诉讼法授权委托特定政府技术专员进行调查;

——要实行逮捕拘留,公诉调查人员需在24小时内向当地法院首席法官申

请授权。

11. 第十一章：刑罚，第 45 条至第 52 条

—任何人犯下禁止行为的将被处以监禁和罚金。

12. 第十二章：过渡条款，第 53 条

13. 第十三章：最终条款，第 54 条

除上述条文外，关于网络犯罪还需遵从刑事诉讼法（KUHP），2008 年第 44 号法律关于儿童色情的规定，2002 年 19 号法律关于知识产权法案，刑法典，以及恐怖主义法案（第 15 号法律）的相关条款。

三、技术手段和程序

应用标准对于加强维护网络安全能力非常关键，印尼政府采用了安全管理国际标准（ISO 27001）。

四、组织结构

印尼网络安全由以下机构负责：

管理

1. 信息安全委员会（KOMINFO）

KOMINFO 为保护未成年人关闭了所有色情网站。

2. 印尼网络应急反应小队（IDSIRTII）—KOMINFO

3. 国家保密局

国防和军事

1. 国防部（KEMENHAN）

2. 印尼国家武装部队（TNI）

3. 印尼国家反恐委员会（BNPT）

印尼国家反恐委员会（BNPT）会对可能损害或危及国家利益的网络恐怖主义行为进行监控。

执法

1. 警察

印尼国家警察每年能接收到 800000 份有关网络犯罪的报告。

2. 检察官

3. 法官

情报

1. 国家情报局（BIN）

2. 印尼陆军战略情报局（BAIS TNI）

五、能力建设

能力建设指获取资金再投入信息安全保障的能力。可通过以下渠道获得：

1. 产业及贸易

2. 公私合伙

3. 认证

4. 意识教育

六、国际合作

印尼在网络安全方面采取了积极自由的原则，并就此进行了国际合作。印尼参加的国际组织有：

1. 东盟网络安全行动会议工作组

2. 国际电信联盟（ITU）

3. 双边网络安全合作

4. 亚太计算机应急反应小队指导委员会（APCERT）

5. FIRST（事件应对和安全小队论坛）

七、结语

信息技术的发展给印尼带来了巨大的网络威胁，印尼政府和相关各方为了应对都付出了巨大努力。只有看到现实和理想的差距，并不断努力才能为印尼创建一个良好的网络环境。

Using Internet in the Lao PDR

Phimchanthaphone Sinthavong [*]

1. Introduction

The Internet in Laos was first introduced in 1997. The introduction of mobile broadband has significantly increased the use of the Internet in Laos since 2008. On 4 July 2013, The Lao Ministry of Post and Telecommunication's National Internet Center announced that it had launched the Lao Computer Emergency Response Team (Lao CERT), a branch of government focused on battling cyber-crime. the country's first body dedicated to fighting cyber-crime. Training kicked off on July 1 and will continue until October 11, [①] Laos is included in the open Net initiative (ONI) Regional Overview for Asia (2009). ONI found no evidence of Internet filtering in the political, social, conflict/security, and tools areas based on testing performed in 2011.

The government controls domestic Internet servers and sporadically monitors Internet usage, but by the end of 2012 it apparently did not have the ability to block access to Web sites. Authorities have developed infrastructure to route all Internet traffic through a single gateway, enabling them to monitor and restrict content. However, they apparently had not utilized this increased capability as of the end of 2012. The National Internet Committee under the Prime Minister's Office administers the Internet

---

[*] Head of Division of Research (foreign legal), Ministry of Justice, Lao PDR.
[①] Vietianetime Report.

system. The office requires Internet service providers to submit quarterly reports and link their gateways to facilitate monitoring, but the government's enforcement capability appears limited.

Mobile broadband is the marketing term for wireless Internet access through a portable modem, mobile phone, USB wireless modem, tablet or other mobile devices. The first wireless Internet access became available in 1991 as part of the second generation (2G) of mobile phone technology. Higher speeds became available in 2001 and 2006 as part of the third (3G) and fourth (4G) generations. In 2011, 90% of the world's population lived in areas with 2G coverage, while 45% lived in areas with 2G and 3G coverage. And 5% lived in areas with 4G coverage. By 2017 more than 90% of the world's population is expected to have 2G coverage, 85% is expected to have 3G coverage, and 50% will have 4G coverage.

2. Local Operators Internet in Laos

In 2008 two operators, Lao Telecom and Unitel, were granted 3G licenses. Another two licenses were issued to ETL and Beeline in 2011. In 2012, the main ways to access Internet in Laos are a factual comparison of the different Internet Service Providers (ISP) in Laos.

3. Consideration Policies of Using Internet in Laos

Although the factors elaborated above have presented considerable obstacles to connectivity in Laos, they have been compounded by broader social issues. The slowness with which Internet connectivity has been established in Laos is, in many respects, a result of the hesitancy of the Lao government in allowing access to this new global medium. The government has remained very cautious in its approach to the Internet and slow in formulating the required policies. At the same time the government recognizes the benefits to be gained for the country's socioeconomic development, it is concerned with how to maintain control over the information flowing into the country and the risk of cultural pollution this entails. Over the years, the government's stance has loosened up somewhat, as reflected in the history of Internet development discussed above. Nonetheless, social and cultural concerns continue to influence access to the Internet.

As in many other communist countries, the policies of the Lao government regarding media as well as information and communications technologies have in general been highly restrictive. In the early 1990s fax machines and satellites were not allowed and IDD was nonexistent. Over the years these restrictive policies have loosened up somewhat, especially with regard to access to information from the outside world. Faxes are now readily available, in both private and public sectors. IDD is widespread and is even available from public telephone booths throughout the country. And satellite dishes abound in the country. Foreign newspapers and journals are still illegal.

4. Dissemination of Information on the Internet

In Article 6 of Decree Information Management on the Internet of Laos, the dissemination of information through the Internet is the posting of messages, animations, photos, voices, and videos on the website in order to present, to have comment, to share, to send, and to forward message to one or many people. And article 7 of Decree Information Management on the Internet of Laos, Regulations for Disseminating Information on the Internet Individuals, legal entity, and organizations are able to disseminate information through social media but they must identify the source of information correctly. Information, which has not gone through official media or legal media offices, cannot be used as official information.

Website owners or website managers have the responsibility of checking content and information thoroughly before allowing others to disseminate it through their website.

The law has placed strict if not excessive regulations on how Internet users can share or disseminate information online. Article 6 recognizes the right of individuals to exchange online data but obliges website administrators "to check content before disseminating it on their web page. " this sounds impractical. The same provision states that "information which is not (approved) from official media or media offices; organizations legally cannot be used officially. " does this mean that Lao citizens can only share news reports approved by the State?

According Article 7 in this Decree prohibits the creation of anonymous or pseudonymous social media accounts, instead requiring individuals to register by giving their "name, surname and current address in (compliance with official documents). " This is a blow to citizens who seek to expose wrongdoings in the government through the Internet.

5. Prohibition Using Internet

The government of Laos has signed an Internet law that claims to support the growth of the Internet but actually contains numerous contradictory provisions that undermine free speech and other citizen rights. The concern of many was the broad and vague cybercrimes enumerated in the law. At the time, though, a text of the law had yet to be made public. We now have an unofficial English translation of the law and after reading the document, they can confirm that there are grounds to worry about the negative impact of the new law in media freedom and democracy in Laos. The law has placed strict if not excessive regulations on how Internet users can share or disseminate information online. Example article 6 and 7 above, And article 9 of Decree Information Management on the Internet of Laos, Security of Information Usage Individuals, legal entity, or organizations, who use information through the Internet shall save and change their password often to assure the security of using their personal information. They also won't create conditions for others to use their personal information illegally.

On Article 9 explicitly bans the posting and sharing of content that feature the following:

—Disseminating false and misleading information against the Lao People's Revolutionary Party, undermining the peace, independence, sovereignty, unity, and prosperity of Lao PDR;

　　—Circulating information that encourages citizens to become involved in terrorism, murder, and social disorder;

　　—Supporting online campaigns that seek to divide solidarity among ethnic groups and countries;

　　—Spreading information that distorts the truth or tarnishes the dignity and rights of individuals, sectors, institutions or organizations;

　　—Sharing of comments whose content are in line with the above-mentioned prohibitions.

　　We seem that legitimate criticism of government programs and policies could be interpreted as a criminal act if it creates division, confusion, or "disorder" among the public. It is not hard to see how authorities could use the law to prosecute journalists, activists, and other critics of the government.

　　On Articles 11 and 13 require Internet service providers and website administrators to "terminate access" and "temporarily or permanently block users" who are found to be violating government decrees and other regulations. They are also expected to "cooperate and provide information" to agencies conducting investigations. Meanwhile, article 14 prohibits Internet service providers from providing assistance or opportunities to individuals, legal entities or organizations who seek to undermine the Party and government policies.

　　The law also identified several agencies that have been given the mandate to conduct widespread online surveillance. Article 18 empowers the Information, Culture and Tourism Sector to "monitor (follow and inspect), diagnose and analyze the Internet-based information content" of individuals, legal entities and organizations.

　　Internet users will be prohibited from circulation untrue information related to the Lao government or the Lao people's revolutionary Party for the purposes of undermining peace, independence, sovereignty, unity, and national prosperity.

　　The decree also prohibits content which could be interpreted as an incitement to murder, social disorder, or acts of terrorism. Content that sullies Lao tradition and culture is pornographic in nature or is designed to diminish solidarity between ethnic groups or countries will also be prohibited. It will also be prohibited to publish classified or sensitive material online.

Despite the new prohibitions, the government is hopeful that the vast majority of lawful internet users will continue to embrace constructive and positive use of digital platforms.

6. The Law Protection Internet

The law generally protects privacy, including that of mail, telephone, and electronic correspondence, but the government reportedly continues to violate these legal protections when there is a perceived security threat. The law prohibits unlawful searches and seizures. While the law requires that police obtain search authorization from a prosecutor or a panel of judges, policedo not always obtain prior approval, especially in rural areas. Security laws allow the government to monitor individuals' movements and private communications, including via cell phones and e-mail.

On Article 19 gives the Public Security Sector the authority to "collect, check and analyze Internet-based information (disrupting) national stability and social security". It can also "conduct an investigation" into individuals and organizations suspected of breaching the law.

The government believes that this kind of Internet regulation is needed. While acknowledging the positive contributions of the Internet to the local e-conomy, Lao officials also warned that the medium can be used to cause panic in society. But the new law will obviously discourage citizen from using online forums to engage public officials and challenge public policies. It is hardly conducive to a free and open Internet. What Laos needs is a law that will encourage Internet commerce and online innovation; not something that will unfairly penalize critics, activists, and even ordinary Internet users.

7. Measures toward Violators

In Laos PDR，the measures toward violators includes Article 26 of Decree Information Management on the Internet of Laos，providing individuals，legal entity or organizations that violate this decree will be warned，educated，penalized，fined，and subjected to civil or criminal charges depending on the severity of the case.

Plaintiff may bring common law civil action for passing off or a civil action，May seek an injunction，damages for losses，May institute criminal case under Penal Code，Laos Merchandise Act，the Court can confiscate all goods and things.

8. Education Measures toward Violators

According Article 56 of Law on Telecommunication (Amended) No. 09/NA Vientiane Capital，Date 21 December，2011，Any individual，legal entity or organization that has slighting violated any provision of this law shall be educated in such instances as：

1. A service providers deny to fix technical failing if an installation，repair or other telecommunication services in a timely manner and failed to comply with technical standard；

2. Users avoid paying for their service charges on a regular basic and others.

• Civil Measures

Any individual，legal entity or organization Who has violated this law which caused damaged to the state，collective or other persons shall pay for such damages one's caused.

• Measure for applying penalties or crime law

Any person who has violated any provision to this law that is penal offences shall be penalized according to penal code.

Any person who has adjusted the radio frequency to other radio stations or use their telecommunication equipment or networks to interconnect to other networks to block, interfere, hack, destroy, change, delete, wire, tap, eavesdrop or detect information of others shall be imprisoned from three to six months and shall be fined from 500, 000 Kip up to 5,000,000 Kip.

In case of offences against paragraph two of this Article occurs repeatedly, or collectively offence, the offenders shall be imprisoned from one to three year and shall be fined from 1,000,000 up to 10,000,000 Kip.

老挝的网络服务

Phimchanthaphone Sinthavong[*]

余胜男　译

一、概述

与很多社会主义国家一样,老挝高度制约媒体以及信息通信技术的发展。90 年代初期,传真及卫星通信被禁止,亦无 IDD。近年随着政策松绑,私人及公共传真逐步投入使用,IDD 也受到广泛使用,卫星天线遍布全国,但访问外国报纸和期刊仍被禁止。老挝在 1997 年允许提供网络服务,当地网络服务供应商为 2008 年取得 3G 运营执照的 Lao Telecom 与 Unitel,以及于 2011 年取得营业执照的 ETL 和 Beeline。在 2012 年,服务供应商(ISP)则需通过竞争进入老挝市场。

老挝政府意识到网络对社会经济发展的益处,但担心信息传播不受控制及其对文化的侵害,因此对网络服务提供非常警惕。现在,老挝政府对社会稳定及文化保护的忧虑仍影响着网络监管。老挝政府建造了能够监测并限制访问内容的设施,但至 2012 年底仍未投入使用,因此不能有效控制网络访问。老挝总理办公厅要求网络服务提供者提交季度报告并进行联网以便监管,但执行效果十分有限。2013 年 7 月 4 日,老挝成立了首个专门打击网络犯罪的政府部门。在此过程中,老挝政府也出台了规制网络行为的法律。

---

[*] 老挝司法部外国法律研究中心主任。

二、老挝规制网络行为的法律体系

1.《老挝网络信息管理法案》

老挝政府签署了《老挝网络信息管理法案》以鼓励网络发展,但该法的多个条款均有削弱言论自由和其他公民权利的嫌疑。该法对网络犯罪的模糊广泛定义引起了民众担忧。当时该法案文本未公布,但一份非官方英文译本,能体现民众对新法对言论自由及民主制度可能造成的不良影响的合理担忧。该法严格限制网络使用者在线分享或散布信息,如下述第6条、第7条。

《老挝网络信息管理法案》第6条规定了通过网络散布信息的内涵。第7条规定,个人、法人及组织发布信息或允许他人散布前必须正确辨认来源,非经官媒或合法媒体发布的信息不能作为官方信息,且网站所有者或管理人允许他人散布信息前应全面检查信息。

第6条确认了个人交换数据的权利但第7条要求网页管理人"允许他人散布信息前应全面检查信息及其内容",这是不现实的。第7条还规定"没经过官方媒体或机构合法发布(证实)的信息,不能正式使用",是否意味着老挝人民只能分享国家准许的新闻报道?此外,禁止用户匿名注册,必然会打击公民通过网络曝光政府的错误的积极性。

除第6条、第7条,有可能损害言论自由及民主制度的条款还有第9条、第11条、第13条、第14条。

第9条规定使用网络信息的个人、法人或组织应经常保存并更改密码保护个人信息,且不为他人非法使用个人信息创造条件,并明确禁止发布或分享包含危害国家安全、社会稳定的内容的信息及评论。如果对政府的合法批评在公众间产生了分歧、误解或"混乱",可被解释为犯罪行为,政府可起诉记者、活动家或其他政府批评者。第11条、第13条规定网络服务提供者及网页管理人对违法使用者"终止接入"及"暂时或永久禁止进入",也需与调查机关"合作并提供信息"。同时,第14条禁止网络服务提供者帮助损害党及政府政策的个人、法人或组织。

此外,该法赋予了某些机构广泛监控的权力。第18条规定信息文化及旅游部对个人、法人及组织"监控(跟踪及调查),评价及分析网络信息内容"。该法禁止网络用户传播有可能损害老挝国家安全、社会稳定的信息,禁止线上发布分级或敏感内容。同时希望合法的网络用户可以继续建设性地、积极地使用数字平台。

再次，该法保护包括邮件、电话和电子通讯的隐私，禁止非法搜查及扣押，要求警察从检察官或法官处获得搜查许可。但同时，与国家安全相关的规定则允许政府监控个人包括通过手机和电子邮件进行的活动及私人通信。《老挝网络信息管理法案》第19条也规定公共安全部门可"收集、检查并分析（扰乱）国家稳定和社会安全的网络信息"，也可对有嫌疑的个人和机构"进行调查"。

最后，除上述规定以外，《老挝网络信息管理法案》第26条还规定，个人、法人或组织违反本法案，会被警告、教育、受刑罚、罚款并依据违法严重性受到民事或刑事控告。原告可提起民事诉讼，申请强制令、赔偿损失；也可依据《刑法》、《老挝商法》提起刑事诉讼，由法院没收所有货物及物品。

2.《电信法》

根据《电信法》（已修订）第56条，服务提供者不能及时解决技术失灵，及违反技术标准或用户不定期缴纳服务费用及其他行为应受批评教育。并规定了损害国家、集体或第三人利益，赔偿损失的民事措施及构成犯罪的应依据刑法受罚。

该法还针对把无线电频率调至其他基站或利用通信工具或网络连接到其他网络来阻止、干扰、攻击、破坏、更改、删除、偷听或窃取他人信息的行为，设置了具体的刑罚。

三、结论

老挝政府清楚地意识到网络对当地地经济的贡献，但也担心其会带来社会动乱，因此制订新法、修订旧法监控国内网络服务提供者及网络使用情况。但新法妨碍了市民在论坛抨击政府官员及政策的自由，不利于网络自由与开放。现阶段，笔者认为，老挝真正需要的是能鼓励电子商务和创新的法律，而不是惩罚抗议者甚至普通网络使用者的法律。

Cyber Laws in Malaysia

Charlie Ng Zheng Hui[*]

Abstract   Technology waits for no one including the law. Since the last decade, we have witnessed the rapid pace of development of the Internet driving changes in various every day activities including the way people do business. Today, almost every medium and large sized organization in the world has a web site. Given the nature of technology and the Internet, the lawwill continue to shift and change. This short essay examines the existing legal framework in Malaysia in protecting the interest of the stakeholders in the world of cyber.

A. INTRODUCTION

The definition or scope of "Cyber laws" has been generalised to a set of laws that deal with the utilisation of Internet as converging tools of information and communications technology ("ICT"). The term Cyber laws has been interchangeably used for other similar terms such as Internet law, information technology law, or ICT law for indicating the wide range scope of the terms.

Generally speaking, cyber laws in Malaysia can be divided into two distinctive categories as follow:

(1) Those legislation that address solely on specific issues related to the ICT tools and utilisations ("Category I");

---

* Legal Associate of Lee Sok Wah & Co.

(2) Those legislation that do not solely address on specific ICT aspects, but rather a general law but applicable, in part or in totality, to the cyberspace and online environment ("Category II").

The structure of cyber laws in Malaysia is described by Diagram 1 as below.

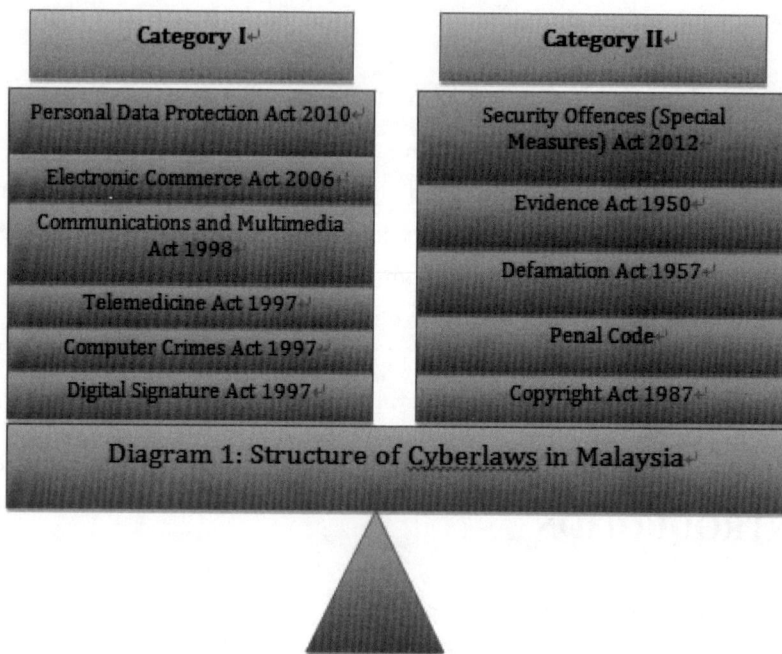

Category I	Category II
Personal Data Protection Act 2010	Security Offences (Special Measures) Act 2012
Electronic Commerce Act 2006	Evidence Act 1950
Communications and Multimedia Act 1998	Defamation Act 1957
Telemedicine Act 1997	Penal Code
Computer Crimes Act 1997	
Digital Signature Act 1997	Copyright Act 1987

Diagram 1: Structure of Cyberlaws in Malaysia

The first cyber laws of Malaysia relating to Category I were passed in 1997 and Malaysia has been hailed as one of the first ASEAN countries to have done so. Among the others, these include are the Digital Signature Act 1997 (Act 562), Computer Crimes Act 1997 (Act 563), Telemedicine Act 1997 (Act 564), the Communications and Multimedia Act 1998 (Act 588) and the Malaysian Communications and Multimedia Commission Act 1998 (Act 589). The rise of information and communication technologies has indeed not only revolutionized how people interact with each other but also force the Malaysia to operate in significantly altered business landscapes. Thus, there have been various amendments to current legislation to adapt to modern Internet situations, and new cyber laws have been passed, such as the Electronic Commerce Act 2006 (Act 658), Electronic Government Activities Act 2007 (Act 680) and the Personal Data Protection Act 2010 (Act 709).

On the other hand, the cyber laws of Malaysia relating to Category II are included but not limited to Copyright Act 1987 (Act 332), Penal Code (Act 574), Defamation Act 1957 (Act 286), Evidence Act 1950 (Act 56) and Security Offences (Special Measures) Act 2012 (Act 747).

It is important to note that the Malaysian Communications and Multimedia Commission (MCMC) has been established pursuant to the Malaysian Communications and Multimedia Commission Act 1998 as a regulator for the communications and multimedia industry in Malaysia, which include Internet.

B. BRIEF OVERVIEW OF CYBERLAWS IN MALAYSIA—CATEGORY I

1. Digital Signature Act 1997 (Act 562)

The Digital Signature Act 1997, enforced on the 1st of October 1998, is an enabling law that allows for the development of, amongst others, e-commerce by providing an avenue for secure on-line transactions through the use of digital signatures.

For the purpose of this Act, the digital signature does not refer specifically to a signature that is sent electronically, but rather to an asymmetric cryptosystem that is used when sending a message. This system uses a pair of "keys" held by the sender (known as the private key) and the receiver (known as the public key) of the message. When the sender uses his key to send his message, the message gets encrypted and only the person who has the corresponding key can decrypt it. To ensure the system is trustworthy, only a licensed Certification Authority is able to issue the keys recognized as being legally valid.

Thus, the Digital Signature Act is essentially a statute that provides for the licensing and regulation of the Certification Authorities, and the Commission that is responsible for administering the Act and ensuring that it is being complied with.

In addition，the Digital Signature Act makes a digital signature a legally valid signature as long as the basic requirements are met；that is，it used a digital signature that was certified by a licensed certification authority. In essence，a digital signature has the same effect in law as a person who had signed on a piece of paper.

2. Computer Crimes Act 1997（Act 563）

The Computer Crimes Act 1997，effective as of the 1st of June 2000，created several offences relating to the misuse of computers computer criminal activities such as unauthorised use of programmes，illegal transmission of data or messages over computers and hacking and cracking of computer systems and networks. Among others，it deals with unauthorised access to computer material，unauthorised access with intent to commit other offences and unauthorised modification of computer contents. It also makes provisions to facilitate investigations for the enforcement of the Act.

The punishment meted out for the above offenses differ according to the intent of the perpetrator's actions. In addition，a person who abets such an act receives the same punishment as the perpetrator while a person who attempts such an offense would only receive half of the maximum term provided for under the offence. Essentially，it makes it a crime for a person（or to help such a person）to access or attempt to access any computer in Malaysia without permission.

Interestingly，the Acthas extra-territoriality effect and applies to everyone，anywhere，and is regarded as if he had been present within Malaysia during the commission of the offence. So long as the person had committed such offenses，then his actions are deemed as if they had been committed in Malaysia even though he may not be physically in Malaysia.

3. Telemedicine Act 1997（Act 564）

The Telemedicine Act 1997 was enacted in March 1997，providing a framework to enable licensed medical practitioners to practice medicine using audio，visual and data communications. As at 30 November 2014，the Act has yet to be enforced.

Telemedicine can be described as providing healthcare through the means of technology，making distance not an issue. Under this Act，telemedicine can only be practiced by a "fully registered medical practitioner holding a valid practicing certificate". This would refer to any person who is fully registered under the Medical Act 1971 (Act 50) and is certified to practice medicine in Malaysia by the Malaysian Medical Council. In other words, a doctor who has the license to practice medicine in Malaysia.

The Act provides for other persons who may practice telemedicine, but such persons can only do so through a fully registered medical practitioner holding a valid practicing certificate. It can be stated that such persons can fall under two categories. The first would refer to a medical practitioner (that is, a doctor), who is registered or licensed outside of Malaysia. For a "foreign" doctor, he must first obtain a certificate to practice telemedicine as is issued by the Malaysian Medical Council.

The second category would be the other persons involved in providing healthcare, such as a provisionally registered medical practitioner, a registered medical assistant, a registered nurse, a registered midwife or any other person providing healthcare. They may only practice telemedicine in Malaysia. The Director General of Health (Malaysia) permits it in writing once he deems it suitable, after reviewing the application which had been made on their behalf by the fully registered medical practitioner holding a valid practicing certificate. Anyone who practices telemedicine in contravention of this Act, shall be guilty of an offence which is punishable to a fine not exceeding RM500,000 or to an imprisonment term not exceeding 5 years, or both.

One of the main weaknesses of the Telemedicine Act is that there are no provisions within it regarding liability of conducting telemedicine as it is more focused on regulating who may practice telemedicine.

The only other aspect of interest is that a patient must give informed consent, in writing, before telemedicine can be conducted on the patient. If this is not done, then the medical practitioner is guilty of an offence which is punishable by a fine not exceeding RM 100,000 or imprisonment not exceeding 2 years, or to both.

4. Communications and Multimedia Act 1998 (Act 588)

The Communications and Multimedia Act 1998 which came into effect on the 1st of April 1999, provides a regulatory framework to cater for the convergence of the telecommunications, broadcasting and computing industries, with the objective of, among others, making Malaysia a major global centre and hub for communications and multimedia information and content services.

The Act and its subsidiary legislation has extraterritorial application as it "shall apply to any person beyond the geographical limits of Malaysia and her territorial waters if such person—(a) is a licensee under this Act; or (b) provides relevant facilities or services under this Act in a place within Malaysia."

A licensee under the Act refers to a person who has a license for owning or providing network facilities, or for providing network services, or for providing application services. Here, "application services" would also include "content application services", that is, an application service that provides content. In essence, the Act covers the communications industry as the network facilities are the physical infrastructure needed to provide the network services (which uses e-lectromagnetic radiation) required by the application services to provide its service. In other words, this Act would apply to telecommunications providers (such as MAXIS, Digi), satellite television providers (such as Astro) and internet service providers (such as MAXIS, TM NET, Digi).

The Act has extra-territorial effect, as it applies to one who "provides relevant facilities or services under this Act in a place within Malaysia". There are two aspects to be considered here. First, "relevant facilities or services under this Act" had not been defined. If one is to follow the concept of the Act, however, it is assumed that such "facilities" and "services" would denote a network facilities provider, network service provider, applications service provider and content application services, as these categories are regulated under the Act.

Secondly, "in a place within Malaysia" has been defined broadly. It encompasses everything above and below the Malaysian boundaries, be it its geo-graphical boundaries or the territorial waters. As long as it is within the boundaries of Malaysia, it does not matter whether it is in the air, outer space, underwater or underground. Therefore, the Act can apply to a person outside of Malaysia as long as he provides services under this Act "in a place" within Malaysia. It does not matter if he is not physically within Malaysia; so long as the services he provides is enjoyed in Malaysia.

The interesting thing to note about this section is that it makes it an offence that can be committed both by the person making the such statements and the service provider. This section is applicable to anything, as long as it relates to "content", for example, websites, sms and email. This offence is punishable with a fine not exceeding RM50,000 or to an imprisonment term notexceeding 1 year, or both. In addition, the person shall also be liable for a further fine of RM1,000 for each day (or part of it) that the content is still available, after conviction.

Furthermore, the Act also covers fraudulent use of network facilities and network services. Essentially, it refers to situations whereby one either obtains the use of such network facilities or services without paying for it, or creates a system in order to obtain its use without having the proper authorization to do so. In short, "stealing". Such offences are punishable with a fine not exceeding RM300, 000 or an imprisonment term not exceeding 3 years, or both.

5. Electronic Commerce Act 2006 (Act 658) & Electronic Government Activities Act 2007 (Act 680)

The Electronic Commerce Act 2006 came into effect on the 19th October 2006, is to apply to any commercial transaction conducted through electronic means, and is generally dealing with electronic messages. The Electronic Government Activities Act 2007 is to convey legal recognition of electronic messages in dealings between the Government and the public. The statutes are dealt with together as its contents regarding the legal effect of an electronic message are strikingly similar.

It is not mandatory to "use, provide or accept" electronic messages, but it can be implied from his conduct that he had agreed to it. The legislation deals specifically with commercial transactions, and is thus focusing on the validity of an electronic message in certain scenarios, such as creating a contract, the requirement of "writing", "signature", "seal", "witness", validity of information contained in an electronic message, and so forth.

In addition, it clarifies the position as to when an email is deemed sent, and received: "an electronic message is deemed sent when it enters an information processing system outside the control of the originator." Thus, the position is similar to one posting a letter. This provision has been worded broadly, and a different position may be reached if the originator utilizes an internal server. In such a case, the message may only be deemed "sent" once it has been processed by

253

the internal server and sent out. In other words, as long as it is within the internal server system, it is not "outside the control" of the originator and the email cannot be deemed to have been sent. In most cases, this would not be an issue, but it would be in situations where the internal server malfunctions and has not sent the email out even though the originator has already "sent" it.

As for when an email is deemed received, two scenarios are provided for. If the person receiving the electronic messages has an email that he uses regularly, then it is deemed "received" once the system receives it. If the person does not have an email system that he checks regularly, then it is only deemed as being received once he is aware of it.

Regardless, please be noted that this Act shall not apply to the transactions or documents such as power of attorney, the creation of wills and codicils, the creation of trusts and negotiable instruments.

6. Personal Data Protection Act 2010 (Act 709)

The Personal Data Protection Act 2010 that was gazetted back in July 2010 has just recently come into force on15th November 2013. The main purpose of the Act is to regulate the processing of personal data of individuals (known as data subjects in the Act) involved in commercial by data users so as to provide protection to the individual's personal data, by upholding the rights and interests of such individuals.

The Act defines "personal data" as any information in respect of commercial transactions, which—

(a)is being processed wholly or partly by means of equipment operating automatically in response to instructions given for that purpose;

(b)is recorded with the intention that it should wholly or partly be processed by means of such equipment; or

(c)is recorded as part of a relevant filing system or with the intention that it should form part of a relevant filing system, that relates directly or indirectly to a data subject, who is identified or identifiable from that information or from that and other information in the possession of a data user, including any sensitive personal data and expression of opinion about the data subject.

This would thus include the obvious information such as name, email address, national identification registration number, mobile number etc. that is directly related to a data subject. It is interesting to note that any information as to the physical or mental health or condition of a data subject, his political opinions, his religious beliefs or other beliefs of a similar nature will also fall within the meaning of personal data.

The world "processing" has been defined as collecting, recording, holding or storing the personal data or carrying out any operation or set of operations on the personal data. Not to mention that this include the organization, adaptation, retrieval, consultation, alteration, combination, correction, erasure or destruction and even alignment of personal data.

Be mindful that the Act applies to any person who has control over or authorizes the processing of any personal data in respect of commercial transactions, e. g. outsourced processing. Data users are defined as a party who processes personal data either alone or jointly or in common with others or has control over or authorizes the processing of any personal data. The Personal Data Protection (Class of Data Users) Order 2013 (P. U. (A) 336) highlights that certain organisations are required to register as data users with Personal Data Protection Commissioner ("Commissioner"). These include:

- Banking and financial institutions
- Communications service providers
- Tourism and hospitality providers
- Insurers
- Real estate firms
- Education bodies
- Direct marketing organisations
- Transportation firms

C. BRIEF OVERVIEW OF CYBERLAWS IN MALAYSIA— CATEGORY II

1. Copyright Act 1987 (Act 332)

The Copyright Act 1987 came into force on the 1st of December 1987, to make unauthorised transmission of copyright works over the Internet an infringement of copyright. It is also an infringement of copyright to circumvent any effective technological measures aimed at restricting access to copyright works. These provisions are aimed at ensuring adequate protection of intellectual property rights for companies involved in content creation in the ICT and multimedia environment.

2. Penal Code (Act 574)

Penal Code stipulates criminal offence and therespective punishments in Malaysia. These offences apply in general circumstance as long as there is no exception to such generality. Some provisions of Penal Code do apply for online environment. These include the offences of fraud (e. g. for online fraud or fraud by email), impersonation, extortion, obscenity and pornography with commercial intent, as well as criminal defamation.

3. Defamation Act 1957 (Act 286)

The Act provides offences of libel and slander and other malicious falsehoods involved in content creation in the ICT and multimedia environment.

4. Evidence Act 1950 (Act 56)

The Evidence Act 1950 has been made some amendments so as to adapt to changing online environment. For instance, the provision of computer-generated documents that now can be used as original copy of a document provided that its integrity is duly proven.

5. Security Offences (Special Measures) Act 2012 (Act 747)

This piece of legislation seeks to prevent any act or conduct that may cause detriment to the security of the country or any part of it via online platform such as Facebook, Twitter , blogspot etc.

D. OTHER CYBERLAW INITIATIVES

Other than the above-mentioned laws, the stakeholders of the Internet industry have also taken a proactive approach by initiating regulations, codes and guidelines in the areas of ICT andelectronic commerce activities. These initiatives constitute another ground for establishing legal and regulatory framework for ICT developments and e-commerce in Malaysia. For instance, General Consumer Code of Practice for the Communications and Multimedia Malaysia issued under the MCMC to set service provider benchmarks for a wide range of issues ranging from advertising and representation of services charging and billing and privacy to the setting up of a complaints handling system.

Another important initiative is the Content Code Malaysia released by the Communications and Multimedia Content Forum (CMCF) of Malaysia as another industry body designated by the Communications and Multimedia Act 1998. This Content Code sets out the guidelines and procedures for good practice and standards of content disseminated to audiences by service providers in the communications and multimedia industry in Malaysia.

E. CONCLUSION

According to Helsinki-headquartered security solutions firm F-Securer's Threat Report H1 2014, the first half of 2014 saw a global increase in online attacks on various platforms and devices, and included a significant increase of cyber-attacks in Malaysia. [1]Eighty-one [81] percent of all threats detected in H1 2014 globally were found to be in Malaysia as well. These threats include Downadup/Conficker worms, redirect malware and the Sality virus.

Regardless of the above-mentioned fact, the current legislation of Malaysia is still able to cope with the arising cyber crimes so long as the cyber laws enforcement is being taken promptly.

---

[1] See more at: http://www. computerworld. com. my/resource/security/troubling-cyber-threat-growth-in-malaysia-f-secure-study/ # sthash. e0JtZ2tR. dpuf

马来西亚网络法

Charlie Ng Zheng Hui[*]

陈卿铨　译

摘要　过去十年见证了互联网的高速发展给人们日常活动(包括经商方式在内)带来的变化。目前,世界上几乎每个中等或大型的组织都有网站。考虑到技术和互联网的性质,这些和互联网相关的法律还将持续改变。这篇文章主要分析了当前马来西亚有关保护利益相关者在网络世界的利益的法律架构。

一、引言

"网络法"的定义被概括为:调整作为信息通信技术("ICT")融合工具的互联网的使用的一系列法律规范。"网络法"和其他类似术语如"互联网法"、"信息技术法"或"信息通信技术法"等可以相互替代使用。

一般而言,马来西亚网络法可分成以下两种不同的类型:

(1)仅调整与信息通信技术的工具及使用有关的具体问题的法律("类型Ⅰ");

(2)不仅调整信息通信技术的具体方面,而是可以全部或部分地适用于网络空间和在线环境的一般法("类型Ⅱ")。

---

[*]　马来西亚李素桦律师事务所法务助理。

二、马来西亚网络法简述之类型 I

1. 1997 年《数字签名法》(第 562 号法案)

1997 年《数字签名法》于 1998 年 10 月 1 日实施,它是一部授权法,除其他事项外,还考虑到了电子商务的发展,并通过使用数字签名以保障在线交易的安全。

在该法中,"数字签名"并不是具体指采用电子方式发送的签名,而是指采用非对称加密系统发送信息。该系统使用一串钥匙,由信息发送者持有的称为"私钥",由信息接收者持有的称为"公钥"。

2. 1997 年《预防计算机犯罪法》(第 563 号法案)

1997 年《预防计算机犯罪法》于 2000 年 6 月 1 日生效,规定了几项不当使用计算机的行为为犯罪行为,例如未经授权使用程序、使用计算机非法传输数据或信息以及黑客行为和破解计算机系统和网络。

根据行为人行为的目的,对上述犯罪行为适用不同的处罚。该法具有域外效力,并适用于任何地方的任何人。

3. 1997 年《远程医疗法》(第 564 号法案)

1997 年《远程医疗法》于 1997 年 3 月颁布,该法允许经过许可的执业医师通过音频、视频及数据交流从事医疗工作。

根据本法,远程医疗仅能由"经过充分注册的、持有有效证件的执业医师"开展。

4. 1998 年《通信和多媒体法》(第 588 号法案)

1998 年《通信和多媒体法》于 1999 年 4 月 1 日生效。该法规定了监管框架,以满足电信、广播和计算机行业融合发展的需要。其目标是使马来西亚成为全球通信和多媒体信息及内容服务的中心。

该法具有域外效力,因为它可适用于"在马来西亚境内的地方根据本法提供相关设施或者服务"的人。

5. 2006 年《电子商务法》（第 658 号法案）、2007 年《电子政府活动法》（第 680 号法案）

2006 年《电子商务法》于 2006 年 10 月 19 日生效。它适用于任何通过电子方式进行的商业交易，并广泛涉及电子信息。2007 年《电子政府活动法》在法律上承认了政府和公众之间的交易所使用的电子信息。

立法特别针对商业交易，关注特定情况下电子信息的有效性。此外，澄清了电子邮件发送和接收的情形："当电子信息进入信息处理系统、脱离信息发送者的控制时，视为已发送。"

6. 2010 年《个人信息保护法》（第 709 号法案）

2010 年《个人信息保护法》于 2010 年 7 月发布，2013 年 11 月 15 日生效。该法的主要目的在于规制对商业广告中包含的个人信息的处理，维护个人权利和利益，保护个人信息。

根据该法对个人信息的定义，个人信息包括姓名、电子邮件地址、身份证号码、手机号码、有关身体或精神健康、政治观点、宗教信仰的信息等等。

三、马来西亚网络法简述之类型 II

1. 1987 年《版权法》（第 332 号法案）

1987 年《版权法》于 1987 年 12 月 1 日生效，规定在互联网上未经授权传播版权作品的行为侵犯版权的行为。规避旨在限制访问版权作品的有效技术措施也属于侵权行为。这些规定旨在保护在信息通信技术和多媒体环境中参与创建内容的公司的知识产权。

2.《刑法典》（第 574 号法案）

《刑法典》中的某些条文适用于网上环境，规制包括诈骗（例如网上诈骗或使用电子邮件诈骗）、假冒、勒索、带有商业目的的淫秽物品以及刑事诽谤的犯罪行为。

3. 1957 年《诽谤法》（第 286 号法案）

该法规定了在信息通信技术和多媒体环境的内容创建中的书面和口头诽

谤以及其他恶意造假的违法行为。

4. 1950 年《证据法》(第 56 号法案)

为了适应不断变化的网上环境,1950 年《证据法》作了修改。例如,现在计算机生成的文件可作为原件使用,只要其完整性得到及时证明。

5. 2012 年《安全罪行(特别措施)法》(第 747 号法案)

该法试图防止任何通过在线平台(例如 Facebook,、Twitter、blogspot 等等)可能对国家安全或国家的任何部分造成损害的行为。

四、其他网络法倡议

除了上述法律,互联网产业的利益相关者也通过在信息通信技术和电子商务活动领域倡导规章、行为准则、指南,采取积极的措施。这些倡议构成了马来西亚信息通信技术发展和电子商务的另一个法律和监管框架的基础。

五、结论

F-ecure 公司《2014 年威胁报告 H1》指出,2014 年上半年,针对不同平台和设备的网上攻击在全球范围内增加,其中,针对马来西亚网络攻击也大量增长。在该报告中测出的 81% 的此类威胁在马来西亚均有发现。这些威胁包括了 Downadup/Conficker 蠕虫病毒、重导向恶意软件和 Sality 病毒。不论如何,只要马来西亚的网络法迅速实施,就足以应付出现的网络犯罪。

The Republic of the Union of Myanmar's Internal Law

Kay Thee Hlaing[*]

A. Introduction

The Republic of the Union of Myanmar is South-East Asian nation. It has friendly relations with all the nations in the region. It is also committed to regional peace and stability. All of the neghbouring countries have Cyber Law or Internet Law.

In Myanmar have Electronic Transaction Law and the Computer Science Development Law. Laws regulating the Internet include the Computer Science Development Law (1996), the wide Area Network Order (2002), and the Electronic Transactions Law (2004). These laws and associated regulations are broadly worded and open to arbitrary or selective interpretation and enforcement. The Electronic Transactions Law covers to any act detrimental. And specifically "receiving or sending and distributing any information relating to"—state security, law and order, community peace and tranquility, national solidarity, the national economy, or national culture. Violators face fines and prison terms of 7 to 15 years. The importing and use of a modem without official permission is banned, with penalties for violations of up to 15 years in prison.

---

[*] Additional Township Judge, the Tamwe Township Court, Myanmar.

B. The Internet in Myanmar

The Internet in Myanmar has been available since 2000 when the first Internet connections were established. Beginning in September 2011, the historically pervasive levels of Internet censorship in Myanmar were significantly reduced. Prior to September 2011 the military government worked aggressively to limit and control Internet access through software-based censorship, infrastructure and technical constraints, and laws and regulations with large fines and lengthy prison sentences for violators. At Bagan Cybertech, there are data communication operations and functions of projected e-Commerce and Internet. So far, ten private companies have already made arrangements to offer e-Shopping, e-Banking, e-Reservation, e-Media, e-Journal and e-Book services. Concerning the Internet, there are system programmes, rates, aims and services of the V-set networking system of the information communication technology park.

C. Telecommunication

Telecommunications is becoming one of the most dynamic sectors in Myanmar's gradual transition from military rule to democracy. In June 2013, the government granted two international telecommunications companies the opportunity to provide services and infrastructure alongside local firms. Besides creating jobs, the move drove much-needed legal reform. In October, the government passed a Telecommunications Law drafted with input from the international community. Under the new framework, Norway's Telenor Group established the country's first independent connection to the international internet in March 2014. Qatar's Ooredoo introduced mobile phone service in much of the country in August.

D. The Computer Science Development Law

The Computer Science Development Law enacted by the State Law and

Order Restoration Council in 1996.

1. Objectives

The Objectives of this Law are as follows :

(a) to contribute towards the emergence of a modern developed State through computer science;

(b) to lay down and implement measures necessary for the development and dissemination of computer science and technology;

(c) to create opportunities for the youth, especially students, to study computer science;

(d) to study computer science, which is developing internationally and to utilize the same in a manner which is most beneficial for the State;

(e) to cause extensively development in the use of computer science in the respective fields of work;

(f) to supervise the import and export of computer software or information.

2. Prior Sanction and Licence

The Ministry of Communications, Posts and Telegraphs Council may determine by notification the types of computer to be imported kept in possession or utilized only with the prior sanction.

Under Section-28, 29, 30,31 divided into:

—A person desirous of importing, keeping in possession or utilizing the type of computer prescribed in sub-section (a) of section 26 shall apply to the Ministry of Communications, Posts and Telegraphs in accordance with the stipulations to obtain prior sanction.

—A person desirous of setting Lip a computer network or connecting a link inside the computer network shall apply to the Ministry of Communications, Posts and Telegraphs in accordance with the stipulations to obtain prior sanction.

The Ministry of Communications, Posts and Telegraphs may, after scrutinizing the applications submitted under section 27 or section 28 in accordance with the stipulations, grant prior sanction or refuse to grant prior sanction.

A person desirous of keeping in possession or utilizing the type of computer prescribed under sub-section (a) of section 26, shall comply with the orders and directives issued from time to time by the Ministry of Communications, Posts and Telegraphs with respect to issuance of licence, prescribing the term of licence, licence fee and licence conditions.

E. The Electronic Transactions Law

The State Peace and Development Council enacts by Electronic Transactions Law in 2004.

1. Definition

(a) Information includes data, texts, images, sounds, codes, computer programmes, software and databases;

(b) Electronic record means a record generated, sent, received or stored by means of electronic, magnetic, optical or any other similar technologies in an information system or for transmission from one information system to another;

(c) Electronic data message means an information generated, sent, received or stored by means of electronic, optical or any other similar technologies, including electronic data interchange, fax, e-mail, telegraph, telex and telecopy;

(d) Computer means a device capable of receiving, transmitting, storing, processing or retrieving information and records, using arithmetic and logical means by manipulation of electronic, magnetic, optical or any other similar technologies;

(e) Computer network means the network system of the interconnection of computers through use of satellite or by any other technologies;

(f) Electronic signature means any symbol or mark arranged personally or on his behalf by electronic technology or any other similar technologies to verify the authenticity of the source of the electronic record and the absence of amendment or substitution;

(g) Certification authority means a person or an organization that has been granted a licence by the Control Board under this Law for services in respect of the electronic signature;

(h) Certificate means the certificate issued to a subscriber by the certification authority as an electronic data message or other record identifying the relation between the signer of an electronic signature and the electronic data message;

(i) Originator means a person by whom or on whose behalf the electronic record or electronic data message purports to have been created, generated or sent. This expression does not include a person acting as an intermediary with respect to electronic record or electronic data message;

(j) Addressee means a person who is intended by the originator to receive the electronic record or electronic data message. This expression does not include a person acting as an intermediary with respect to electronic record or electronic data message;

(k) Subscriber means a person who is by any technologies identified as an authentic signer of an electronic signature in the certificate;

(l) Central Body means the Central Body of Electronic Transactions formed under this Law;

(m) Ministry means the Ministry of Communications, Posts and Telegraphs;

(n) Control Board means the Electronic Transactions Control Board formed under this Law.

2. Aims

The aims of this Law are as follows:

(a) to support with electronic transactions technology in building a modern, developed nation;

(b) to obtain more opportunities for all-round development of sectors including human resources, economic, social and educational sector by electronic transactions technologies;

(c) to recognize the authenticity and integrity of electronic record and electronic data message and give legal protection thereof in matters of internal and external transactions, making use of computer network;

(d) to enable transmitting, receiving and storing local and foreign information simultaneously, making use of electronic transactions technologies;

(e) to enable communicating and co-operating effectively and speedily with international organizations, regional organizations, foreign countries, local and foreign government departments and organizations, private organizations and persons, making use of computer network.

3. Application

(a) The provisions contained in this Law shall apply to any kind of electronic record and electronic data message used in the context of commercial and non-commercial activities including domestic and international dealings, transactions, arrangements, agreements, contracts and exchanges and storage of information;

(b) This Law shall apply to any person who commits any offence actionable under this Law within the country or from inside of the country to outside of the country, or from outside of the country to inside of the country by making use of the electronic transactions technology.

The provisions contained in this Law shall not apply to the following matters:

(a) "Will" defined in sub-section (h) of section 2 of the Succession Act;

(b) "Negotiable instrument" defined in section 13 of the Negotiable Instruments Act;

(c) "Trust" defined in section 3 of the Trusts Act;

(d) "Power of Attorney" granted under the Powers of Attorney Act;

(e) Documents relating to title;

(f) Instruments prescribed in any existing law to be registered;

(g) Matters exempted by the Ministry by issuing notification, with the approval of the Government.

And then Myanmar is connected to the international internet via the SEA-ME-WE 3 submarine cable, and satellite and cross-border cable links with China and Thailand. China Unicom and MPT signed a Memorandum of Understanding in July 2013 to build a link from the SEA-ME-WE 5 cable through Mandalay and into China. Low bandwidth is largely responsible for the congestion experienced by local internet users, especially during peak afternoon hours.

The Posts and Telecommunications Department regulates Myanmar's telecommunications industry under the MCIT. Under the junta, the MCIT and intelligence agencies implemented arbitrary and ad hoc censorship decisions. Other state institutions tasked with information and communications technology (ICT) development and management are largely inactive. The Myanmar Computer Federation, formed under the 1996 Computer Science Development Law and comprised of industry professionals, is the designated focal point for coordination with the ITU. Critics say it failed to take advantage of the 2011 political change to play a more active role in the ICT sector.

F. The Telecommunications Law

The Telecommunications Law passed on October 12, 2013, providing a foundation for the privatization of the industry. In March 2014, the Norway-based Telenor Group established an independent connection to the international internet.

Until this year, the Ministry of Communications and Information Technology (MCIT) controlled the country's international connection to the internet through two main ISPs, the state-owned Myanmar Post Telecommunication (MPT), and the military-linked Yatanarpon Teleport (YTP). Redlink, SkyNet, and other FTTH providers operate under YTP.

In 2012, the government announced plans to liberalize its telecom sector and invite foreign investment. In June 2013, the government awarded international licenses to Norway's Telenor and Qatar's Ooredoo, allowing them to offer services and infrastructure alongside local firms. The tender and selection processes were widely applauded as fair and transparent. After the Telecommunications Law was enacted in October 2013, operator licenses for the two companies followed in January 2014. Both subcontracted other international companies to build infrastructure. MPT also plans to cooperate with Telenor, Ooredoo, and other operators to expand the telecoms network and build over 80,000 transmission towers across the country.

To compete with Telenor and Ooredoo, MCIT officials said MPT would transform from a state-owned to a public firm. Local news reports said MPT invited Orange and Vodafone, two leading telecommunication companies that did not win the operating licenses, to enter into a private partnership.

YTP, now 49 percent private-owned, began transforming into a public company in 2012, though the process has been opaque. The other 51 percent remains government-controlled. On January 30, 2014, the government granted YTP a telecommunications license, making it the fourth service provider after state-owned MPT, Telenor and Ooredoo.

On 8 October 2013 a new Telecommunications Law was issued in Myanmar, which revokes the previous Myanmar Telegraph Act (1885) and the Myanmar Wireless Telegraphy Act (1934). The new Law outlines the duties and rights of telecommunications service providers who are licensed under the Law, as well as how the Ministry (the Union Ministry of Communications and Information Technology) and the Regulator (the Department of Posts and Telecommunications) will work together in facilitating the development and regulation of the telecommunications services sector.

As one of the last untapped telecommunications markets in the world, the opening of Myanmar's telecommunications market has attracted the attention of many foreign investors. On June 27, the Ministry of Communications and Information Technology ("MCIT") announced that Norway's Telenor and Qatar's Ooredoo (also known as Qatar Telecom or Q-Tel) had been awarded licenses to build Myanmar's telecommunications network and run a nationwide wireless network in Myanmar for 15 years.

The Telecom Law provides that any local or foreign person, department, or individual who desires to possess or use any telecommunications equipment will require a telecommunications equipment license. It appears that these exceptions are targeted at the private use of telecommunications equipment such as mobile phones and the use of telecommunications equipment by contractors who are building the telecommunications network.

G. Conclusion

The objectives of the Computer Science Development Law are to define and implement measures necessary for the development and dissemination of computer science and technology and to supervise the import and export of computer software or information.

This Commentary summarizes the key provisions of the Telecom Law that may interest prospective foreign investors. And it also summarizes the Computer Science Development Law, and the Electronic Transactions Law.

Myanmar is a signatory to the e-ASEAN agreement. It will have to work with might and main for progress of computer technology. It has founded the Myanmar Computer Technology Development Council and is promoting the computer science stage by stage to the best of its capacity.

缅甸联邦共和国网络法

Kay Thee Hlaing[*]

陈卿铨　译

一、引言

缅甸的网络法主要有《计算机科学发展法》、《电子交易法》、《广域网令》和《电信法》等。但是,这些法律法规用词宽泛,可能会被任意或选择性地加以解释和执行。例如,《电子交易法》涵盖任何有害行为,特别是"接收或发送、散布任何有关"国家安全、法律和秩序、社会和平与安宁、民族团结、国民经济、民族文化等信息的行为。违者将面临罚金和 7 到 15 年刑期。禁止进口或使用未经官方许可的调制解调器,违者将面临高达 15 年的刑期。

二、缅甸互联网和电信

自 2000 年以来,缅甸第一次建立了互联网连接。2011 年 9 月开始,历史性的大规模互联网审查制度大大减少。2011 年 9 月之前,军政府通过基于软件的审查制度、基础设施以及技术限制等严格控制互联网接入。同时,法律法规对违法者设置了巨额罚款和漫长的刑期。八甘网络技术公司拥有数据通信业务和开展电子商务和互联网的职能。到目前为止,有十家私营公司已经计划提供电子购物、电子银行、电子预定、电子媒体、电子杂志和电子书服务。

在缅甸由军事统治向民主转变过程中,电信成为最有活力的部门之一。在 2013 年 6 月,政府准许两家国际电信公司和当地公司一起提供服务和建设

---

[*]　缅甸塔姆威法院法官。

基础设施。除创造工作之外，该举动推动了法制改革。2013年10月，政府通过了国际社会协助起草的《电信法》。在新框架下，挪威电信集团在2014年3月建立了缅甸第一次独立的互联网连接。2014年8月，卡塔尔电信公司Ooredoo在缅甸大部分地区引进移动电话服务。

三、缅甸网络法简述

（一）《计算机科学发展法》

《计算机科学发展法》由国家法律与秩序恢复委员会于1996年颁布。

1. 目标

该法目标如下：通过计算机科学使缅甸成为现代发达国家；（2）为计算机科技的发展和传播规定和实施必要措施；（3）为年轻人（特别是学生）学习计算机科学创造机会；（4）研究计算机科学，并以最有利于本国的方式使用计算机；（5）使用计算机科学促进各领域工作的广泛发展；（6）监督计算机软件或信息的进出口。

2. 事先批准和许可证

电信部、邮电委员会有权发布通知决定进口计算机的类型，此类计算机经事先批准才可持有或使用。

根据第28条至第31条的规定：（1）进口、持有或使用第26条（a）款规定的计算机的，应当按照规定向电信部、邮电委员会申请，以获得事先批准；（2）设立计算机网络或者在计算机网络内部建立连接的，应当按照规定向电信部、邮电委员会申请，以获得事先批准；（3）电信部、邮电委员会审查依照第27或第28条规定提交的申请书之后，给予或拒绝事先批准；（4）持有或使用第26条（a）款规定的计算机的，应当遵守电信部、邮电委员会发布的有关颁发许可证、许可证期限、许可证费用以及许可证条件的命令和指令。

（二）《电子交易法》

国家和平和发展委员会于2004年颁布了《电子交易法》。

1. 定义

该法对"信息"、"电子记录"、"电子数据"、"计算机"、"计算机网络"等术语进行了界定。

2. 目标

该法的目标主要有:(1)用电子交易技术支持缅甸建设现代化发达国家;(2)通过电子交易技术全面发展各部门;(3)给予使用计算机网络在国内和涉外交易法律保护;(4)使用电子交易技术,实现同时传输、接收、存储本地和国外的信息;(5)使用计算机网络,实现和国际组织、区域组织、外国、当地和外国政府部门和组织、民间组织和个人迅速有效的交流和合作。

3. 适用

该法适用于:

(1)在商业和非商业活动中使用的任何种类的电子记录和电子数据信息,包括国内和国际交易、安排、协议、合同和信息交换和存储。

(2)在国内或者从国内到国外,或者从国外到国内的任何利用电子交易技术做出可被起诉的违法行为的人。

但是,该法不适用于某些法定的事项,例如"遗嘱"、"可转让票据"、"信托"等。

(三)《电信法》

《电信法》于 2013 年 10 月 12 日通过,为电信业私有化奠定基础。在2014 年 3 月,挪威电信集团建立了一条通向国际互联网的独立连接。

直到今年,通信和信息技术部通过两大主要互联网服务提供商——缅甸国有通信公司(MPT)和与军方有关联的雅达娜蓬电信公司(YTP)——控制着全国国际互联网连接。

2012 年,政府宣布计划放宽电信部门限制,邀请外国投资。2013 年 6 月,政府授予挪威电信公司和卡塔尔 Ooredoo 公司国际许可,允许它们和当地公司一起提供服务和基础设施。2013 年《电信法》颁布后,经营者执照于 2014年发给了这两家公司。两公司均将基础设施建设业务转包给其他跨国公司。

缅甸电信市场的开放吸引了众多外国投资者的关注。《电信法》规定任何当地或外国的企业或个人持有或使用任何电信设备的,均需电信设备许可证。

四、结论

本文简要总结了《计算机科学发展法》、《电子交易法》、《电信法》的主要规定。潜在的外国投资者可能对这些法律抱有兴趣。另外,值得一提的是,缅甸是《电子东盟协议》的签字国,缅甸将尽全力发展本国的计算机技术;而且,缅甸目前已设立计算机技术发展委员会,并尽其所能逐步促进计算机科学的发展。

The Virtual World: the Philippine Experience

Everlene O. Lee[*]

Abstract　With the advent of modern technology and the more adept people are in using the world wide web, there is a need to put into place laws, rules and regulations to ensure the protection of netizens, to prevent the commission of crimes in cyber space and to provide a mode of redress for those whose rights have been violated. In the Philippines, two main laws regulate cyber space—the E-Commerce Act and the Cybercrime Prevention Act of 2012. Under the E-Commerce Act, the acts of hacking or cracking, introduction of computer viruses and piracy are considered criminal acts. The Cybercrime Prevention Act of 2012, on the other hand defined certain acts, when committed using the internet or through similar means to be criminal acts. These are categorized into three main areas: Offenses again the confidentiality, integrity and availability of computer data and systems; Computer-related offenses; and Content-related offenses. Aiding or abetting and attempt in the commission of cybercrime are also punishable acts under the Cybercrime Prevention Act of 2012.

A. Introduction

The development in our technology have changed the way people live their lives. In the last ten to fifteen years, what we had only thought possible

---

＊　Senior Associate, Angara Abello Concepcion Regala & Cruz Law Offices.

in movies like "James Bond 007" or "Mission Impossible" have become possible—watches that act like telephones, video conferencing, talking cars, etc.

Today, people actually live and operate in two worlds—a physical world and a virtual world. In fact, many of our daily activities involve the virtual world—from the way we conduct our business, communicate with others, socialize and shop. Today, business correspondences are just one press of the "send button"; contracts can be signed by parties thousands of miles apart; fund transfers and payments are similarly just a "click" away. Facebook, Twitter, Instagram keep friends (and enemies) updated on each others lives. Information, is literally, at the tips of our fingers.

However, just as this virtual plane provides us so many conveniences, there are also many dangers that lurk around this virtual playgrounds. As the development in technology speed through the information highway, current laws become obsolete as it fails to address the problems presented in the virtual plane. Cyber space presents problems which are not encountered in the physical environment or magnifies them to an extent current laws are unable to address. These problems include, among others, cyber bullying[①] through the use of social media, invasions of privacy, identity theft and destruction of property through the propagation of malwares and viruses. The problem is magnified due to the fact that "the online medium is borderless, hard to control and police. Law enforcement in such an environment poses

---

① Cyber Bullying refers to any severe or repeated use by one or more students of electronic expresions (or any bullying done through the use of technology or any electronic means) directed at another student that has the effect of actually causing or placing the latter in reasonable fear of physical or emotion harm or damage to his property; creating a hostile environment at school for the other student; infringing on the rights of the other student at school; or materially and substantially disrupting the education process. (Republic Acxt No. 10627, otherwise known as the "Anti-Bullying Act of 2013").

steep challenges not only to resources, but to personnel and equipment as well. "[①]

B. A World Without Laws

"Natura dedit omnia omnibus, that Nature hath given all things to all men; insomuch, that jus and utile, right and profit, is the same thing. But that right of all men to all things, is in effect no better than if no man had right to any thing. For there is little use and benefit of the right a man hath, when another as strong, or stronger than himself, hath right to the same"[②]

~Thomas Hobbes, 1640

Laws exist to ensure order in society. Without laws, anarchy would rule and people will not feel safe in their lives and property. Laws are necessary to "prevent violence and rapine, than to punish the same when it is committed; and all violence proceeded from controversies that arise between men concerning meum and tuum, right and wrong, good and bad, and the like, which men use every one to measure by their own judgments. "[③] Thus the government has the responsibility to set forth these laws, and "make known the common measure by which every man is to know what is his, and what another's, what is good and what is bad; and what he ought to do, and what not; and to command the same to be observed". [④]

However, in the early days of "cyber space" or the "virtual world", there were no rules to speak of or to follow, no sovereign nor government to state the law that will rule the conduct of men in the virtual world. It is each man for himself, to determine if his actions are right or wrong. No standard

---

① Hofilena, Chay F. "Libel in the Age of Like", 24 February 2014. http://www.rappler.com/thought-leaders/51184-cybercrime-libel-age-like, last accessed 10 December 2014.

② Hobbes Thomas, "The Elements of Law Natural and Politic", 1640.

③ Hobbes Thomas, "The Elements of Law Natural and Politic", 1640.

④ Hobbes Thomas, "The Elements of Law Natural and Politic", 1640.

to measure when the exercise of a right is a breach of another, and in case of breach, there is no recourse or means to obtain justice for the violation.

Many would recall that on 4 May 2000, a computer worm virus called the "I LOVE YOU" virus was released, attacking millions of Windows personal computers worldwide. It was spread through the corporate email systems and further propagated through the mailing lists of its source targets. [1] The malicious virus was touted as one of the world's most destructive computer-related disasters affecting over 45 million computers worldwide. [2] It affected both public and private sectors around the world including commercial and financial hubs like Hong Kong, Europe, and the United States. The outbreak was estimated to have caused US $ 5. 5 to 8. 7 billion in damages worldwide and another US $ 15 billion to remove the worm. [3]

Based on investigation conducted by Philippine internet service provider, Sky Internet and the Philippines National Bureau of Investigation (the "NBI"), it was discovered that the virus, which caused massive damage globally, was the creation of a young Filipino computer programmer, Onel de Guzman. [4] Unfortunately, at the time the virus was released by De Guzman, there was yet no law criminalizing the act of creating and propagating computer virus causing damage to others. Investigators thus tried to charge De Guzman with traditional crimes such as theft and violation of the Access Device Regulation Act[5], a law covering credit card fraud[6].

---

[1]   http://en. m. wikipedia. org/wiki/ILOVEYOU. Last accessed 9 December 2014.

[2]   Weinberger Sharon, "Top Ten Most-Destructive Computer Viruses", 19 March 2012. http://www. smithsonianmag. com/science-nature/top-ten-most-destructive—computer viruses.

[3]   http://en. m. wikipedia. org/wiki/ILOVEYOU. Last accessed 9 December 2014.

[4]   http://en. m. wikipedia. org/wiki/ILOVEYOU. Last accessed 9 December 2014.

[5]   Republic Act No. 8484, An Act Regulating the Issuance and Use of Access Devices, Prohibiting Fraudulent Acts Committed Relative Thereto, Providing Penalties and for Other Purposes, 11 February 1998.

[6]   "Charges Dropped in 'Love Bug' Virus Case", http://abcnews. go. com/Technology/sotry? id-119536&page=1.

However, the Department of Justice dismissed these charges on the ground that the same either did not apply to computer hacking, or there was insufficient evidence to back up the crime charged. [①] This applies the basic principle in Philippine criminal law of the legal maxim "*nullum crimen, nulla poena sine lege*" which translates to "there is no crime if there is no penal law punishing it". Thus, an "act or omission is punishable only if there is a law prohibiting the performance of the act or a law that commands a person to do an act but he failed to perform"[②].

The "I LOVE YOU" virus was considered as the first socially engineered computer virus. [③]

C. Philippine Internet and Cybercrime Laws

1. The E-Commerce Act

More than a month after the "I LOVE YOU" virus incident, or on 14 June 2000, the Philippines passed into law Republic Act No. 8792, otherwise known as the "Electronic Commerce Act of 2000" (the "E-Commerce Act").

The objective of the law was to facilitate domestic and international dealings, transactions, arrangements, agreements, contracts and exchanges and storage of information through the utilization of electronic, optical and similar medium, mode, instrumentality and technology to recognize the authenticity and reliability of electronic documents related to such activities and to promote the universal use of electronic transactions in the government

---

① "Charges Dropped in 'Love Bug' Virus Case", http://abcnews. go. com/Technology/sotry? id-119536&page=1.

② "Criminal Law in the Philippines", The Round Table, 26 December 2009. http://attheroundtable. wordpress. com/2009/12/26/criminal-law-in-the-philippines/ Last accessed 12 December 2014.

③ Weinberger Sharon, "Top Ten Most-Destructive Computer Viruses", 19 March 2012. http://www. smithsonianmag. com/science-nature/top-ten-most-destructive—computer viruses.

and the general public. [1] It applies to any kind of data message and electronic document used in the context of commercial and non-commercial activities to include domestic and international dealings, transactions, arrangements, agreements, contracts and exchanges of storage of information. [2] The law recognized the validity of electronic transactions and contracts, provided it complies with certain formalities. [3] It also recognized the admissibility of electronic data messages or electronic documents as evidence. [4]

The law also provided for penalties for certain acts, which included the act of introducing computer viruses such as those made by De Guzman through the "I LOVE YOU" virus. These acts are:

a. Hacking or cracking which refers to unauthorized access into or interference in a computer system/server or information and communication system, or any access in order to corrupt, alter, steal, or destroy using a computer or other similar information and communication devices, without the knowledge and consent of the owner of the computer or information and communication system, including the introduction of computer viruses and the like, resulting in the corruption, destruction, alteration, theft or loss of electronic data messages or electronic document shall be punished by a minimum fine of one hundred thousand pesos (P100,000) and a maximum commensurate to the damage incurred and a mandatory imprisonment of six (6) months to three (3) years;

b. Piracy or the unauthorized copying, reproduction, dissemination, distribution, importation, use, removal, alteration, substitution, modification, storage, unloading, downloading, communication, making available to the public, or broadcasting of protected material, electronic signature or copyrighted works including legally protected sound recordings or phonograms or information material on protected works, through the use of telecommunication networks, such as, but not limited to, the internet, in a

---

[1] Section 3, E-Commerce Act.
[2] Section 4, E-Commerce Act.
[3] Section 16, E-Commerce Act.
[4] Section 12, E-Commerce Act.

maner that infringes intellectual property rights shall be punished by a minimum fine of One hundred thousand pesos (P100,000) and a maximum commensurate to the damage incurred and a mandatory imprisonment of six (6) months to three (3) years;

c. Violations of the Consumer Act, or Republic Act No. 7394 and other relevant or pertinent laws through transactions covered by or using electronic data messages or electronic documents, shall be penalized with the same penalties as provided in those laws;

d. Other violations of the provisions of the E-Commerce Act shall be penalized with a maximum penalty of one million pesos (P1,000,000) or six (6) years imprisonment. [①]

2. The Cybercrime Prevention Act of 2012

More than a decade after the passing of the E-Commerce Act, and the further development of various technologies that uses the internet such as mobile phones, tablets, phablets and wearable technology, people have become more attuned to using the internet than they were ten years ago. A major controversy which rocked thePhilippine public was the uploading in cyber space of sex videos involving several celebrity personalities, evoking outrage. The need therefore for more stringent laws to address the growing concerns for cybercrime prevention becomes urgent. Thus, on 12 September 2012, Republic Act No. 10175, "An Act Defining Cybercrime, Providing for the Prevention, Investigation, Suppression and the Imposition of Penalties Therefore and for Other Purposes", otherwise known as the "Anti Cybercrime Prevention Act of 2012" was passed into law.

Under the Cybercrime Prevention Act of 2012, it is the declared policy of the law that the State recognizes the vital role of information and communications industries such as content production, telecommunications, broadcasting electronic commerce, and data processing, in the nation's overall social and economic development, however, with such advancements in information technology, the State realized the importance of providing an

---

① Section 33, E-Commerce Act.

environment conducive to the development, acceleration, and rational application and exploitation of information and communications technology (ICT) to attain free, easy, and intelligible access to exchange and/or delivery of information; and the need to protect and safeguard the integrity of computer, computer and communications systems, networks, and databases, and the confidentiality, integrity, and availability of information and data stored therein, from all forms of misuse, abuse, and illegal access by making punishable under the law such conduct or conducts. [1] It is in this light that the Philippine lawmakers passed the Cybercrime Prevention Act of 2012, to adopt sufficient powers to effectively prevent and combat such offenses by facilitating their detection, investigation, and prosecution at both the domestic and international level. [2]

The Cybercrime Prevention Act of 2012 identified three general areas of cybercrime offenses: [3]

1. Offenses against the confidentiality, integrity and availability of computer data and systems.

Under this category, the following acts are punishable:

(1) Illegal Access. —The access to the whole or any part of a computer system without right.

(2) Illegal Interception. —The interception made by technical means without right of any non-public transmission of computer data to, from, or within a computer system including electromagnetic emissions from a computer system carrying such computer data.

(3) Data Interference. —The intentional or reckless alteration, damaging, deletion or deterioration of computer data, electronic document, or electronic data message, without right, including the introduction or transmission of viruses.

(4) System Interference. —The intentional alteration or reckless

---

① Section 2, Cybercrime Prevention Act of 2012.

② Section 2, Cybercrime Prevention Act of 2012.

③ Section 4, Cybercrime Prevention Act of 2012.

hindering or interference with the functioning of a computer or computer network by inputting, transmitting, damaging, deleting, deteriorating, altering or suppressing computer data or program, electronic document, or electronic data message, without right or authority, including the introduction or transmission of viruses.

(5)Misuse of Devices—

①The use, production, sale, procurement, importation, distribution, or otherwise making available, without right, of:

a. A device, including a computer program, designed or adapted primarily for the purpose of committing any of the offenses under this Act; or

b. A computer password, access code, or similar data by which the whole or any part of a computer system is capable of being accessed with intent that it be used for the purpose of committing any of the offenses under Cybercrime Prevention Act of 2012.

②The possession of an item referred to in paragraphs 5(i)(aa) or (bb) above with intent to use said devices for the purpose of committing any of the offenses under this section.

(6) Cyber-squatting. —The acquisition of a domain name over the internet in bad faith to profit, mislead, destroy reputation, and deprive others from registering the same, if such a domain name is:

(1)Similar, identical, or confusingly similar to an existing trademark registered with the appropriate government agency at the time of the domain name registration;

(2)Identical or in any way similar with the name of a person other than the registrant, in case of a personal name;

(3)Acquired without right or with intellectual property interests in it.

2. Computer-related Offenses, which includes:

(1) Computer-related Forgery. —The input, alteration, or deletion of any computer data without right resulting in inauthentic data with the intent that it be considered or acted upon for legal purposes as if it were authentic, regardless whether or not the data is directly readable and intelligible; or

The act of knowingly using computer data which is the product of computer-related forgery as defined herein, for the purpose of perpetuating a fraudulent or dishonest design.

(2)Computer-related Fraud. —The unauthorized input, alteration, or deletion of computer data or program or interference in the functioning of a computer system, causing damage thereby with fraudulent intent.

(3)Computer-related Identity Theft. —The intentional acquisition, use, misuse, transfer, possession, alteration or deletion of identifying information belonging to another, whether natural or juridical, without right.

3. Content-related Offenses:

(1) Cybersex. —The willful engagement, maintenance, control, or operation, directly or indirectly, of any lascivious exhibition of sexual organs or sexual activity, with the aid of a computer system, for favor or consideration.

(2)Child Pornography. —The unlawful or prohibited acts defined and punishable by Republic Act No. 9775 or the Anti-Child Pornography Act of 2009, committed through a computer system.

(3) Unsolicited Commercial Communications. —The transmission of commercial electronic communication with the use of computer system which seek to advertise, sell, or offer for sale products and services are prohibited unless:

a. There is prior affirmative consent from the recipient;

b. The primary intent of the communication is for service and/or administrative announcements from the sender to its existing users, subscribers or customers;

c. The following conditions are present:

. The commercial electronic communication contains a simple, valid, and reliable way for the recipient to reject. receipt of further commercial electronic messages (opt-out) from the same source;

. The commercial electronic communication does not purposely disguise the source of the electronic message;

. The commercial electronic communication does not purposely include misleading information in any part of the message in order to induce the recipients to read the message.

It is worth mentioning at this juncture that the Philippine Supreme Court declared this provision on Unsolicited Commercial Communications as unconstitutional. Further details on this will be discussed later.

(4) Libel. —The unlawful or prohibited acts of libel as defined in Article 355[1] of the Revised Penal Code, as amended, committed through a computer system or any other similar means which may be devised in the future.

In addition to the above three main categories of cybercrime offenses, the law also identified the following as constituting an offense under the Cybercrime Prevention Act of 2012:

a. Aiding or Abetting in the Commission of Cybercrime—Any person who willfully abets or aids in the commission of any of the offenses enumeratedunder the Cybercrime Prevention Act of 2012 shall be held liable. [2]

b. Attempt in the Commission of Cybercrime—Any person who willfully attempts to commit any of the offenses enumerated inthe Cybercrime Prevention Act of 2012 shall be held liable. [3]

c. All crimes defined and penalized by the Revised Penal Code of the Philippines, as amended, and special laws, if committed by, through and with the use of information and communications technologies shall be covered by the relevant provisions of the Cybercrime Prevention Act of 2012. [4]

It must be noted that a prosecution under the Cybercrime Prevention

---

[1] Revised Penal Code Article 355 "Libel by writings or similar means—A libel committed by means of writing, printing, lithography, engraving, radio, phonograph, painting, theatrical exhibition, cinematographic exhibition, or any similar means, shall be punished by prison correctional in its minimum and medium periods or a fine ranging from 200 to 6,000 pesos, or both, in addition to the civil action which may be brought by the offended party. "

[2] Section 5(a), Cybercrime Prevention Act of 2012.

[3] Section 5(b), Cybercrime Prevention Act of 2012.

[4] Section 6, Cybercrime Prevention Act of 2012.

Act of 2012 shall be without prejudice to any liability which an accused may incur for violation of any provision of the Revised Penal Code, as amended, or special laws. [1]

Other notable provisions of the Cybercrime Prevention Act of 2012 is the provision on "Real-time Collection of Traffic Data[2]", where law enforcement authorities, with "due cause", are authorized to collect or record by technical or electronic means traffic data in real-time associated with specified communications transmitted by means of a computer system. However, it must be noted that the real-time collection only refers to "Traffic Data", all other data to be collected or seized or disclosed will require a court warrant. [3] This provision was later struck down by the Philippine Supreme Court for being unconstitutional, a discussion on the constitutional challenge against the Cybercrime Prevention Act of 2012 is discussed in the latter part of this paper.

Another notable provision, which was laterstruck down as unconstitutional by the Philippine Supreme court was the provision on "Restricting or Blocking Access to Computer Data". Under this provision, when a computer data is prima facie found to be in violation of the provisions of the Cybercrime Prevention Act of 2012, the Department of Justice (the "DOJ") shall issue an order to restrict or block access to such computer data. [4]

The Regional Trial Court shall have jurisdiction over violations of the provisions of the Cybercrime Prevention Act of 2012, including any violation committed by a Philippine national regardless of the place of commission. Jurisdiction shall lie if any of the elements was committed within the Philippines or committed with the use of any computer system wholly or partly situated in the country, or when by such commission any damage is caused to a natural or juridical person who, at the time the offense was com-

---

[1]   Section 7, Cybercrime Prevention Act of 2012.

[2]   Traffic data refer only to the commication's origin, destination, route, time, date, size, duration, or type of underlying service, but not content nor identities.

[3]   Section 12, Cybercrime Prevention Act of 2012.

[4]   Section 19, Cybercrime Prevention Act of 2012.

mitted, was in the Philippines. ①

The law also provided for international cooperation where all relevant international instruments on international cooperation in criminal matters, arrangements agreed on the basis of uniform or reciprocal legislation, and domestic laws, to the widest extent possible for the purposes of investigations or proceedings concerning criminal offenses related to computer systems and data, or for the collection of evidence in electronic form of a criminal, offense shall be given full force and effect. ② The law created an Office of Cybercrime within the DOJ which was designated as the central authority in all matters related to international mutual assistance and extradition. ③

D. The Constitutional Challenge Against the Cybercrime Prevention Act of 2012

Immediately upon the passage of the Cybercrime Prevention Act of 2012, fifteen (15) petitions were filed before the Philippine Supreme Court to declare the same unconstitutional. On 9 October 2012, the Supreme Court issued a 120-day temporaryrestraining order ("TRO") to enjoin the government from implementing the cybercrime law. This 120-day TRO was later on extended indefinitely until the final adjudication of the case.

The petitioners challenge the constitutionality of the Cybercrime Prevention Act of 2012 claiming that the means adopted by the cybercrime law for regulating undesirable cyberspace activities violate certain of their

---

① Section 21, Cybercrime Prevention Act of 2012.
② Section 22, Cybercrime Prevention Act of 2012.
③ Section 23, Cybercrime Prevention Act of 2012.

constitutional rights. [1]

The following provision of the Cybercrime Prevention Act of 2012 were challenged by the petitioners:

1. Illegal Access;

2. Data Interference;

3. Cyber-squatting;

4. Identity Theft;

5. Cybersex;

6. Child Pornography;

7. Unsolicited Commercial Communications;

8. Libel;

9. Aiding or Abetting and Attempt in the Commission of Cybercrimes;

10. Penalty of One Degree Higher;

11. Prosectuion under both the Revised Penal Code and the Cybercrime Prevention Act of 2012;

12. Penalties;

13. Realt-time Collection of Traffic Data;

---

[1]   Jose JesusM. Disini, Jr. et al. Vs. The Secretary of Justice, et al. G. R. No. 203335, Louis "Barok" C. Biraogo vs. National Bureau of Investigation, et al. G. R. No. 203299, Alab ng Mamamahayag (ALAM), et al. vs. Office of the President, et al. G. R. No. 203306, Senator Teofisto DL Guingona III vs. Executive Secretary, et al., G. R. No. 203359, Alexander Adonis, et al. Vs. The Executive Secretary, et al., G. R. No. 203378, Hon. Raymond V. Palatino, et al. vs. Paquito N. Ochoa, Jr., et al., G. R. No. 203391, Bagong Alyansang Makabayan Secretary General Renato M. Reyes, Jr., et al. vs. Benigno Simeon C. Aquino III, et al. G. R No 203407, Melencio S. Sta. Maria, et al. vs. Honorable Paquito Ocoha, et al., G. R. No. 203440, National Union of Journalists of the Philippines (NUJP), et al. vs. The Executive Secretary, et al. G. R. No. 203453, Paul Cornelius T. Castillo, et al. vs. The Hon. Secretary of Justice, et a., G. R. No. 203454, Anthony Ian M. Cruz, et al. vs. His Excellency Benigno S. Aquino III, et al., G. R. No. 203469, Philippine Bar Association, Inc. vs. His Excellency Benigno S. Aquino III, et al., G. R. No. 203501, Bayan Muna Representative Neri J. Colmenares vs. The Executive Secretary Paquito Ochoa, Jr., G. R. No. 203509, National Press Club of the Philipines, Inc. vs. Office of the President, et al. G. R. No. 203515, Philippine Internet Freedom Alliance, et al. vs. The Executive Secretary, et al., G. R. No. 203518, 11 February 2014.

14. Preservation of Computer；

15. Data；

16. Disclosure of Computer Data；

17. Search，Seizure and Examination of Computer Data；

18. Destruction of Computer Data；

19. Restricting or Blocking Access to Computer Data；

20. Obstruction of Justice；

21. Creation of the Cybercrime Investigation and Coordinating Cener (the "CICC")；

22. CICC's powers and functions. [1]

The various grounds for the challenge include the violation of the equal protection clause，violation of the right to privacy and correspondence，violation of the right to due process of law，over breadth and creation of a chilling and deterrent effect on freedom of speech and expression，and vagueness，among others. [2]

However，despite the challenge，the Supreme Court declared that the Cybercrime Prevention Act of 2012 is valid，except for the following void and unconstitutional provisions：

1. Unsolicited Commercial Communications[3]

The Supreme Court found the provision on Unsolicited Commercial Communications to be unconstitutional. The Court ratiocinated that "to prohibit the transmission of unsolicited ads would deny a person the right to read his emails，even unsolicited commercial ads addressed to him. Commercial speech is a separate category of speech which is not accorded the same level of protection as that given to other constitutionally guaranteed forms of expression but is nonetheless entitled to protection. The State cannot rob him of this right without violating the constitutionally guaranteed freed of expression. Unsolicited advertisements are legitimate forms of ex-

---

① *Ibid.*

② *Ibid.*

③ Section 4(c)(3). Cybercrime Prevention Act of 2012.

pression. "①

2. The provision on Aiding and Abetting as it relates to Libel, Unsolicited Commercial Communications and Child Pornography

The Supreme Court found the provision on "aiding and abetting" as it relates to the crime of libel, to constitute broad sweep that generates a chilling effect on those who express themselves through cyberspace posts, comments and other messages. The provision was found to be invalid for being overbroad or vague. As the Court noted, "a person who does not know whether his speech constitutes a crime under an overbroad or vague law may simply restrain himself from speaking in order to avoid being charged of a crime. The overbroad or vague law thus chills him into silence. "②

Thus, the Court ruled that the provision on "aiding and abetting" as it relates to the crimes of Libel,③ Unsolicited Commercial Communication④ and Child Pornography,⑤ cannot stand scrutiny. "Its vagueness raises apprehension on the part of internet users because of its obvious chilling effect on the freedom of expression, especially since the crime of aiding or abetting ensnares all the actors in the cyberspace front in a fuzzy way. What is more, formal crimes such as libel are not punishable unless consummated. " ⑥

However, the crime of aiding and abetting the commission of cybercrimes, other than the three (3) specifically mentioned above, were held by the High Court to be valid. ⑦

3. Libel as it Relates to Persons Who Receive the Post and React to It

Although the Court did notstruck down as unconstitutional the provision on Libel, it took the limited view that the same applies only to the original author of the libelous statement or article and does not extend to

---

① *Ibid*, Note 34.
② *Ibid*.
③ Section 4(c)(4). Cybercrime Prevention Act of 2012.
④ Section 4(c)(3). Cybercrime Prevention Act of 2012.
⑤ Section 4(c)(2). Cybercrime Prevention Act of 2012.
⑥ *Ibid*.
⑦ *Ibid*.

persons who merely "react", "like" or "retweet" the same. The Court took cognizance of the fact that "the internet is characterized as encouraging a freewheeling, anything-goes writing style. In a sense, they are a world apart in terms of quickness of the reader's reaction to defamatory statements posted in cyberspace, facilitated by one-click reply options offered by the networking site as well as the speed with which such reactions are disseminated down the line to other internet users. " ①

4. Real-Time Collection of Traffic Data

The Court recognized that, "undoubtedly, the State has a compelling interest in enacting the cybercrime law for there is a need to put order to the tremendous activities in cyberspace for public good. To do this, it is within the realm of reason that government should be able to monitor traffic data to enhance its ability to combat all sorts of cybercrimes. " ② The Court also recognized that under the Budapest Convention on Cybercrimes, signatory countries are required to adopt legislative measures to empower state authorities to collect or record "traffic data", in real time, associated with specified communications. ③ However, the Court finds that the provision on Real-Time Collection of Traffic Data is vague as it fails to hint as to the meaning it intends for the phrase "due cause". Thus the Court held that the authority that the provision gives to law enforcement agencies is too sweeping and lacks restraint. The court found that "while it says that traffic data collection should not disclose identities or content data, such restraint is but an illusion. Admittedly, nothing can prevent law enforcement agencies holding these data in their hands from looking into the identity of their sender or receiver and what the data contains. This will unnecessarily expose the citizenry to leaked information, or worse, to extortion from certain bad elements in these agencies. " ④

Furthermore, the Court acknowledged that "advances in technology

---

① *Ibid.*
② *Ibid.*
③ *Ibid.*
④ *Ibid.*

allow the government and kindred institutions to monitor individuals and place them under surveillance in ways that have previously been impractical or even impossible. " Thus, the Court recognizes that it is its role to "ensure that laws seeking to take advantage of these technologies be written with specificity and definiteness as to ensure respect for the rights that the Constitution guarantees. " ①

5. Restricting or Blocking Access to Computer Data

The Court found the provision providing authority to the DOJ to issue an order to restrict or block access to computer data which is prima facie found to be in violation of the cybercrime law to be a violation of the freedom of expression and right against reasonable searches and seizure. ②

The Supreme Court found that the provision not only preclude judicial intervention, but also disregarded jurisprudential guidelines established to determine the validity of restrictions on speech. Restraints on free speech are generally evaluated on one of or a combination of three tests: (a) the dangerous tendencydoctrine; (b) the balancing of interest test; and (c) the clear and present danger rule. The Court, however, noted that the provision merely requires that the data to be blocked be found prima facie in violation of any provision of the cybercrime law. It does not take into consideration of the three tests aforementioned. ③

6. Prosecution of the Crimes of Libel and Child Pornography under the Revised Penal Code and the Anti-Child Pornography Act of 2009, respectively and under the Cybercrime Prevention Act of 2012

The Court ruled that with respect to the crimes of Libel and Child Pornography, the provision allowing prosecution under the cybercrime law and under the Revised Penal Code and other special laws is unconstitutional as the same constitutes a violation of the proscription against double jeopardy. ④

---

① Ibid.
② Ibid.
③ Ibid.
④ Section 7, Cybercrime Prevention Act of 2012.

E. Conclusion

The length and breadth of what technology can do is still unmeasured. It can, as the popular TV series say, "boldly go where no man has gone before". [1] Cyberspace is that massive open space where anything is possible and people can hide behind anonymity, without the need to take responsibility for their words or actions. Where "defamatory information shared or stored online can be more virulent and can inflict more harm". [2] As one writer said, "In the online world where social media is pervasive and has become the platform and means by which to spread information rapidly, it is understandable how the online medium can be regarded as a more dangerous place that should offer heavier penalties to those who abuse it." [3]

Certainly, the need for a cybercrime law is necessary to ensure the protection of the life, liberty and property of individuals and to ensure that there is recourse against those who abuse the internet. However, at present, the Philippine cybercrime law is yet untested. Although passed in 2012, it did not come into effect immediately in light of the constitutional challenge against it. It remains to be seen on whether the same will be an effective deterrent against criminal elements in victimizing netizens and an effective remedy to those who seek justice against violators or, will it be, as those opposed to the cybercrime law fear, be merely a tool to restrain the citizenry from the exercise of their constitutionally guaranteed freedom and rights.

---

[1] Star Trek: the Next Generation.

[2] Hofilena, Chay F. "Libel in the Age of Like", 24 February 2014. http://www. rappler. com/thought-leaders/51184-cybercrime-libel-age-like, last accessed 10 December 2014.

[3] Hofilena, Chay F. "Libel in the Age of Like", 24 February 2014. http://www. rappler. com/thought-leaders/51184-cybercrime-libel-age-like, last accessed 10 December 2014.

网络虚拟世界：菲律宾的经验

Everlene O. Lee[*]

余胜男　译

摘要　菲律宾有两项监管网络空间的法律——《电子商务法》及《2012 年网络犯罪防范法》；前者规定黑客或制造病毒、窃取隐私是犯罪行为。后者规定通过网络或类似方法的特定行为是犯罪行为。主要涉及三方面：侵害计算机数据及系统的保密性、完整性和可用性；与计算机相关；与内容相关的犯罪行为。此外，协助或教唆及意图网络犯罪的也会被处罚。

一、引言

科技改变了我们的生活模式，带来很多便利，但也引来诸多威胁。法律因滞后性不能及时解决虚拟世界的问题。包括：网络暴力、侵犯隐私、盗取身份信息及财产。这些问题因"线上媒介难于监管，执法需要资源、人员及装备的支持而被放大"。

2000 年 5 月 4 日，通过邮件传播的"我爱你"计算机病毒攻击了成千上万的 Windows 系统电脑。该病毒造成巨大损失。调查结果显示病毒为菲律宾计算机程序员制造，但当病毒散播时，并无法律惩罚制造及传播计算机病毒造成他人损害的行为。因此只能以盗窃并违反《接入设备管理法》起诉。但司法部因法律不适用且没有足够证据撤销控告。因此，亟需监管网络行为的法律。

---

[*]　菲律宾安加拉·阿贝罗·雷加拉·克鲁斯律师事务所高级法务助理。

二、菲律宾网络及网络犯罪法

1.《电子商务法》

"我爱你"病毒事件后，菲律宾颁布了《电子商务法》以促进电子交易，适用于涉及交易中商业或非商业活动的所有信息及电子文档。该法承认符合特定要求的电子交易及合同的有效性，允许电子数据信息或电子文档作为证据。此外，该法也规定了对"黑客"行为、剽窃或侵害知识产权的行为的具体处罚，也规定《消费者保护法》及其他法律有特殊规定的，优先适用。

2.《2012年网络犯罪防范法》

《电子商务法》颁行后，菲律宾又出台了《2012年网络犯罪防范法》。该法是为保护信息与数据的安全制定，力求运用足够力量通过便利侦查、调查和起诉有效防止与打击国内及国际网络犯罪。

该法禁止如非法接入、拦截等损害计算机数据及系统的保密性、完整性和可用性的行为；与计算机相关的伪造、诈骗行为；以及诽谤、传播网络色情与儿童色情作品及垃圾商业信息的行为3类网络犯罪。

三、《2012年网络犯罪防范法》的违宪审查

15名请愿者向最高法院提起违宪审查，认为该法的非法接入、数据扰乱、域名抢注等22个条款违宪，侵害了公民宪法性权利。审查理由包括违反平等保护、正当程序的权利，损害言论自由等。最终，最高院裁定《2012年网络犯罪防范法》除涉及垃圾商业信息的规定、涉及诽谤、垃圾商业信息及儿童色情作品行为的"协助和教唆"的规定、关于诽谤的规定、涉及流量数据的实时搜集的规定、赋予政府颁布限制或阻止计算机数据接入的命令的权力的规定、涉及诽谤及儿童色情作品的起诉的规定这6个条款违宪而无效，并裁定除此以外的规定均有效。

四、结论

网络空间使一切皆有可能，人们可以通过匿名企图对自身言行免责，因此

《网络犯罪法》是保护生命安全、自由和个人财产所必需的。其虽于 2012 年通过，但因合宪性审查并没有即时生效。该法能否有效打击网络犯罪补偿受害者或只是限制公民宪法性自由与权利的工具，仍有待观察。

The Kingdom of Thailand's Internet Law

Yanaphak Mantarat[*]

Abstract   The Kingdom of Thailand's Internet Law was one of the most important socio-economic part of Thailand. We gave importance to the development of Information Technology, which could clearly be seen, since the establishment of the Ministry of Information and Communication Technology (MICT) by the Bureaucratic Restructuring Act of B. E. 2545 (2002). The Ministry of ICT has the agencies and state enterprises to be under. Moreover, Thailand as the members of the ASEAN community has already sign an important framework agreement called E-ASEAN framework agreement, whichaware of the opportunities offered by the revolution in information and communications technology (ICT) and electronic commerce. The Kingdom of Thailand already has the obligation on this agreement. Moreover, we also look at other countries internet laws. According to the Information Technology in Thailand, it divided into three subjects. Firstly, the Electronic Transaction Act B. E. 2544 (2001). Secondly the Computer Crime Act, B. E. 2550 (2007). Thirdly, the Data Privacy Protection. However, in the present the Computer Crime was Act on Computer-Related Offences played an important role in the Kingdom of Thailand to define the computer offences against Confidentiality, Integrity and Computer Related Forgery and Computer Related Fraud, Content Related offences. The further issues are on internet telecommunications on Intellectual Property, telecommunications on In-

---

* Judge, The Central Intellectual Property and International Trade Court of Thailand.

ternational Trade and the role of telecommunication regulators.

Keywords Information Technology; Computer-Related; Telecommunication; E-ASEAN; MICT

The Institution Structure of Thailand's Organizations on Internet Law

The Kingdom of Thailand, in 3 October 2002 established the Ministry of Information and Communication Technology (MICT) by the Bureaucratic Restructuring Act of B. E. 2545 (2002). The agencies and state enterprises; Office of the Minister, Office of the Permanent Secretary, Meteorological Department, National Statistical Office, Software Industry Promotion Agency (Public Agency), TOT Public Company Limited, CAT Telecom Public Company Limited and Thailand Post Company Limited was under MICT. [1]

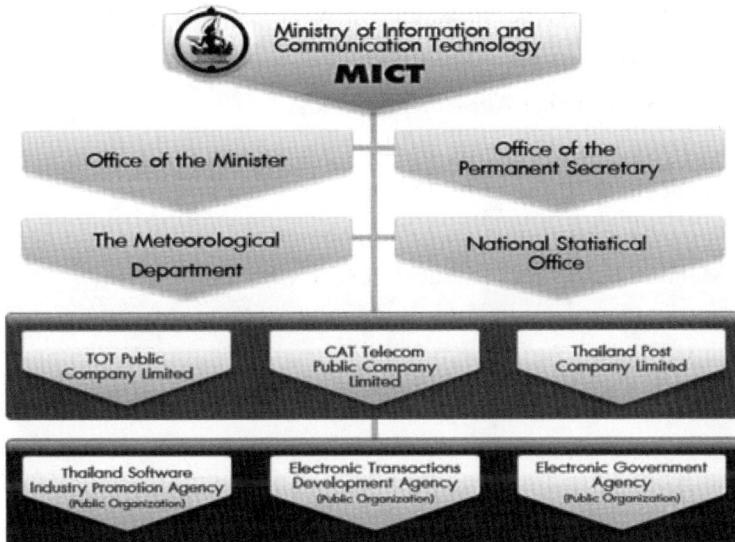

---

[1] About MICT, Ministry of ICT Smart Thailand, http://www. mict. go. th/view/10/About%20Us.

International influence on Thailand's Internet Law

In the Tenth United Nations Congress on the Prevention of Crime and the Treatment of Offenders, at Vienna 10-17 April 2000, divide the computer crime into 5 kind: enter without permission, establish damaged to information and computer programme, plague or interrupt the computer system or network, to cease information that send or from the internal system or network without permission and espionage information on computer. The Kingdom of Thailand as one of the ASEAN countries signed the E-ASEAN framework agreement, on 24 Nov 2000, in Singapore. The member state that sign this agreement includes; State of Brunei Darussalam, the Kingdom of Cambodia, the Republic of Indonesia, the Lao People's Democratic Republic, Malaysia, the Union of Myanmar, the Republic of the Philippines, the Republic of Singapore, the Kingdom of Thailand, and the Socialist Republic of Viet Nam. The objective of the Agreement was state on the Article 2[1]:

The objectives of this Agreement are to:

(a) promote cooperation to develop, strengthen and enhance the competitiveness of the ICT sector in ASEAN;

(b) promote cooperation to reduce the digital divide within individual ASEAN Member States and amongst ASEAN Member States;

(c) promote cooperation between the public and private sectors in realising e-ASEAN;

(d) promote the liberalisation of trade in ICT products, ICT services and investments to support the e-ASEAN initiative.

When the Kingdom of Thailand was on the Computer-Related Crime Act B. E. 2550 (2007) drafting process we studied other countries the Computer Crime law and related law. These countries included the

---

① E-ASEAN Framework Agreement, The ASEAN Secretariat, http://www.asean. org/news/item/e-asean-framework-agreement.

Philippines Electronic Commerce Act 2000, the Malaysia Computer Crime Act 1997, the SingaporeComputer Misuse Act, The Japan Unauthorized Computer Access Law 2000, The India Information Technology Act 2000 and The Council of Europe Convention on Cybercrime. [1]

Challengesof Thailand's Policy and Regulation on Information Technology

Regulator faced these three expectations from stakeholders on regulator; Industry section they expects light-touched regulations or no intervention and let the market decide, Consumers section expects variety of services with low price, the character of telecoms market is always evolving and has rapid growth. Finally the answer for these was no absolute single pricing model that fits for all IP-based interconnection charging like one-size-fits-all model. Role of telecommunication regulators in promoting protection; Encourage and promote industry self-regulation approaches with stakeholders; ensure balance, proportionate and robust mechanism for content owner and copy right infringement; ensure protection of consumer right privacy; encourage the removal of market barriers; facilitate legal service as part of solution to managing; Promote and encourage innovation of new services.

Thailand's Internet Law and Related Law

The Internet law, in Thailand, was known as the law in the area of Information Technology. It divided mainly into three subjects. Firstly, the Electronic Transaction Act B. E. 2544 (2001), secondly the Computer Crime Act, B. E. 2550 (2007) and thirdly, the Data Privacy Protection. The other related laws are the Radio Communication Act, the Telecommunications

---

① The Criminal Justice Response to Cybercrime: Thailand, Santipatn Prommajul, p. 89.

Business Operation Act, the Frequency Allocation Act and the Broadcasting Business Act. These law was applies in these area telecoms, internet sector, and audio-visual media distribution. In the Kingdom of Thailand, the Computer Crime Act, B. E. 2550 (2007) has the important role in the Information Technology, which aim to specify the person who will be responsible for such crime and the person who have to share the responsibility, more clearly and concise. The essence of this act, it define kind of Computer-Related Offences and define the officer who have authority operated this act. The Computer Crime Act, B. E. 2550 (2007)[①] define offenses against the Confidentiality, Integrity and Availability of Computer Data and Systems, Computer Related Forgery and Computer Related Fraud and Content Related offences, such as crime, as said bellow:

1. Section 5 Any person illegally accessing a computer system for which a specific access prevention measure that is not intended for their own use is available shall be subject to imprisonment for no longer than six months or a fine of not more than ten thousand baht or both.

2. Section 7 If any person illegally accesses computer data, for which there is a specific access prevention measure not intended for their own use available, then he or she shall be subject to imprisonment for no longer than two years or a fine of not more than forty thousand baht or both.

3. Section 8 Any person who illegally commits any act by electronic means to eavesdrop a third party's computer data in process of being sent in a computer system and not intended for the public interest or general people's use shall be subject to imprisonment for no longer than three years or a fine of not more than sixty thousand baht or both.

4. Section 9 Any person who illegally damages, destroys, corrects, changes or amends a third party's computer data, either in whole or in part, shall be subject to imprisonment for no longer than five years or a fine of not more than one hundred thousand baht or both.

---

① The Computer Crime Act, B. E. 2550 (2007), Transalation by Chaninat & Leeds, Thailand Law Forum.

5. Section 10 Any person who illegally commits any act that causes the working of a third party's computer system to be suspended, delayed, hindered or disrupted to the extent that the computer system fails to operate normally shall be subject to imprisonment for no longer than five years or a fine of not more than one hundred thousand baht or both.

6. Section 11 Any person sending computer data or electronic mail to another person and covering up the source of such aforementioned data in a manner that disturbs the other person's normal operation of their computer system shall be subject to a fine of not more than one hundred thousand baht.

7. Section 14 If any person commits any offence of the following acts shall be subject to imprisonment for not more than five years or a fine of not more than one hundred thousand baht or both:

(1) that involves import to a computer system of forged computer data, either in whole or in part, or false computer data, in a manner that is likely to cause damage to that third party or the public;

(2) that involves import to a computer system of false computer data in a manner thatis likely to damage the country's security or cause a public panic;

(3) that involves import to a computer system of any computer data related with an offence against the Kingdom's security under the Criminal Code;

(4) that involves import to a computer system of any computer data of a pornographic naturethat is publicly accessible;

(5) that involves the dissemination or forwarding of computer data already known to be computer data under (1) (2) (3) or (4);

8. Section 15 Any service provider intentionally supporting or consenting to an offence under Section 14 within a computer system under their control shall be subject to the same penalty as that imposed upon a person committing an offence under Section 14.

9. Section 16 Any person, who imports to a computer system that is publicly accessible, computer data where a third party's picture appears either created, edited, added or adapted by electronic means or otherwise in a manner that is likely to impair that third party's reputation or cause that

third party to be isolated, disgusted or embarrassed, shall be subject to imprisonment for not longer than three years or a fine of not more than sixty thousand baht, or both.

The Enforcement and Implementation of Internet Law

When the Computer Crime Act B. E. 2550 (2007) was in force, on July 2007, the Computer-Related Crimes that was reported to the Royal Thai Police was in these areas, as illustrate by the picture bellow:[1]

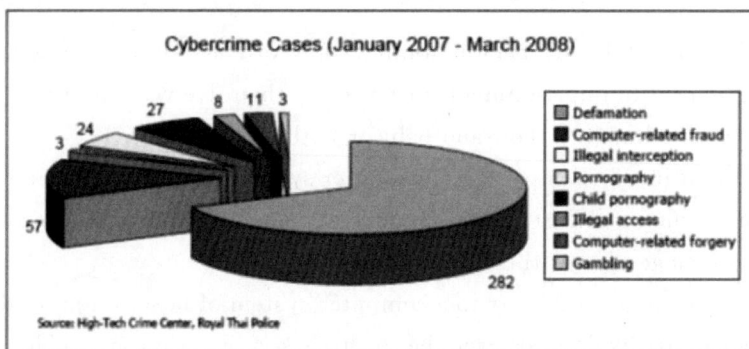

Moreover, the issue on internet or telecommunication had expands its issue into Intellectual Property and International Trade areas.

Telecommunications and Intellectual Property

There is an important issue on internet, which had connect between Intellectual Property and Telecommunications section. The Copyright and Telecoms which serve as platform through Internet for each player to delivered services. The Patent include group of Telecoms devices and group of Technology Deployment, they play their role through internet by creating smartphone patents and patent on designing aircard. These current issues on

---

① Cited from The Criminal Justice Response to Cyber Crime : Thailand by SantipatnPrommajul.

Telecommunication and Intellectual Property in Thailand, the regulators promoting the protection by encourage and promote industry self-regulation approaches with stakeholders, ensure balance, proportionate and robust mechanism for content owner and copy rightinfringement, ensure protection of consumer right privacy, encourage the removal of market barriers, facilitate legal service as part of solution to managing Intellectual Property Right and Promote and encourage innovation of new services.

Telecommunications and International Trade

The International Trade on internet issues included these areas; Free trade, Discourage Monopoly, eliminate trade barriers, non-discrimination. Telecommunications according to the World Trade Organization (WTO), it is a part of International service, globalization, generating huge amount of revenue, creating spectrum allocation resulting related services and creating of works and investment domestically and internationally. Telecommunications Convergence between infrastructures, services and companies. The challenge can said in three section, firstly private content as privacy safety. Secondly, Information Content as responsibility accuracy pluralism. Thirdly, the Entertainment as copyright piracy. These current issues on Telecommunications and International Trade in Thailand, the regulators emphasize on the public interest. This can be see through the Thailand Radio Communication Act, the Telecommunications Business Operation Act, the Frequency Allocation Act and the Broadcasting Business Act. The protection of Thailand public interest according to the International Trade, Thailand made clauses on Limitation on Market Access, Limitation on National Treatment and Additional Commitment. For instance, the announcement on the prohibition of alien overshadow Thailand Telecommunications Business Operation, implement under Article 8 of Thailand Telecommunications Business Operation Act. This announcement had already made an consultant to the WTO body for such limitation.

Summary

Nowadays，the global socio-economic run with the Information Technology. The sufficiency economy on Information Technology will be the primary basic of the global socio-economic. The law and mority of Information Technology should be the secondary choice. The development and the Internet law of Thailand could said that had move alongside with the global trend，according to the worldwide connection. These evidence seen through the obligation on E-ASEAN framework agreement and Thailand Internet law and other related law，which accordance with international standard according one of the member of the United Nation（UN）and the World Trade Organization（WTO）. Especially，when Thailand start on drafting the Computer-Related crime Act，we already overview other countries internet law. In the future it is necessary，that all countries should move together. The International Cooperation on Internet law will need to be more urgently tighten to be able to consistent to the global socio-economic development.

泰国的互联网法

Yanaphak Mantarat[*]

刘俊杰　译

摘要　泰国对互联网法高度重视,并采取各类举措促进互联网法的发展。泰国建立了互联网法的监管机构信息与通讯技术部,借鉴国际先进立法,完善了国内互联网相关法律,同时对互联网相关知识产权和国际贸易领域进行监管保护。

关键词　互联网法;信息技术;计算机相关;信息与通讯技术部

一、泰国互联网法的监管机制

泰国互联网法的主要监管机构是信息与通讯技术部,该机构于 2002 年 10 月 3 日根据 B.E. 2545(2002)官僚体制重组法案建立,下设部长办公室、常务秘书办公室、气象部、国家统计局,还包括 3 个公共有限公司,即 TOT 公共有限公司、CAT 电信公共有限公司以及泰国邮政有限公司,以及 3 个协会,即软件产业促进协会、电子交易发展协会、电子政府协会。

监管机构的职责在于提供保护、鼓励和促进产业自律,确保信息保有与著作权侵权间的平衡和健康机制,确保保护消费者隐私,促进和鼓励新服务的创新。实际上,监管者在监管过程中受到各方利益的制约,产业方面希望监管能更加透明,减少国家干预,由市场去决定。消费者希望各类服务的价格能更低,电信市场能一直快速发展,因此互联网监管面临着一定的挑战。

---

[*]　泰国中央知识产权与国际贸易法院法官。

二、泰国互联网相关法律的现状

泰国积极参与和互联网相关的国际立法。2000年11月24日,泰国在新加坡签订了电子东盟框架协议,旨在促进东盟各国的合作,减少成员国数字鸿沟,促进信息通讯技术产品、服务、投资的贸易自由化,加强东盟的信息通讯技术的竞争力,以支持电子东盟计划。同时,在起草国内法律时也考量了国际立法现状,如2000年第十届联合国预防犯罪和犯罪待遇大会上对计算机犯罪的定义,以及其他国家,如菲律宾、新加坡、马来西亚、日本互联网相关法律。

泰国关于信息技术的法律可以分为三个主题:第一是B.E.2544(2001)电子交易法;第二是B.E.2550(2007)计算机犯罪法案;第三是数据隐私保护。其他相关的法律包括广播通讯法,电信业务操作法,频率分配法,广播商业法。

在泰国,B.E.2550(2007)计算机犯罪法案在信息技术中占有重要地位,因为该法清晰明确地规定了承担网络犯罪责任的主体。此部法律的本质在于确立了计算机相关犯罪的类型以及监管者,定义了针对机密性和完整性的计算机犯罪以及计算机相关的伪造和欺诈行为,如下所述:

第五节:非法访问计算机系统应当被处以不超过6个月的监禁或者不超过10,000铢的罚金或两者并罚。

第七节:非法获取计算机数据,应当被处以不超过2年的监禁或者不超过40,000铢的罚金或两者并罚。

第八节:非未以公共利益或公众的使用为目的,非法采用电子手段窃听属于第三方的计算机,应当被处以不超过3年的监禁或者不超过60,000铢的罚金或两者并罚。

第九节:非法破坏、损毁、纠正、改变、修正第三方的计算机数据,应当被处以不超过5年的监禁或者不超过100,000铢的罚金或两者并罚。

第十节:由于行为人的非法行为,导致第三方的计算机被中止、迟延、妨碍、干扰而不能使用,应当被处以不超过5年的监禁或者不超过100,000铢的罚金或两者并罚。

第十一节:用扰乱他人计算机系统正常操作的方式向他人发送计算机数据和电子邮件以及隐藏上述提及数据的来源的应当被处以不超过100,000铢的罚金。

第十四节:下列犯罪行为应当被处以不超过5年的监禁或者不超过100,000铢的罚金或两者并罚:

（1）以可能损害第三方或公众的方式向计算机系统导入全部或部分伪造或虚假的计算机数据。

（2）以可能损害国家安全或造成公众恐慌的方式向计算机系统导入虚假数据；

（3）向计算机系统导入与刑法典下影响国家安全的犯罪行为相关的任何计算机数据。

（4）向计算机系统导入可公开访问的色情性质的计算机数据；

（5）散播或转发以上提及的计算机数据；

第十五节：任何服务提供者在其可控制的计算机系统内，故意支持或允许第十四节规定的犯罪行为，应当被处以与第十四节犯罪相同的处罚。

第十六节：任何人以可能会损害第三方名誉或者使第三方被孤立、憎恶、尴尬的方式，向计算机系统导入可公开访问的数据或是通过电子手段或其他方式对第三方的形象进行编辑、修改、添加、改编的，应当被处以不超过 3 年的监禁或者不超过 60,000 铢的罚金或两者并罚.

当 B. E. 2550（2007）计算机犯罪法案实施后，泰国皇家警察对 2007 年 1 月—2008 年 3 月计算机犯罪案件的类型进行了统计，网络诽谤、欺诈、儿童色情属于计算机犯罪的高发领域，另外还包括计算机相关伪造、非法访问、非法窃听、赌博等网络犯罪类型。

三、泰国互联网法的发展

随着网络向传统领域如知识产权和国际贸易的渗透，互联网法不再局限于计算机领域的规制，也开始对这些交叉领域进行监管和保护。

知识产权与互联网的交叉体现在著作权人通过互联网平台向公众传递服务，专利包括一系列的电信设备和技术手段，通过创建智能手机专利和上网卡的设计来发挥着作用。此时互联网监管者的功能在于提供保护、鼓励和促进产业自律；确保运营商与著作权侵权间的平衡恰当健康的机制；确保保护消费者隐私；促进作为管理知识产权手段的法律服务；促进和鼓励服务创新。

根据世界贸易组织的规定，与互联网相关的国际贸易属于国际服务、全球化的一部分，会产生巨大的经济利益，为国内国际上带来公众创建工作机会。但也带来了隐私安全、信息内容责任多元化、娱乐产品盗版等问题。泰国的监管者制定了以下法案来应对上述问题：泰国广播通讯法、电信业务操作法、频率分配法、广播商业法。同时，泰国还对市场准入、国民待遇以及附加承诺进行限制。例如,根据电信业务操作法第8条,禁止外国人从事电信业务。该规定已被置于WTO框架下进行磋商。

四、总结

当前,信息技术已成为全球社会经济发展的基础。泰国通过重组互联网监管机构,积极参与国际立法,完善国内立法,关注互联网交叉领域来促进互联网法的发展。在未来,泰国希望与各国更紧密合作,以满足全球社会经济发展的趋势。

Cyber Law in Vietnam

Pham Thi Minh Hau[*]

In Vietnam, from 2011 to date, the domain name ". vn", the country's national domain name, has been registered as being the most widely used in the ASEAN region. In addition to ". vn" being ranked as the most popular domain name in the ASEAN region, it was also considered a significant domain name registered in Asia. [2] On 25 August 2014, the Ministry of Information and Communications, the Vietnam Internet Network Information Center[3] held a program named "Celebration for the millionth registration of the national domain name". This event recognized Vietnam as a country with a domain name of significant national reach and a domain name popularly used internationally. The millionth registration of the national domain name is evidence of the development of the internet in Vietnam and supports local users as an efficient tool to advertise Vietnamese products. [4]

---

[*] Associate, Vinh An Law Office—Rajah & Tann LCT Lawyers.

[2] Report on Internet Resource 2014 made by the Vietnam Internet Network Information Center.

[3] the Vietnam Internet Network Information Center is established from 2000 and is a supporting department of the Ministry ofInformation and Communications

[4] http://vnnic. vn/tenmientiengviet/tintuc/vnnic-t％E1％BB％95-ch％E1％BB％A9c-ch％C6％B0％C6％A1ng-tr％C3％ACnh-ch％C3％A0o-m％E1％BB％ABng-s％E1％BB％B1-ki％E1％BB％87n-t％C3％AAn-mi％E1％BB％81n-ti％E1％BA％BFng-vi％E1％BB％87t-th％E1％BB％A9-1-tri-0

I. Overview of Internet Development and Usage in Vietnam

Internetdevelopment and its significant application in Vietnam over recent years

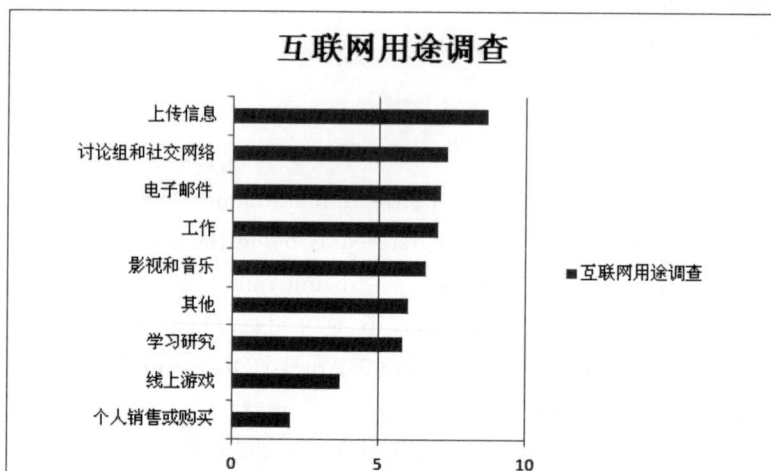

互联网用途调查

上传信息
讨论组和社交网络
电子邮件
工作
影视和音乐
其他
学习研究
线上游戏
个人销售或购买

■互联网用途调查

0   5   10

On 10 August 2005, the Prime Minister of Vietnam promulgated Decision No. 777/QD-TTg to approve the Feasibility Report on the Project of Information Technology and Media Development in Vietnam. This is a loan project granted by the World Bank in order to boost the application of information technology and media by both public and private organizations, as well as educate and amend some issues related to telecommunications policies and information technology for the purpose of socioeconomic development and integration requests.

The total project investment was USD 107,030,000, including 5 dependent mini-projects run by the Ministry of Post and Telecommunications, State General Statistics Office, and the People's Committees of Hanoi, Da Nang and Ho Chi Minh City. At that time, the target for 2010 was that at least 10% to 15% of Vietnamese citizens were to be provided with public electronic services, 80% of websites and communications port automatically provided, 30% of documentation publicly uploaded, and 30% to 40% of enterprises applying information technology and media for their operational activities and business transactions. [1]

To date, in Vietnam, together with the application of information technology, internet has shown significant development and made remarkable achievements. The internet has played an important role in connecting all life aspects and business sectors, and has become a key tool for business and social activities of enterprises and individuals.

According to a survey made by the Vietnam E-commerce and Information Technology Agency [2] in 2013, among 781 internet-user respondents in Vietnam, 92% (702 respondents) often use the internet every day. Laptops and hand phones were the most common means of accessing the internet. Also, according to this survey, 87% of respondents shared that their purposes of using the internet was to be updated on information, while 73% used it to participate in forums and social networks, 71% used it to check emails and 20% used it for personal sales and purchasing. [3]

The development and increasing use of the internet has impacted societies and businesses nationwide.

Thanks to the application of the internet, business can happen across national boundaries via electronic commerce without the need to physically be at a location ("e-commerce"). The year 2005 was the last year of the period where the e-commerce system had been formed and is also officially recognized under the law of Vietnam. This has given recent rise to business efficiencies and opened up trade avenues in Vietnam. For years after the implementation of the master-plan on e-commerce development set forth by the Vietnamese Government, the country has witnessed a number of changes relating to e-commerce, such as the reformation to its legal system, the appearance of the electronic business index and the transformation of a number

---

[1]   The data is cited from the Report on E-commerce 2005 of the Ministry of Industry and Trade of Vietnam.

[2]   The Vietnam E-commerce and Information Technology Agency was established in 2008 and is a supporting department of the Ministry of Industry and Trade of Vietnam.

[3]   The data is cited from the Report on E-commerce 2013 of the Ministry of Industry and Trade of Vietnam.

of types of e-commerce.

II. Overview of the Vietnamese Legal System

The legal system of Vietnam is based on socialist legal theory and inherits the French civil law system. The National Assembly is the highest office responsible for law-making activities. The Legal Committee and various subordinate offices play roles in assisting the National Assembly in its lawmaking functions. The competent agencies, such as ministries or ministerial agencies, in the relevant fields take charge in drafting the law. Depending on the level of legalization of drafted documents (as stipulated by the Constitution), they will be submitted to the appropriate levels for consideration, revision, and approval.

The highest-ranked legal document in Vietnam is the Constitution passed by the National Assembly on April 1992. Under the Constitution are laws, ordinances, decrees and other subordinate legal documents that deal with different aspects of social life. The authority to issue these legal documents and the hierarchy in application of some main legal documents are detailed as follows:[1]

No.	Type of legal document	Competent authority
1	Laws	passed by the National Assembly
2	Ordinances	passed by the Standing Committee of the National Assembly
3	Decrees	passed by the government to generally implement laws and ordinances in detail
4	Circulars	Issued by ministriesto usually providing guidance as to how a particular ministry will administer a law, ordinance or decree

---

[1] In practice, in case the municipal authorities are not able to verify whether the application of the regulation in some specific cases are in compliance with the laws or not, ministries will issue official letter to give instruction.

Ⅲ. Legal Framework

Vietnamese lawmakers have not legislated a law that directly governs activities through the internet (internet law, cyber law, etc.). However, Law No. 67/2006/QH11 dated 29 June 2006 regarding information technology (the "Law on Information Technology") has in its major governing scope matters in relation to the internet, and this law has played a key role in the legal framework of governing the internet and its associated activities, including e-commerce activities in Vietnam. The Law on Information Technology provides overall regulations regarding application activities and information technology development as well as measures and solutions to secure provision of technology infrastructure to all relevant activities.

In addition to the Law on Information Technology, the Vietnamese legal system also has various other related laws and guidance to govern trading activities via the internet specifically. For example, Law No. 51/ 2005/QH11 dated 29 November 2005 regarding e-transactions (the "Law on E-transactions") currently directly governs e-transactions.

The Law on Information Technology and Law on E-transactions are implemented concurrently with detailed guidance provided under numerous decrees and circulars.

1. Overview of the primary internet laws (Law on Information Technology)

The Law on Information Technology provides extensive activities related to the internet and includes 6 chapters and 79 articles. The brief structure and contents are as follows:

Chapter I (General Provisions) outlines the issues of scope, the applicable law, interpretation on terms and policies of the State on information technology, the rights and responsibilities of organizations and individuals involved in the application and development of information technology, information technology inspection and prohibited acts.

Chapter II(The application of information technology) creates the basic legal framework for promoting the application of information technology in all socioeconomic aspects.

Section 1. General provisions on the application of information technology—providing the principle of operation of information technology applications, including rights and obligations of agencies, organizations and individuals in the management, use, transmission of digital information; collecting, handling, use, storage, supply personal information in the network environment and establishing electronic information page.

One basic rule is that organizations and individuals are free to apply information technology in sectors that are not prohibited by law. For organizations and individuals using the national domain of Vietnam. "vn" when setting up a website, they may bypass the notice requirement to the Ministry of Post—Telecommunications. For those establishing electronic information pages with a domain name that is not ". vn", they will need to inform the network environment with the agency.

Section 2. The application of information technology in the activities of agencies—creating significant legal framework to promote an "e-government" in Vietnam. The law provides, in principle, conditions and contents of information technology applications in the activities of state agencies, the activities of state agencies in the network environment, and electronic information pages of state agencies.

Section 3. All organizations and individuals have the right to participate in commercial activities in the network environment. This section provides for the object, the principle of the application of information technology in business. It also provides information on contracts in the network environment, the handling of consequences of wrong trade information in the network environment and payment in the network environment.

Section 4. The application of information technology in a number of areas, such as education, health, culture, defense and security, are regulated in this section. The application of information technology in specialized fields not only must comply with the provisions of this law but also must comply with the relevant laws governing such fields.

Chapter III (Development of information technology) regulates the study of the development of information technology, human resource development in information technology (including development policy), and the development of information technology services (including types of policy development and information technology services).

Chapter IV (Measures to ensure the application and development of information technology)

Section 1. The infrastructure for the application and development of information technology.

Section 2. Investment in information technology. This section is important in order to promote the development of information technology. This section specifies the investment of organizations and individuals into information technology and the investment into information technology for agriculture and rural development.

Section 3. International cooperation on information technology. This section defines principles and sets out contents on international cooperation on information technology in order to create conditions for economic sectors to expand cooperation in information technology, to promote the development of information technology Vietnam to meet the requirements of industrialization, modernization and international economic integration.

Section 4. Protection of rights and legitimate interests and support for use of products and services in information technology. This section provides the responsibility of the State and society in protecting the legitimate rights and interests of users, protects national domains, protects intellectual property rights in the information technology field, anti-spam, computer virus and other malicious software, and ensures the safety and confidentiality of information.

Chapter V. (Settlement of disputes and handling violations of provisions) provides jurisdiction to resolve disputes in information technology in general and dispute in registration and use of national domain name ". vn".

Chapter Ⅵ. (Terms of execution).

2. Legal framework: Law on Information Technology and its detailed regulations for implementation

Date	Legal Document	Main contents
29 June 2006	Law on Information Technology	provides for information technology application and development activities, measures to ensure information technology application and development, and the rights and obligations of agencies, organizations and individuals engaged in information technology application and development activities
15 July 2013	Decree no. 72/2013/ND-CP regarding internet services and provision information via internet	specifies the management, provision and use of internet services, online information, and online games, and assurance of information security; and the rights and obligations of organizations and individuals on the management, provision and use of internet services, online information, online games, and assurance of information security
10 April 2014	Decree no. 64/2007/ND-CP on information technology application	Providesfor information technology application in the state agencies' operations
13 June 2011	Decree no. 43/2011/ND-CP on online information provision and public services via the website of state authorities	Providesthe provision of online information and public services on websites or web portals and conditions to assure operations of web portals of state agencies
15 February 2007 13 November 2013	Decree no. 26/2007/ND-CP detailing the implementation of the Law on E-Transactions on digital signatures and digital signature certification services and Decree no. 170/2013/ND-CP amending a number of articles of Decree no. 26/2007/ND-CP	Details provisions on digital signatures and digital certification, and the management, provision and use of digital signatures certification services

Continued

Date	Legal Document	Main contents
13 August 2008 5 October 2012	Decree no. 90/2008/ND-CP against spam Decree no. 77/2012/ND-CP to amend a number of articles under Decree no. 90/2008/ND-CP	Provides for the fight against spam, and the rights and obligations of concerned agencies, organizations and individuals
13 November 2013	Decree no. 174/2013/ND-CP	Regulates violations, forms of administrative sanctions, limits on fine, injunctive relief and authority to apply administrative sanctions
30 December 2008	Circular no. 12/2008/TT-BTTTT	Guides some contents of Decree no. 90/2008/ND-CP against spam in detail
14 December 2009	Circular no. 37/2009/TT-BTTTT prescribing dossiers and procedures for licensing, registration and accreditation of institutional providers of digital signature certification services	Guides Decree no. 26/2007/ND-CP in detail
15 November 2010	Circular no. 25/2010/TT-BTTTT on collection, use, sharing, security assurance and protection of personal information on websites or portals of state agencies	Guides Decree no. 64/2007/ND-CP in detail

3. Legal framework: Law on E-Transactions and its detailed regulations for implementation

Date	Legal Document	Main contents
29 November 2005	Law onE-Transactions	Provides for e-transactions in the operations of state agencies, and in civil, business, commercial and other sectors prescribed by law The provisions of thislaw do not apply to the granting of certificates of land use rights, ownership of houses and other immovable properties, inheritance documents, marriage certificates, divorce decisions, birth certificates, death certificates, bills of exchange and other valuable papers. General principles in e-transactions To voluntarily select electronic means for transactions To mutually agree on the selection of type of technology for e-transactions No technology shall be considered the sole one in e-transactions To ensure equality and security in e-transactions To protect lawful rights and interests of agencies, organizations, individuals, interests of the State and public interests E-transactions ofstate agencies must comply with the principles stipulated in Article 40 of the law Prohibited acts in e-transactions Obstructing the selection of the use of e-transactions Illegally obstructing or preventing the process of transmitting, sending and receiving data messages Illegally modifying, deleting, canceling, counterfeiting, copying, disclosing, displaying or moving part or whole of a data massage Creating or disseminating software programs that trouble, change or destroy operating systems or committing other acts to destroy the technological infrastructure on e-transactions Creating data messages in order to commit illegal acts Tricking, wrongly identifying, appropriating or illegally using e-signatures of others
23 February 2007	Decree no. 27/2007/ND-CP one-transactions in financial activities	Provides for e-transactions in financial activities
8 March 2007	Decree no. 35/2007/ND-CP on bankinge-transactions	Provides for banking e-transactions

Continued

Date	Legal Document	Main contents
16 May 2013	Decree no. 52/2013/ND-CP on E-commerce	Provides the development, application and management of e-commerce activities Subjects of application Traders, organizations and individuals engaged in e-commerce activities in the territory of Vietnam, including: Vietnamese traders, organizations and individuals Foreign individuals residing in Vietnam Foreign traders and organizations present in Vietnam through investment operations, establishment of branches and representative offices or websites with a Vietnamese domain name On the basis of economic and social conditions and management requirements of each period, the Ministry of Industry and Tradewill assume the prime responsibility for and coordinate with the Ministry of Information and Communications in guiding management measures for foreign traders, organizations and individuals that carry out e-commerce activities with Vietnamese parties Subjects involved in e-commerce activities: Traders, organizations or individuals that develop e-commerce websites by themselves to serve their commercial promotion, sales or service provision (owners of sales e-commerce websites) Traders, organizations or individuals that develop e-commerce websites to provide an environment for other traders, organizations or individuals to conduct their commercial promotion, sales or service provision (traders or organizations providing e-commerce services) Traders, organizations or individuals that use websites of traders or organizations providing e-commerce services to serve their commercial promotion, sales or service provision (sellers) Traders, organizations or individuals that purchase goods or services on sales e-commerce websites and e-commerce service provision websites (customers) Traders or organizations providing technical infrastructure for owners of sales e-commerce websites and for traders and organizations providing e-commerce services (traders or organizations providing infrastructure) Traders, organizations or individuals that use electronic equipment connected to other networks for carrying out commercial activities

Continued

Date	Legal Document	Main contents
16 May 2013	Decree no. 52/2013/ND-CP on E-commerce	Forms of organization of e-commerce activities A sales e-commerce website is an e-commerce website developed by traders, organizations or individuals by themselves to serve their commercial promotion, sales or service provision E-commerce service provision website is an e-commerce website developed by traders or organizations to provide an environment for other traders, organizations or individuals to conduct their commercial activities E-commerce service provision websites can be of the following types: E-commerce trading floor; Online auction website; Online promotion website; Other types of website as stipulated by the Ministry of Industry and Trade For applications installed on electronic devices connected to the network that allow users to access the databases of other traders, organizations and individuals to purchase and sell goods, provide or use services, depending on the utilities of these applications, traders or organizations shall comply with this decree's provisions on sales e-commerce website or e-commerce service provision websites The Ministry of Industry and Tradewill stipulate e-commerce activities conducted on mobile telecommunications networks Principles of e-commerce activities Principle of free and voluntary agreement in e-commerce transactions Parties to e-commerce activities are free to reach agreement not contrary to the provisions of law to establish the rights and obligations of each party in the transaction. This agreement is a ground for the settlement of disputes arising in the transaction process Principles of determination of the scope of business in e-commerce If traders, organizations or individuals conducting their activities of sales, service provision or commercial promotion on e-commerce websites do not specify geographical limits of these activities, these activities are regarded to be conducted on a national scale Principles of determination of the obligation to protect consumer interests in e-commerce

Continued

Date	Legal Document	Main contents
16 May 2013	Decree no. 52/2013/ND-CP on E-commerce	The owners of sales e-commerce websites and the sellers on e-commerce service provision website shall comply with the Lawon Protection of Consumer Interests when providing the goods or services to customers The customers on e-commerce service provision websites are e-commerce service consumers and consumers of goods and services provided by the sellers on these websites In case the sellers directly post information about their goods and services on e-commerce websites the traders or organizations providing e-commerce services and the traders or organizations providing infrastructure are not the third party providing information as prescribed by the Law on Protection of Consumer Interests Principles of trading in goods and provision of services restricted from trading or provision or goods and services subject to business conditions through e-commerce The subjects applying e-commerce for trading in goods and providing services restricted from trading or provision, or goods and services subject to business conditions shall comply with relevant regulations on the trading in those goods and provision of those services
22 November 2012	Decree no. 101/2012/ND-CP regarding non-cash payments	Deals with non-cash payments, including opening and using payment accounts, non-cash payment services, payment intermediary services, and organizing, managing and supervising the payment systems
15 November 2013	Decree no. 185/2013/ND-CP providing the penalties on administrative violations in commercial activities, the production of and trading in counterfeit or banned goods, and protection of consumer rights	Provides for acts of administrative violations, forms of sanction, levels of sanctions, remedial measures, competency to make records and to impose sanctions on administrative violations in commercial activities, the production of and trading in counterfeit or banned goods and protection of consumer rights

Continued

Date	Legal Document	Main contents
15 September 2008	Circular no. 78/2008/TT-BTC	Guides Decree no. 27/2007/ND-CP regarding requirements on parties entering into e-transactions in financial activities, the use of the Ministry of Finance's e-data, the use of e-signatures, the legal validity of and specific signs on converted documents, procedures for the grant, suspension or revocation of papers of recognition of value-added network (VAN) service providers, VAN service charges, and relationships between VAN service providers and their partners
28 June 2013	Circular no. 87/2013/TT-BTC guiding e-transactions on the securities market	Regulates the principles and procedures for conducting e-transactions in online securities trading activities, exchanging e-information relevant to public offers of securities, securities depository, listing, registering and trading, administration of securities companies, fund management companies and securities investment companies, and disclosure and announcement of information and other securities market activities in accordance with the Law on Securities no. 70/2006/QH11 dated 29 June 2006 and the Law Amending and Supplementing a Number of Articles of the Law on Securities no. 62/2010/QH12 dated 24 November 2010
9 November 2010	Circular no. 23/2010/TT-NHNN regulating the management, operation and use of inter-bank electronic payment systems	Regulates the management, operation and use of the Inter-bank Electronic Payment System to implement payment and settlement in VND among units participating in this payment system
10 November 2010	Circular no. 180/2010/TT-BTC guiding electronic transaction in the field of tax	Guides: electronic transactions in tax registration (not applicable for tax registrations as prescribed in Decree no. 43/2010/ND-CP of the Government on enterprise registration), electronic transactions in tax declaration, and electronic transactions in tax payment procedures for granting, temporarily suspending, and revoking thecertificate for the recognition of value-added service providing organizations on electronic transactions in the field of tax, and performing electronic transactions in the field of tax via the value added service providing organizations on electronic transactions in the field of tax

4. Legal Framework: other laws governing activities performed via the internet

Date	Legal Document	Main contents
14 June 2005	Civil Code no. 33/ 2005/QH11	Provides the legal status and legal standards for the conduct of individuals, legal persons, other subjects, and the rights and obligations of subjects regarding personal identities and property in civil, marriage and family, business, trade, labor relations (*civil relations*) The Civil Code has the task of protectingthe legitimate rights and interests of individuals and organizations, the State's interests and public interests, as well as ensuring legal equality and safety in civil relations, contributing to the creation of conditions for meeting the material and spiritual demands of people, and to the promotion of socioeconomic development
29 November 2005 19 June 2009	Lawno. 50/2005/QH11 on Intellectual Property Law no. 36/2009/QH12 amending a number of articles of Law no. 50/ 2005/QH11	Regulates copyright, copyright-related rights, industrial property rights and rights to plant varieties, and the protection of such rights
23 September 2009	Law no. 41/2009/QH12 on Telecommunications	provides for telecommunications activities, including telecommunications investment and business, public-utility telecommunications, telecommunications management, construction of telecommunications works, and rights and obligations of organizations and individuals engaged in telecommunications activities

Continued

Date	Legal Document	Main contents
14 June 2005	Law no. 36/2005/QH11 on Commerce	Governing scope: Commercial activities conducted in the territory of Vietnam Commercial activities conducted outside the territory of Vietnam in cases where the involved partiesagree to this law for application, or where a foreign law or a treaty to which Vietnam is a contracting party stipulates the application of this law. Activities not for profit purposes conducted by a party in its transactions with traders in the territory of Vietnam in cases where the party conducting such not-for-profit activities chooses to apply this law
14 June 2005	Law no. 42/2005/QH11 amending a number of articles of Law no. 29/2001/QH10 on Customs	Provides online customs procedures
19 June 2009	Law no. 37/2009/QH12 amending a number of articles of Penal Code no. 15/1999/QH10	Provides regulations on crimes involving internet and information technology

Ⅳ. Conclusion

So far, the Vietnamese legal system governing activities associated with the internet is sufficient, despite the regulations being scattered in various legal instruments. Under the current legal system, the development of the internet and activities performed via internet are progressively being improved. Therefore, the legal framework governing the internet and its associated activities play an important role in the Vietnamese legal system, resulting from the extensive impact of the internet to almost all aspects of society and the economy.

越南的网络法

Pham Thi Minh Hau*

赵韦翰 译

自 2011 年以来,".vn"作为越南国家域名已经成为了东盟内最为广泛注册的域名。不仅如此,".vn"还是亚洲的重要域名之一。2014 年 8 月 25 日,隶属信息通信部的越南互联网信息中心①举办了"庆祝国家域名注册超百万"的活动。这意味着越南国家域名作为重要域名成为了国际通用域名之一。第一百万个国家域名的成功注册是越南互联网产业发展的铁证,也为产品宣传提供了一项利器。

一、越南互联网发展及应用概述

近年来越南的互联网发展和重要应用

2005 年 8 月 10 日,越南总理颁布了 No.777/QD-TTg 决议批准了越南信息技术和媒体发展工程的可行性报告。这是由世界银行批准的贷款项目,出于社会经济学和一体化要求,旨在通过类公共和私人机构促进信息技术和媒体的应用,加强教育和解决电信政策和信息科技相关的问题。

本项目投资额达到了 107,030,000 美金,包括附带的 5 项小型项目。届时,到 2010 年将会有 10%到 15%的越南市民享有公共电子服务,80%的网站和通信站将自行运营,30%的文件会公开上传,30%到 40%的企业会利用信息技术和媒体来扩展其运行和业务。

---

* 越南文瀚法律办公室 罗杰·谭律师事务所法律助理。

① the Vietnam Internet Network Information Center is established from 2000 and is a supporting department of the Ministry of Information and Communications.

目前,越南的信息技术和网络应用已经有了长足的发展。互联网成为了日常生活中一个必不可少的工具。

根据 2013 年越南电子商务和信息技术局①的调查,在 781 名被访的互联网用户中,92%(702 位)的用户每天使用互联网,而笔记本电脑和手机是最为普遍的上网方式。同时,根据调查显示,受访者中 87% 的用户通过网络更新信息,73% 的用户参与了网上讨论和社交网络,71% 的用户使用了电子邮件,20% 的用户进行了网上销售或购物。

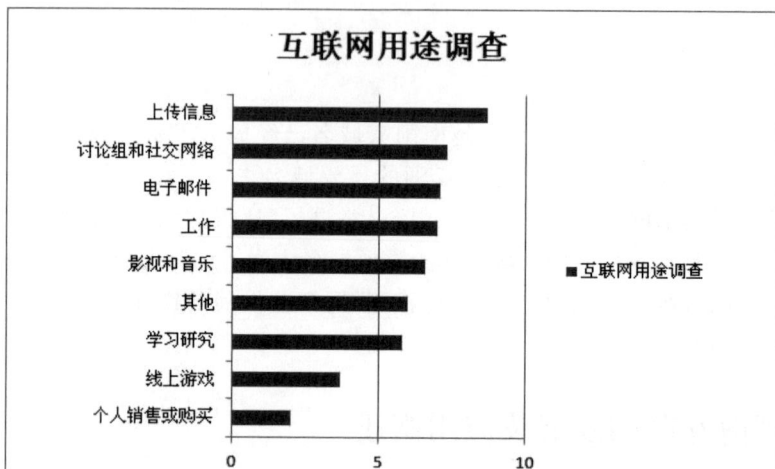

互联网用途调查

上传信息	
讨论组和社交网络	
电子邮件	
工作	
影视和音乐	
其他	
学习研究	
线上游戏	
个人销售或购买	

■互联网用途调查

2005 年,越南电子交易系统构建成形并正式纳入法律体系。随着近年来越南政府贯彻落实电子交易发展总计划,越南的电子商务有了显著的进步。同时相关法律也得到了一定完善,电子商务形式也愈发多样。

二、越南法律体系概述

越南法律体系根基于社会主义法律理论并借鉴了法国民法体系。国民大会是最高立法机关,法务委员会及其附属机构协助国民大会履行立法职能。立法草案则会由适格的部门或部级机构负责。法律或文件的起草、修正和批准需根据其级别提交相应层级的部门。

---

① The Vietnam E-commerce and Information Technology Agency was established in 2008 and is a supporting department of the Ministry of Industry and Trade of Vietnam.

越南最高级别的法律文件是 1992 年 4 月由国民大会通过的宪法。在宪法之下有法条、条例、法令以及其他次级法律文件,它们分别规制社会生活的各个层面。其批准部门和法律层级状况具体如下:

No.	法律文件类别	批准部门
1	法条	国民大会
2	条例	国民大会常务委员会
3	法令	政府用以具体履行法条和条例
4	通告	各部门用以解释法条、条例和法律如何具体实施

三、法律框架

越南并没有就互联网事宜直接单独立法(如互联网法、网络法等),但是在 2006 年 6 月 29 日实施的 No.67/2006/QH11 法案却作为主要规制互联网相关问题的法律,在互联网法律框架确立和具体事务管理上发挥着关键作用。该法律除了对信息技术的相关事务应用和发展做出了规制外,还提出了相应的保护措施。

除上述法律外,还有其他相关法律和指南用以特别管理互联网贸易,例如 2005 年 11 月 29 日的 No.51/2005/QH11 法案("电子交易法案")。

目前,信息技术和电子商务相关的法律已经在许多相关法令和通告的指导下开始实施。

1. 主要互联网法律(信息技术法)概况

信息技术法包含 6 章共 79 条,以下是其简要结构和内容:

第一章 总论:概况,适用法律,信息技术相关术语和政策解释,信息技术应用和发展中组织和个人的权利和义务,信息技术调查和禁止行为。

第二章 信息技术的应用:规定了社会经济层面上信息技术应用的基础法律框架。

第一节 信息技术应用的总则——规定了信息技术应用的原则,包括了相关部门和组织及个人的权利和义务。

其中一个基本原则是信息技术法无禁止即可应用,组织或个人申请国内域名".vn"的无需向国家电信出版总局报告,若不是".vn"则需向该局通报有关情况。

第二节政府部门的信息技术应用和政府信息化的构建。对政府部门的信息技术应用及其应用环境、条件和原则进行了规定。

第三节任何组织和个人均有权参与网络商业行为。对信息技术在商业应用中的客体和原则进行了规定,同时还对电子合同、互联网环境下的贸易信息错误的后果与解决,以及偿付事宜进行了进一步规定。

第四节对其他领域,如教育、医疗、文化、国防安全等的信息技术应用进行了规制,除本法外也需遵从其他相关立法。

第三章(信息技术的发展)对信息技术的研究、人力资源、服务的发展事宜进行了规定。

第四章(确保信息技术应用和发展的措施)

第一节 信息技术应用和发展的基础设施

第二节 信息技术的投资。本节规定了组织和个人可参与的信息技术投资和农业、农村信息技术投资。

第三节 信息技术的国际合作。为了契合越南工业化、现代化以及世界经济一体化需求,本节对信息技术国际合作的原则和内容作出了规定。

第四节 信息技术合法权益保护和对相关产品与服务的扶持。本节规定了国家和政府保护信息技术使用者的各项法定权益的义务。

第五章(争端解决和违反条约的后果)规定了一般信息技术争端和注册域名".vn"相关争端的管辖权。

第六章(执行条款)

2. 信息技术法及其实施细则

日期	法律文件	主要内容
2006 6.29	信息技术法	对信息技术的应用和发展进行了规制,规定了保障信息技术发展的措施,确定了政府部门、个人和组织的相关权利与义务
2013.7.15	No. 72/2013/ND-CP 互联网信息与服务法令	列举了互联网相关服务的管理、供应和使用方式;并规定了组织和个人的相关权利和义务

续表

日　期	法律文件	主要内容
2014.4.10	No.64/2007/ND-CP 信息技术应用法令	规定了国家机关的信息技术应用事宜
2011.6.13	No.43/2011/ND-CP 国家机关的在线信息和公共服务网站法令	规定了国家机关的门户网站上的信息和服务,以及其运行的确保措施
2007.2.15 2013.11.13	No.26/2007/ND-CP 电子商务法的具体实施细则 No.170/2013/ND-CP 的 No.26/2007/ND-CP 修正案	规定了电子签名和电子认证及其服务和管理的法律实施细则
2008.8.13 2012.10.5	No.90/2008/ND-CP 反垃圾邮件法令 No.77/2012/ND-CP 法令,对 No.90/2008/ND-CP 法令进行了修订	明确打击垃圾邮件,并规定了相关部门、组织和个人的权利与义务
2013.11.13	No.174/2013/ND-CP 法令	规定了行政处罚的形式、违反和权限,罚金以及指令性救济的限制
2008.12.30	No.12/2008/TT-BTTTT 通告	对 No.90/2008/ND-CP 反垃圾邮件法令的内容细节发布了执行指南
2009.12.30	No.37/2009/TT-BTTTT 通告,规定了电子签名认证机构的事务相关档案及流程	No.26/2007/ND-CP法案的具体实施指南
2010.11.15	No.25/2010/TT-BTTTT 通告,规定了国家机关所属网站中的个人信息收集、公布、保护等问题	No.64/2007/ND-CP法令的具体实施指南

3. 电子交易法及其实施细则

日期	法律文件	主要内容
2005 11.29	电子交易法	规定了电子交易在政府部门以及民事商业领域中的运作 本法不适用于本法规制内容外的其他文件 电子交易的一般原则 电子交易形式选择意思自治 电子交易技术的类型需双方同意 不可规定某项技术为电子交易唯一方式 平等、安全原则 维护各方合法权益 政府机关的电子商务行为须遵从本法第40条 禁止行为 妨碍形式选择的意思自治 非法阻碍信息传输 非法修改、删除、撤销、伪造、复制、公开数据 编写或散布能对电子商务平台和系统产生危害的软件程序 出于犯罪目的创建数据信息的 非法使用他人电子签名
2007 2.23	No. 27/2007/ND-CP 财政电子交易法令	对政府财政的电子交易进行了规制
2007 3.8	No. 35/2007/ND-CP 银行电子交易法令	对银行业的电子交易进行了规制

续表

日期	法律文件	主要内容
2013 5.16	No. 52/2013/ND-CP 电子商务法令	规定了商业领域的电子交易发展、管理和应用事宜 应用 越南境内的电子商务用户包括: 越南贸易商、组织和个人 定居越南的外国人 在越南投资,建立分支机构和代表处,或拥有越南网站域名的外国贸易商和组织 工业贸易部应在信息通信部的合作下负责引导外国贸易商、组织和个人的电子商务事宜 电子商务活动包括: 建立提供自己的产品或服务的电子商务网站 建立为他人的商业行为提供电子服务的电子商务平台 通过电子贸易网站提供自己的产品或服务 通过电子商务网站进行购物 贸易商或组织向电子商务网站拥有者提供相关技术设施 使用移动终端开展电子贸易 电子商务活动的组织形式 电子商务网站是建立者用以提供商业推广、销售或服务的网站 电子服务平台是建立者用以他人的商业行为提供电子环境的网站 电子服务平台可有以下几种: 电子商务平台 在线拍卖网站 在线推广网站 通商产业局规定的其他网站 安装在电子设备中,用以完成贸易或提供服务的联网应用软件 工业贸易部会对移动终端上的电子商务行为作出进一步规定 电子商务活动的原则 意思自治原则 保护消费者利益原则(须遵从消费者权益保护法) 货物与服务贸易受到电子商务商业条件的限制

续表

日期	法律文件	主要内容
2012 11.22	No. 101/2012/ND-CP 非现金支付法令	规定了非现金支付的账户设立使用、服务、中介、管理和监督等相关事宜
2013 11.15	No.185/2013/ND-CP 法令	规定了商业中的有关行政违法行为、产品伪造、禁止性货物的处罚,以及消费者权益保护
2008 9.15	No.78/2008/TT-BTC 通告	No.27/2007/ND-CP 财政电子商务法令的具体执行指南
2013 6.28	No. 87/2013/TT-BTC 通告(证券市场电子商务法律执行指南)	规定了证券市场中涉及电子商务的相关事宜的法律执行问题,并规定还需遵从 2006 年 6 月 29 日的证券法 70/2006/QH11 和 2010 年 11 月 24 日的证券法修正案 no. 62/2010/QH12 的相关法令
2010.11.9 9 November 2010	No. 23/2010/TT-NHNN 通告(跨银行电子支付系统的管理、运营和使用问题)	规定了越南境内跨银行电子支付系统或平台参与支付和支付系统的相关事宜
2010.11.10 10 November 2010	No. 180/2010/TT-BTC 通告(税务领域的电子商务法律执行指南)	对以下事务进行指导: 税务登记、申报以及支付中的电子交易相关事宜 在税务领域电子增值服务执照的准许、暂扣和撤销,以及电子增值服务运行的相关程序

4. 规制其他互联网活动的相关法律框架

日期	法律文件	主要内容
2005 6.14	民法典 no.33/2005/QH11	界定了自然人、法人以及其他主体的法律地位,对人身权利、财产、婚姻家庭、商业贸易以及劳务关系的权利和义务作出了法律规定

续表

日期	法律文件	主要内容
2005 11.29 2009 6.19	No. 50/2005/QH11 知识产权法 No. 36/2009/QH12 的 No. 50/2005/QH11 知识产权法修正案	规定了版权及其相关权利,工业产权,植物专利权,以及上述权利的保护
2009 9.23	No.41/2009/QH12 电信法	对电信活动的相关事宜进行了法律规制
2005 6.14	No. 36/2005/QH11 商法	管理范围: 越南境内的商业行为 越南境外选择适用越南法的 越南境内的非盈利活动行为人选择适用越南法的
2005 6.14	No. 42/2005/QH11 的 no. 29/2001/QH10 海关法修正案	规定了线上海关程序
2009 6.19	No. 37/2009/QH12 的 no. 15/1999/QH10 刑法典修正案	对涉及互联网和信息技术的犯罪作出了规定

四、结语

目前,越南规制互联网相关的法律相对分散却完备,在现有法律制度下,互联网活动将持续发展。鉴于越南互联网相关法律法规所发挥的关键作用,互联网已经深入国家社会经济的各个领域。